Further Praise for *Between Salt Water and Holy Water*

"[Tommaso Astarita] has given us an excellent overview of the past of one of the most fascinating if now overlooked parts of Europe. . . . The curious reader should treasure this book."

— Lou Tanner, *Virginia Quarterly Review*

"A handy reference for curious Italophiles."

— Nathaniel Rich, *Los Angeles Times*

"The history of Italy tends to focus on events from Rome northward, too often giving short shift to the peculiarly named 'Kingdom of the Two Sicilies.' Astarita does a masterful job of correcting this error and bringing to life for English speakers the people and events of these lands so central to the entire Mediterranean basin. . . . A highly readable history, this volume will be enthusiastically received wherever there are concentrations of Italian-Americans."

— Mark Knoblauch, *Booklist*

"There's much drama possible in the many stories Astarita passes along as he offers up his portrait of a still-varied region: here brother betrays brother; there, serfs battled absentee landlords in an obscure Sicilian village that will give its name to two famous English novelists; and there, now and again, a volcano erupts." — *Kirkus Reviews*

"Professor Astarita takes readers where far too few scholars have preceded him, into the strange and wonderful saga of Meridionale Italy. *Between Salt Water and Holy Water* pictures the South in all of its dizzying idiosyncrasy, earning a place on the bookshelf next to the celebrated works of Lord Norwich and Denis Mack Smith."

— Frank Viviano, author of *Blood Washes Blood:*
A True Story of Love, Murder, and Redemption under the Sicilian Sun

"Astarita tells the little-known story of Southern Italy. . . . He brings to life the peasants and the padrone, shamanism and Christianity, the music of the court and the songs of Naples—and all else that lies 'between salt water and holy water.' "

— Mark Rotella, author of *Stolen Figs: And Other Adventures in Calabria*

"Astarita has given us a great look at the sacred and secular stories that helped make the history of this complex and misunderstood region. . . . If you want to understand Italian Americans, you've got to read this book."   —Fred Gardaphe, author of *Leaving Little Italy*

BETWEEN SALT WATER
AND
HOLY WATER

A History
of Southern Italy

TOMMASO ASTARITA

W. W. NORTON & COMPANY

New York · London

For information about permission to reproduce selections from this book, write to
Permissions, W. W. Norton & Company, Inc., 500 Fifth Avenue, New York, NY 10110

Manufacturing by The Haddon Craftsmen, Inc.
Book design by Charlotte Staub
Production manager: Amanda Morrison

Library of Congress Cataloging-in-Publication Data
Astarita, Tommaso.
Between salt water and holy water : a history of Southern Italy / Tommaso Astarita.
p. cm.
Includes bibliographical references and index.
ISBN 0-393-05864-6 (hardcover)
1. Italy, Southern—History. 2. Naples (Kingdom)—History. I. Title.
DG826.A78 2005
945'.7—dc22

2005006085
ISBN-13: 978-0-393-32867-7 pbk.
ISBN-10: 0-393-32867-8 pbk.

W. W. Norton & Company, Inc., 500 Fifth Avenue, New York, N.Y. 10110
www.wwnorton.com

W. W. Norton & Company Ltd., Castle House, 75/76 Wells Street, London W1T 3QT

1 2 3 4 5 6 7 8 9 0

Contents

Preface
& Acknowledgments

I was born and raised in Naples and still spend a part of each year there. Like most Neapolitans I know—and not just those who have left—I have a conflicted relationship with my hometown. Many of us are the city's harshest critics, and yet all of us are fiercely defensive when outsiders speak ill of it, as they often do. Naples's population density today is one of the highest in the Western world, and the city suffers from all the attendant difficulties of dirt, noise, chaos, and crime. Visitors tell us that Naples reminds them of Bombay or Cairo, and we want to remind them that we are Europeans and secretly wish someone would mistake Naples for Stockholm or Bern.

The image of Naples and more generally of the Italian South as at best the end of Europe is a very old one. This rhetoric was a staple of northern Italian patriotic writing in the nineteenth century. Northerners felt the duty to liberate their southern brethren from oppression and were confident that political unification would bring the South into modern Europe and eliminate southern ignorance, poverty, and superstition. In the eighteenth century the philosophers of the Neapolitan Enlightenment wrote that as soon as one exited the gates of Naples, one was among savages. Already in the sixteenth century, Jesuit priests spoke of the southern Italian countryside as "the Indies over here."

This rhetoric is alive and well today, in both popular and scholarly texts. The 1980s English-language Michelin guide to Naples opened by describing Neapolitans as small, dark, friendly, and superstitious. A French historian recently argued that the study of southern Italy requires the same mental tools applied to the study of populations entirely alien to European and modern realities. Yet the identity of the Italian South, and its place in the Western imagination, has always been more nuanced than this common rhetoric indicates, and here is one root of the uneasiness we contemporary Neapolitans feel about our homeland.

Southern Italy was the cradle of early civilization in the western Mediterranean, and significant and beautiful ancient sites still dot the region. Medieval Palermo was one of Europe's wealthiest and most splendid cities. The University of Naples is old and renowned, and the city was one of the largest and most important in Europe from the fifteenth through the nineteenth century. It is difficult to understand European music or art in the seventeenth and eighteenth centuries without considering those produced in Naples. An eighteenth-century gentleman's education was not complete without a prolonged stay in the Italian South, where nature and history taught him the essence of being a cultivated European. In the early twentieth century, Benedetto Croce—passionately attached to his home city—was one of Europe's leading intellectuals, completing a list of great Neapolitan philosophers that begins with Thomas Aquinas.

It is this contradiction—between the centrality of the Italian South to European life and culture on the one hand and the many elements of its distance from what Europeans have long regarded as modern (in economic, social, political, and spiritual terms) on the other— that I believe makes natives and visitors ambivalent in their feelings about the region. In a sense Naples and the South have always been both deeply of Europe and at the same time outside of it.

In late spring of 2003, as I worked on this book and reflected on these themes, the contradictory images of Naples appeared in my daily papers. On May 17, in the *Washington Post*, reporter Daniel Williams wrote of a recent garbage collection strike that was filling Naples with chaos and bad smells. It was a classic, frustrating version of the bad side of the story: crime networks, corrupt or inefficient government, dirt, decay, and a big photo of piles of garbage. Less than a month later, in the travel section of the *New York Times*, the novelist Francine Prose wrote a long article about Naples: after the inevitable mention of the colorful street life and the great food, she focused on the beautiful art, architecture, and archeology found in the city's museums and churches. She left no doubt that she was describing a great European city. As I prepared to review the proofs for this book at the end of 2004, the cycle of good and bad images of the city continued: a spate of gang killings and a great exhibition of Caravaggio's late works brought yet again the attention of the international media to Naples. My hope in the pages that follow is to shed some light on both images, and on the realities behind them.

I am grateful to the staff of the Sezione Napoletana of the Biblioteca Nazionale di Napoli, of the Biblioteca della Società Napoletana di Storia Patria, of Georgetown's Lauinger Library (especially the Inter-Library Loan office), and of the Library of Congress's Rare Book Collection. The Graduate School at Georgetown helped defray the costs of illustrations. Michael Kazin and Aviel Roshwald first suggested that I write an overview of southern Italian history for a general audience. Many colleagues encouraged me and offered useful suggestions when I presented excerpts to our department. My chair, John Tutino, was enthusiastic about the project (and promised to buy a copy of the book). Alane Salierno Mason of W. W. Norton has accompanied the project since its start; though I am not sure that I ever learned to "think like my editor," I hope she is not unhappy with the result of my and her efforts.

Several friends read various parts of the manuscript and gave me the benefit of their comments and corrections. For their help and friendship I am very grateful to Larry Cohen, Thomas Cole and Carol Hartley, Bertrand Forclaz, Gregor Kalas, Josiah Osgood, Silvana Patriarca, Ugo Piomelli, Jeffrey Richter, Gaetano Sabatini, Richard Stites, Wendy Thompson, and especially John McNeill. I began work on this project in the lovely setting of Georgetown's center in Fiesole, where I enjoyed the stimulating company of Marcello Fantoni, Kate Magovern, and the other colleagues and staff members. Bonita Billman, Gregor Kalas, and Thomas Willette helped me to find and choose illustrations. I am also grateful to Trevor Burnard and Deborah Morgan, Alessandra Galizzi, Alison Games, Amy Leonard, Luigina Mattioli, Marco Moracci and Maria Adele Scaramella, Patrick O'Malley, Adam Rothman, Jordan Sand, Francesca Santovetti and David Gillerman, and Paul Young for their friendly support. My family in Naples and Rome were always interested and helpful.

I dedicate this book to my favorite Neapolitan, my mother.

~ Chapter I ~

Where the Romans Met the Greeks
The Italian South in Antiquity

The vast side of the Euboean rock opens up and forms a cave;
one hundred large openings, one hundred doors lead to it,
from it flow out as many voices, the Sybil's responses.

Virgil, *Aeneid*, VI.42–44

*A*t the high point of Roman civilization, in the late first century BC, the great poet Virgil immortalized in his *Aeneid* the heroic journey of Aeneas from Troy to Italy, where his descendants would found Rome, the city destined to universal empire. The first half of the epic follows Aeneas's travels, while the second narrates his struggles once he has reached central Italy. Aeneas sails to Sicily and—after a romantic interlude in Carthage with Queen Dido—up the Italian coast to Latium, the future site of Rome. The story is tightly bound with southern Italy, in particular with Sicily and the Bay of Naples.

The monsters Scylla and Charybdis, perched at the treacherous strait between Sicily and southern Italy, force the Trojans to circumnavigate the island. In Sicily Aeneas's father dies and receives splendid funeral rites. On the island—under the great volcano Aetna—the Trojans also encounter the Cyclops Polyphemus, only recently blinded by Ulysses during his own troubled Sicilian travels. Several of Aeneas's companions—Palinurus, Misenus, Caieta—die during the trip along the Italian coast and give their names to promontories and cities. In Cumae, just north of the Bay of Naples, the Trojans honor Apollo at the temple built by Daedalus. It is also there that Aeneas consults the famous Sybil, who accompanies him on his visit to the

11

underworld—which they access through nearby Lake Avernus—where Aeneas learns of Rome's imperial future.

By Virgil's time, all of southern Italy had been ruled by Rome for about two centuries, and the elite Romans who supported and read Virgil were all very familiar with the region, and especially with the Bay of Naples. For well over a century before Virgil wrote, rich and educated Romans had built themselves elegant residences around the bay. At the start of the second century, one of the first recorded Roman estates in the area belonged to Scipio Africanus, the winner of the Second Punic War. Later in the century Cornelia, the mother of the famous Gracchi brothers whose demands for land redistribution initiated the slow demise of the Roman Republic, lived in the area after her sons' deaths. The dictator Sulla, who ruled the Roman Republic mercilessly after a bloody civil war, retired to the area after relinquishing power in 79 BC. Other owners of villas in the area included all the protagonists of the struggles that ended the Roman Republic: Julius Caesar, his main rival Pompey, and the great orator and politician Cicero, who owned three villas in what he called "the bay of luxury."

In the next generation, Virgil himself wrote his *Georgics* in Naples and was buried just outside the city; the spot believed to be his tomb has been an attraction for visitors ever since. Under Augustus, Virgil's patron and Rome's first emperor, the Roman fleet had one of its greatest ports in Misenum, just a few kilometers south of Cumae (near what is today NATO's largest Mediterranean naval base). Augustus owned villas in Baia, Sorrento, and near Naples, and he sponsored numerous building projects in the area, including a new aqueduct. The area was dotted with lavish Roman villas and prosperous cities well into the imperial age. Capua and Pozzuoli had the two largest amphitheaters in Italy after Rome's own Coliseum. Pozzuoli became the largest imperial harbor for the crucial trade between Italy and Egypt: most of the grains that kept the Roman populace fed and subdued passed through it, as did merchants from across the eastern Mediterranean.

All early emperors spent time in the area. Tiberius ruled the Roman world from his villa in Capri, and from its spectacular cliffs he had his opponents flung into the abyss. Caligula built a bridge of ships between Bacoli and Pozzuoli; Domitian, a road and arch nearby; and, most infamously, Nero had his mother Agrippina murdered on the beach at Baia. In AD 64 Nero also made his first public stage appearance as a musician in Naples; the Greek culture of the city made it the ideal setting for such an unusual performance, one that deeply shocked Roman traditionalists who regarded music and the stage as effeminate and unworthy pursuits. Imperial attention continued in later centuries, and the emperor Hadrian died in the imperial villa in Baia in 138.

The Romans were delighted by the area's great beauty and interesting natural phenomena. Virgil's contemporary Horace wrote that "no bay in the world outshines lovely Baia." Local food was equally delicious, especially the famous shellfish of the Bay of Naples and the area's wines. The peculiar volcanic features fascinated the ancients even before the terrifying eruption of Vesuvius in AD 79 that destroyed Pompeii and Herculaneum. Thanks to volcanic activity, the Bay of Naples also offered celebrated thermal baths: the ones at Baia were especially famous for their curative powers (as well as for the naughty behavior apparently rampant there) and made this little town the main vacation resort of Augustan Rome. Spas were almost as common in the area as villas (today a famous spa operates in Castellammare, near ancient Stabiae).

The Roman elites had other reasons to favor the region. Southern Italy was where the Romans first encountered Greek life and culture. The area had attracted the Greeks since roughly the time of Rome's legendary foundation. The entire Mediterranean, with its limited tides, is generally a friendly sea to sailors, and the Ionian Sea, which links southern Italy to Greece, is especially conducive to navigation thanks to its usually quiet waters. Colonists from numerous Greek cities thus reached southern Italian shores easily when, in the mid-eighth century, overpopulation and social and cultural changes began to push them beyond their peninsula. The entire region indeed became known in antiquity as Magna Graecia, or Greater Greece. The Greeks brought with them their quintessentially urban culture.

Greek cities flourished in Sicily and the continental South. Cumae (the first Greek city on the Italian mainland), Taranto, Reggio, Crotone, Sybaris (whose famously decadent inhabitants made their city's name proverbial), Catania, Taormina, Agrigento (which the poet Pindar called the most beautiful city inhabited by mortals)—all grew as rich, powerful, and cultured as any city in Greece itself. Aeschylus performed in the same Syracuse theater where one can still attend ancient plays. By the end of the fifth century, during the Peloponnesian War, Syracuse even defeated an Athenian invasion and destroyed Athens's dreams of hegemony over the Greek world. The historian Plutarch relates that the Syracusans—though they locked most prisoners in the dreaded caves outside their city—spared Athenian prisoners who could recite the verses of Euripides, of which the Syracusans were especially fond. In the late eighth century the Cumans established the first settlement in Naples, then called Parthenope. Naples itself was founded in 474 BC down the hill from Parthenope and took its name from its proximity to the older site (Neapolis, or New City, was its Greek name).

In Sicily the Greeks initially met the resistance of native farmers who did not know the iron tools and weapons by then familiar to the Greeks. But the Greeks were not the only ones attracted to the Italian and Sicilian shores. Carthage—the Phoenician city of Dido in northern Africa (near today's Tunis)—developed its own colonies in western Sicily. There the Carthaginians founded Palermo, also in the eighth century BC. Carthaginian Palermo—whose Greek name Panormos means "all harbor"—became as prosperous a trading center as any of its Greek rivals. Sicily, with its good waters and natural harbors, and its fertile land for pastures, wheat, wine, and olives, was the object of great conflict between Greeks, Carthaginians, and Etruscans for five centuries. As late as the fourth century, Greek cities prospered in spite of these conflicts, and they fought valiantly against Carthaginians and Romans. During the third century, however, the entire region gradually fell under Rome's dominion, as Rome conquered first its Italian neighbors and then the Greek and Carthaginian areas. In fact, Sicily became the first Roman "province"—a territory ruled by administrative institutions newly developed by the rising Republic.

The Roman conquest did not destroy the area's prosperity or its civilization. Southern Italy continued to be one of the most urbanized areas of the western Roman world well into the imperial age. To the Roman elites, southern Italy appeared to offer the pinnacle of Greek civilization in a gorgeous natural setting. It was a land of wealth, leisure, and style. In the first century BC, Cicero still described Syracuse as "the largest of all Greek cities, and the most beautiful of all cities. . . . It is both strong by its natural situation and striking to behold, from whatever side it is approached, whether by land or sea." Naples remained Greek in language, culture, and style of life into the third century. Most ancient inscriptions from the area are in Greek, and Greek scholars crowded the city. Roman authors typically referred to Naples as "leisurely" and "learned," to reflect what were, to them, fundamentally Greek features.

The southern population was concentrated on the coasts, and rural and inland areas were often poor and isolated. The urban culture and commercial vocation of the coastal centers of southern Italy became perhaps the region's first common denominators. Communication between various areas of the South was always much easier by sea than by the arduous inland routes. In later centuries, other seafaring urban civilizations—the Arabs and the Byzantines—would also be attracted to southern Italy and leave their own legacies there.

The geographic location of the South—so central to all Mediterranean routes—was a primary element of its appeal to ancient cultures. Though southern plains are few and concentrated near the coasts, they are fertile. The Romans called the plain around Naples "happy Campania" because of its fecundity: the lava from Vesuvius, however destructive at times, enriched the soil for agriculture and viticulture. Much of the landscape and coasts are similar to Greece's own, with rocky shores, deep waters, and hilly or mountainous inland regions. Rivers are relatively few and small, compared to central and northern Italy, though many southern rivers used to be navigable before modern deforestation and soil erosion. As in Greece, no area of the South and Sicily is very far from the sea, so the region has little of the harshness of more continental climates.

The patterns of seasons are also similar to Greece's and fairly stable. The climate is generally warm and mild. Winter can be harsh but it is brief and rarely very cold; snow is unusual and has a limited impact on economic activities. The infrequency of ground frost allows the olive tree to thrive. On the other hand, fall and winter rains can be torrential and damage agriculture, and rural areas of the South are often subject to landslides. Spring is beautiful, with lush natural flowers and colors: the broom—a wild shrub that blooms in May and early June—covers many hills and the slopes of Vesuvius with its bright yellow flowers. The summer is hot, long, and largely rainless: temperatures often reach the thirties Celsius, and the hot afternoons make the traditional siesta almost a necessity. This affects work and social patterns, as early morning and evening hours are common for physical labor, and meals and social life are pushed later into the cooler night.

The cuisine of the Italian South is across the globe associated with pasta, tomatoes, and pizza. Yet all these are relatively recent immigrants to the region. Even the prickly pear, which today grows wild and seems, with its jagged branches, so characteristic of the southern landscape, thriving even on Aetna's fiery slopes, came from America not so long ago (its Italian name indeed means "Indian fig," after the "Indies" explored by Columbus). The eucalyptus and palm trees and the bougainvillea, nearly ubiquitous today in the southern countryside, are similarly recent arrivals. On the other hand, the landscape the ancients saw was rich in other resources we have lost: the once famously abundant fish—the Phoenicians began tuna fishing in Sicily—is today much reduced, and the great forests that covered both Sicily and the continental South have long disappeared, with all the attendant environmental consequences. Continuity is represented by the ever-present olive tree and vineyards, and by a few typical southern fruits that have been around since antiquity, such as the sweet medlar in late spring and the fig in late summer.

Christianity began its victorious march through the ancient world in the cities of the Roman empire in the eastern Mediterranean. It spread to the western regions of the empire following the same trade currents that advanced all ancient civilizations, and it entered southern Italy in the first century AD. The spread of Christianity was closely associated with the urban world. The term "pagans" could designate villagers, since the rural areas persisted in practicing the old religion. As southern Italy was the most urbanized region in the western Mediterranean, the new religion quickly took root there, and soon the first dioceses emerged. Southern Italy housed some of the earliest monasteries of western Christianity, which served as outposts of urban, Christian civilization in the countryside. In the late centuries of the Roman empire, the cities of southern Italy and Sicily continued to be Greek in culture and often language, and Christian in religion.

Many also housed communities of Jews displaced by the diaspora of the first century AD. The rural areas remained largely pagan and were increasingly poor and remote from the declining trade economy of late antiquity.

All of Italy suffered terribly in the chaos and warfare that accompanied the dissolution of Rome's rule in the West and continued through much of the fifth and sixth centuries. Different Germanic peoples fought each other in and over Italy. In the sixth century the eastern empire under Justinian (ruled 527–65) attempted to reestablish control over Italy and the western Mediterranean. This resulted in long wars, religious divisions, economic catastrophe, and a steep population decline, caused also by deadly epidemics. The long wars over Italy between Justinian's forces and the Goths were especially destructive: the historian Procopius mentions not only the agricultural wealth of Sicily and the lively economy of Naples, where Syrians and Jews lived and traded, but also the pillaging and devastation wrought by Justinian's forces and their Gothic opponents. Malaria spread in the southern lowlands in the wake of warfare and of the forest clearing long practiced by both Greeks and Romans. Churches also suffered and numerous dioceses and monasteries disappeared.

For the first time since the Roman conquest, the Italian peninsula fragmented politically. By the late sixth century the eastern empire (by now historians call it the Byzantine empire) maintained control over the major islands, most coastal areas, and large urban centers like Rome, Naples, Bari, and Venice; Byzantine power revived the Greek language in Naples and other southern cities. The North and most central inland regions of the peninsula formed a kingdom ruled by the Lombards, Germanic invaders who had come into Italy in 568; separate Lombard principalities ruled the inland mountainous parts of the South.

In the seventh century a slow economic and demographic recovery began. This gradual revival of population and prosperity renewed the traditional vocation of southern Italy as an urban, commercial, and Christian region. Salerno became the capital of an autonomous Lombard principality and was the only significant coastal and commercial center controlled by the Lombards. Naples, Amalfi, Bari, and other cities on both the Tyrrhenian and Adriatic coasts developed active trade economies and enjoyed varied levels of autonomy within the larger Byzantine world. Naples itself was ruled by independent Byzantine dukes since 763.

The economic revival accompanied the renewal of Christian institutions, with new monasteries and dioceses; Christian missionaries attempted to establish their religion in the southern countryside, where paganism had largely survived. Latin and Greek clerics and rites operated side by side, while Rome and Constantinople slowly drifted away from each other in both theological and ecclesiastical matters. In the tenth century the papacy raised Naples and several other southern bishoprics to the status of archdioceses.

In the ninth century the South also came within the sphere of influence and power of Arabic culture. The Arab conquest of Sicily was part of the great sweep of the southern Mediterranean, which from the mid-seventh to the mid-ninth century brought the Arabs and their new religion from the Middle East through North Africa to Spain. The Arab invasion of Sicily began in 827, and in 831 Arab forces conquered Palermo, which became their capital. War with the Byzantines on the island continued for a half-century, until the siege and capture of Syracuse in 878. After the fall of Syracuse, the local monk Theodosius was taken with other captives to Palermo, a city "most famous and most populous." There he met Christians and Muslims, and prisoners of all nations and faiths: "at our entry into the city, we found an immense population of citizens and foreigners. [Palermo] was not inferior to its fame or to our expectations." Over the following century and a half, Arab forces continued to attack, and occasionally occupy, various coastal areas of the continental South.

The Arabs revived the Sicilian economy, which had suffered under heavy Byzantine taxation, just as they revived the economy of the Iberian Peninsula. The new rulers developed irrigation and agriculture on the island, and advanced fishing, mining, and the production of eastern crops such as cotton, sugar cane, rice, citrus fruits, and silk, some of which were grown on plantations in Sicily's interior. These plantations were staffed primarily through the lively slave trade that had crisscrossed the Mediterranean since antiquity. Sicily developed trade links that spanned from Iberia to Egypt, which it maintained even after local emirs took over rule of the island from the distant Baghdad caliphs. Arab Sicily's gold coins circulated across the Christian South of Italy. As they did in Iberia, the Arab rulers of Sicily allowed their new Jewish and Christian subjects to practice their own religions peacefully. Muslim scholars, poets, and musicians flourished in Sicily.

In the 970s the Baghdad merchant Ibn Hawqal visited Palermo. He marveled at its harbors, mills, orchards, gardens, rivers, and canals. He admired its numerous markets and lively economy, and counted 150 butcher shops and over 300 mosques. These served the religious needs of Palermo's estimated 250,000 inhabitants, and they also "serve[d] as meeting-places for the scholars of the country, who gather[ed] there to share their knowledge and augment it." In the largest mosque, a converted church, Ibn Hawqal claimed that local Christians honored a coffin suspended from the ceiling, which they held to contain the body of Aristotle, and that these Christians believed that by praying to the philosopher they could obtain rain and peace. Ibn Hawqal did criticize one feature of Palermo's life: its inhabitants ate "too many raw onions." This "has corrupted their intelligence, altered their brains, coarsened their senses, changed their faculties, narrowed their spirits, spoiled the tint of their faces and altogether changed their temperament." Ibn Hawqal's account shows that, in spite of this deplorable diet, Arab Palermo was one of the wealthiest and largest European cities of the time. He compared its buildings and splendor favorably even to Cordoba's, then the most famous Islamic city in Europe.

Thus, the ninth and tenth centuries confirmed yet another traditional feature of the Italian South: its rich diversity of peoples and cultures. Like their ancient counterparts, both the Byzantines and the Arabs offered southern Italy the benefits of commercial, diverse, and reasonably tolerant empires and cultures, with commercial and cultural links that extended very widely. Though the Byzantines had surrendered Egypt and Syria to the Arabs in the seventh century, their empire still controlled the Balkans and Anatolia. Constantinople also exerted strong cultural and economic influence all the way to Russia over Slavic peoples whom Byzantine missionaries were converting to Greek Christianity. The great religions, languages, and ethnic groups of the early medieval Mediterranean flourished in the Italian South, in relative mutual tolerance and cooperation. A varied population practiced Islam, Judaism, and Christianity in its western and eastern forms, and spoke Arabic, Greek, Latin, the Germanic language of the

Lombards, and early forms of an Italian vernacular. In these same centuries northern Italy was much less diverse: its religion was almost exclusively western Christianity, and the growing tensions between the papacy and the newly formed German empire (later to be known as the Holy Roman empire) created a tense political context that limited contacts between diverse groups. Though both the papacy and the German empire claimed some authority over the South, they were rarely able to exercise significant influence in the region.

At the end of the first millennium, however, the diversity and prosperity of the Italian South were largely limited to its urban, coastal areas. Calabria, Abruzzo, and most inner regions—largely mountainous, difficult to reach, and ungenerous to agricultural efforts—remained poor, rural, and culturally and religiously isolated. The few existing inland towns remained quite different from the dynamic centers on the coasts. They resembled large villages, with little of the commercial vitality, cultural diversity, and varied activities and opportunities of the coastal cities, a difference that one can observe to this day.

This strong contrast between the urban and rural worlds is a prominent element of all Italian history since antiquity, and it was especially conspicuous in the early medieval South. Later, the growth of a strong central state and the spread of the feudal system further reinforced this contrast and reversed the traditional power relations between the two worlds.

Map of Sicily and of the continental South of Italy

~ Chapter II ~

From the Terror of the World to the Wonder of the World
The Kings Who Created the Italian South

This is the light of the great Constance
who by the second blast of Swabia
bore the third and final power.

Dante, *Paradiso*, 3.118–20

In 1016 forty Norman men traveled on pilgrimage to a shrine in Puglia, on the southern Adriatic coast of Italy. While they were in the area, they helped the Lombard prince of Salerno fight the Arabs "not for price of money," wrote Amato of Montecassino, their main historian, but "for the love of God." They liked the place and called on others to join them in the South "for the wealth that was there." They sent home "citrus, almonds, nuts" and urged their fellow Normans to "come to the land that brings forth milk, honey, and so many beautiful things."

The Normans or Northmen, Vikings by origin, had settled in northwestern France in the ninth century and in 912 received recognition of their rule in what we still call Normandy from the king of France. They had by then become Christians, developed feudal institutions, and acquired a reputation for skill in warfare. The warlike pilgrims who came to Puglia in 1016 were part of a vast network. Throughout the eleventh century, groups of Normans traveled to Spain, Italy, Constantinople, and the Levant "to be knightly soldiers"; their greatest success was the invasion of England under William the Conqueror in 1066.

The Normans who came to Puglia entered a world rich not only in milk and honey, but also in diverse people. Arabs, Italians, Greeks, Jews, and Lombards spoke different languages, followed different laws, obeyed different rulers, but lived in relative peace with each other. Cities and coasts participated in both the Byzantine and the Arab craft and trade networks that intersected and spanned the Mediterranean world. When the Normans arrived, as the great eighteenth-century historian Edward Gibbon put it, "the three great nations of the world, the Greeks, the Saracens, and the Franks, encountered each other on the theatre of Italy." From this encounter, the Normans would emerge triumphant.

Their victory was part of a much broader historical change. At the turn of the second millennium western Europe was poorer, weaker, and less culturally advanced than the Byzantine and Arab worlds. Within two centuries or so a new balance of power emerged. The boundaries of western Latin Christendom expanded. The Catholic "Reconquest" of Spain from the Arabs, the Crusades and the establishment of Catholic states in the Balkans and the Levant, the German expansion into eastern Europe, and the Norman creation of a united Catholic kingdom in southern Italy were all elements in this aggressive expansion of western Europe's power, influence, and religion.

After the initial forty pilgrims, more Normans came to Italy to fight for whoever paid them best. This was not the migration of an entire people: almost all who came were men capable of military action. The Normans brought their own language, ideas, and traditions to southern Italy, and these had long-term effects in their new home, but some of the men went back, some moved on to other places, and most of those who stayed married local women and were integrated into local society. Quickly, however, the Normans became protagonists of southern history. In 1030 the Norman knight Rainulf became count of Aversa, near Naples. In 1041 Norman fighters took control of the city of Melfi, in Basilicata, which became their main base of independent power. The next year, since they "did not want any leader of another people or lineage," the Melfi Normans chose as their leader "Iron-Arm" William Altavilla (the Italianized version of the French name Hauteville), "a man most valiant in arms, adorned of all good customs, and handsome, and noble, and young." This accelerated the transformation of the Normans from bands of mercenaries to an autonomous power group with its own interests and leadership.

William was one of a dozen sons of a poor Norman knight. Several brothers followed in his footsteps to seek fortune in the land of milk and honey, including Robert, called Guiscard, or "clever," who arrived around 1046. Robert quickly rose to become the Normans' leader. In the 1050s the Normans' fortunes increased dramatically. In 1053 they defeated an invasion of their territory organized by the pope. The following year, when the pope and the patriarch of Constantinople excommunicated each other, the Catholic and Orthodox Churches finally separated, and the pope began to appreciate potential Norman support against the Byzantines in the South. In 1059, after Robert's forces took the city of Reggio, the pope granted him the title of duke of Calabria and Puglia, elevating Robert to the highest status among his people and recognizing him as a major power in the southern regions.

Robert was no longer a warlord; he was now a prince with no secular superior. This enhanced his feudal and political authority, which resulted in greater military power. He swore an oath to "be from this time forth faithful to the Roman Church," to "remain, insofar as it is in [his] power to be so, the ally of the holy Roman Church," and to pay an annual rent to the Church. These terms became the basis for the papal claim to overlordship of the southern monarchy.

By this time, Robert's youngest brother, Roger, had also come to the South, and the two began to plan an attack on Sicily. In the mid-eleventh century Muslim Sicily—like Muslim Iberia—broke down into smaller separate territories, and in both areas this aided the aggressive plans of neighboring Christian powers. In 1061 the Normans launched an expedition that exploited Arab divisions on the island. The Sicilian adventure gave Roger and Robert a propaganda tool in the Christian world. Roger in particular, wrote the chronicler Malaterra, "always greedy for domination . . . saw [in Sicily] two benefits for himself, namely to soul and body, if he returned to godly worship a land devoted to idols, and if he possessed the fruits and income of this land, which a people inimical to God had usurped for themselves, and which he would spend in the service of God."

Malaterra claimed that St. George fought with the Normans. The forces of Robert and Roger battled effectively for several years on multiple fronts, on the island and the mainland. In April 1071, Robert's forces conquered Bari, the last remaining Byzantine outpost in Italy. The Normans thus inflicted the first of two powerful blows the Byzantines experienced that year: in August their defeat at Manzikert by the Turks would cost the Byzantines most of Anatolia, considerably shrinking their empire. On the Sicilian front, in January 1072 the Normans, led by both brothers, took Palermo "and"—in the words of Amato—"the multitude of the dead covered the earth."

Amato here exaggerates greatly, since the Normans proved actually relatively lenient with Palermo. Then home to about 250,000 people, Palermo was a commercial hub and one of the largest and richest cities in the Mediterranean, still as dynamic and splendid as when Ibn Hawqal visited a century earlier. Its fall shocked Muslims and made the Normans formidable across the Mediterranean. Robert had the Palermo cathedral reconsecrated, to the accompaniment, according to a chronicler, of angels' voices and divine light, and then left Sicilian affairs mostly in the hands of his brother Roger, who from his Sicilian title came to be known as the "Great Count."

In 1076 Robert also took Salerno, the last major city under Lombard rule and another commercial hub: "an illustrious city"—wrote Gibbon—"in which the men were honest and the women beautiful." Within a few years the Normans had conquered the major cities of the South and soundly defeated the three groups that had ruled the region for centuries: the Byzantines, the Arabs, and the Lombards. By the time of Robert's death in 1085 and Roger's in 1101, no serious rival to Norman power remained. In the early twelfth century the few surviving Lombard states and autonomous towns also came under Norman control.

Robert and Roger astonished contemporaries. Dante, not an easy man to please, later placed Robert among the great rulers in *Paradiso* 18. Robert's own epitaph described him as "the terror of the world." Historians from their own lands were effusive with praise of the two leaders. Amato wrote that "[Robert] surpassed all others in piety . . . was humble . . . judged justly all people who had affairs with him, and, while he judged by right and by justice, he also practiced mercy and pity . . . he feared Christ and those who are his servants." One special point of praise was the two Normans' skill away from the battlefield. The historian and bishop Romualdo wrote that Robert "was adorned no less with counsel than with strength," and lauded Roger as "nourisher of the poor, pious, generous with alms." Malaterra describes Roger as "a most handsome youth, tall in stature, elegant of body, most effective in speech, sharp in counsel, provident in attending to what needed to be done, cheerful and affable to all, physically strong, fierce in soldiering."

Opponents were less kind: a German writer referred to the Normans as "the most foul-smelling rubbish in the world." The Byzantine princess and historian Anna Comnena, who witnessed the havoc the Normans caused in her father's dominions, also regarded the Normans as uncouth, dangerous upstarts. Her portrait of "that braggart Robert" includes grudging admiration: "notorious for his power-lust, born in Normandy, but nursed and nourished by manifold Evil . . . of obscure origin, with an overbearing character and a thoroughly villainous mind; he was a brave fighter, very cunning in his assaults on the wealth and power of great men; in achieving his aims absolutely inexorable, diverting criticism by incontrovertible argument . . . admirably well-proportioned and elegant . . . from head to foot the man was graceful . . . [his] bellow, so they say, put tens of thousands to flight." When marking his death, Anna acknowledged "that Robert's manliness, his marvelous skill in war and his steadfast spirit are universally recognized. He was an adversary not readily vanquished, a very tough enemy who was more courageous than ever in the hour of defeat."

Even before their control of southern Italy was complete, the Normans extended their influence farther. Their strength came from their warring vocation, which grew stronger with each success. The first Normans were mercenaries; their early victories and then the triumphs under Robert and Roger attracted to the South from France a steady supply of fighters seeking targets for their greed and bravery. Robert attacked the Byzantines in the Balkans and acquired territory in Albania and Greece, where he died. His son Bohemond, after making war on the Byzantines (Anna Comnena said father and son were like "caterpillars and locusts"), participated in the First Crusade (1096–99) and acquired the principality of Antioch. His descendants ruled parts of the Levant until the thirteenth century. Roger and his successors launched attacks on North Africa from Sicily, and the Normans took Malta in 1091.

Roger completed the conquest of Sicily in 1091 and dealt tolerantly with Muslims and Greeks, founding new Greek monasteries and allowing the free practice of Islam, especially in western Sicily, where Muslims were most numerous. Arabic remained one of the languages of Roger's government, Islamic law continued to apply to Muslims, and coins carried Arabic inscriptions. But Roger also placed the Greek clergy under the jurisdiction of the Catholic hierarchy, and settled Catholic bishops and monasteries across the island. In the 1090s he provided crucial support to Pope Urban II (ruled 1088–99) in the latter's struggle against the Holy Roman emperor. In 1098 the pope granted Roger large powers over Church appointments in Sicily, recognizing— Malaterra said—how Roger had "greatly expanded the Church of God in the land of the Saracens."

The Great Count achieved much, but he had reason to fear for the future: at the age of about sixty he had no surviving legitimate son, though he had sired over a dozen children. His third wife, Adelaide of Montferrat, daughter of a northern Italian prince, finally provided him with an heir, also named Roger, who was only six years old when the Great Count died, at the age of about seventy. Adelaide ruled as regent for Roger II, and it was she who settled the court in Palermo, in part to diminish the influence of her Norman in-laws, who lived primarily on the continent. Her son thus grew up surrounded by Arabs, Greeks, and Italians and acquired the cosmopolitan outlook he would display in his government.

When Roger II came of age, Adelaide accepted an offer of marriage from King Baldwin, who ruled the Christian Kingdom of Jerusalem formed after the First Crusade. Baldwin craved Adelaide's rich dowry and the military support of the Sicilian Normans. Her arrival in Jerusalem was splendid, as a chronicler reported: she came with one thousand soldiers and "seven ships laden with gold, silver, royal purple cloth and great quantities of precious stones and magnificent robes." The marriage proved unhappy, however, and in 1117 Adelaide returned to her son's island, to die the next year. But the Normans gained a claim to the crown of Jerusalem that would later serve their interests in the Levant.

In the 1110s and 1120s Roger II gradually became the indisputable leader of all Normans in the South, taking over the lands of other Norman princes and the few remaining non-Norman territories. Robert Guiscard's heirs proved no match for their Sicilian cousin. Roger began to seek a way to settle his status not only as the sole Norman leader but also as the ruler of a vast and now united territory in both Sicily and the mainland. The political principles of Christian Europe at this time granted limited legitimacy to upstarts like Roger and his family. Sovereignty could not simply be established by force; to guarantee both stability and succession, it needed the legality that came with tradition and recognition by other powers. The highest legitimacy came through the sacredness associated with Christian monarchy.

Roger therefore turned to the papacy, which had already provided the Normans with what formal title to rule they enjoyed. The papacy enjoyed great moral and spiritual authority, and popes were eager to enhance their political influence as well. Popes also needed allies in the papacy's various struggles and whenever the papal office itself became the object of dispute. Roger exploited one such moment, when two papal claimants clamored for the recognition of Christian princes. In 1130 Roger obtained from Anacletus II the title of king of a newly proclaimed Kingdom of Sicily. On Christmas Day in 1130, a papal representative anointed Roger with consecrated oil in the Palermo cathedral, giving the new king a divinely sanctioned legitimacy. The choice of coronation day echoed both Charlemagne, who had been crowned emperor on Christmas Day in 800, and Roger's Norman counterpart, William the Conqueror, crowned king of England on Christmas Day in 1066.

A dubious pope and a wholly new kingdom made Roger's move a bold but shaky one. Alexander of Telese—Roger II's main historian—tried to strengthen Roger's status by claiming that the kingship restored a prior Sicilian monarchy, and ascribed the initiative to Roger's clerics and barons, but the weaknesses of the situation remained. The coronation was in any case splendid, and at the ensuing banquet "nothing was served except in dishes or cups of gold or silver . . . even the waiters wore silk clothes."

Consolidating Roger's power on the mainland took further effort. By 1139 he defeated the forces of Pope Innocent II (ruled 1130–43) and secured the latter's recognition of his status as king. The Kingdom of Sicily was there to stay. It represented a remarkable accomplishment for a band of mercenaries to build, out of a region characterized by long-standing political, religious, and cultural fragmentation, a large new monarchy that vied for preeminence with the papacy, Byzantium, the Holy Roman empire, and the Arab world. The unification of the South also altered the balance of power in medieval Italy. While the northern regions were fragmented politically and each area and city was torn internally by struggles between imperial and papal factions, Roger's kingdom was the only monarchy in Italy and by far the largest Italian state in area and population.

To contemporaries, Roger II's achievement seemed to surpass even his father's and uncle's. Like most Normans, he struck southerners by his imposing appearance, but they also admired his skills, moderation, and mind. The king, wrote Bishop Romualdo, "did not know how to be lazy in time of war or peace . . . he was tall of stature, corpulent, with a leonine face and somewhat hoarse voice, wise, provident, prudent, subtle of mind and great in counsel, he used his reason rather than his forces." Even the historian Falcandus, who despised his successors, presented Roger as the model they failed to follow: "he had a keen intellect and never lacked confidence in himself . . . the application of discretion restrained the impulses of his great spirit . . . it was not easy to judge whether he was wiser in speech or action . . . he made efforts to administer justice in its full rigor on the grounds that it was particularly necessary for a newly-established realm, and to exercise the options of peace and war by turns, with the result that he omitted nothing that virtue requires, and had no king or prince as his equal during his lifetime." An anonymous chronicler described the king in especially flowery language as "the greatest of men, loved and blessed by God . . . admiration of the world, splendor of all virtues." One of the many Arab scholars working for Roger concluded his portrait of the king by saying that "he is such a man that his dreams are worth more than the waking thoughts of ordinary mortals."

Roger II succeeded in both founding and governing his kingdom. Because his father had acquired the island by conquest, he had been able to claim for himself huge tracts of land, so the royal domain in

Sicily was especially rich. Roger II continued Sicily's traditional economic links. He entered commercial agreements with Egypt and
other Muslim states and enforced royal monopolies on Sicily's rich
tuna-fishing industry. His strong finances allowed him to mint gold
coins, even though the kingdom had no gold mines (gold came primarily from Muslim Africa in exchange for Sicily's grain). At the same
time, Sicily's population was not large, and unification under the
Normans resulted in some Arab emigration. Concern over the size of
the population was probably one reason for the king's tolerance of
his Muslim subjects. He and his successors also favored the immigration of Italians, especially from the more populous North. In 1147, a
Norman attack on Byzantine cities in Greece brought to Sicily numerous skilled silk workers. Sicilian agriculture continued to produce
high-quality grain, grapes, olives, and a variety of fruits, especially citrus. The commercial traditions of the southern coastal cities also
endured: a geographer writing under Roger II described Naples as "a
beautiful city, ancient, flourishing, peopled, and provided with markets where one can do useful transactions in all sorts of objects and
goods."

Roger II also built up the royal bureaucracy. In 1140 he issued the
first set of territorial laws for all his subjects. Separate laws applying
to different ethnic and religious groups continued to exist, but only
if not in conflict with new royal legislation. Roger drew his conception of royal power from Roman law, which—thanks mostly to the
Byzantine presence—had never declined in southern Italy as much as
in most of western Europe. In his laws, Roger emphasized the extent
and autonomy of royal authority: "to dispute [the king's] judgements,
decrees, deeds and plans, or [whether] someone whom he has chosen or appointed is worthy, is comparable to sacrilege." Roger's laws
also covered a variety of mundane topics, from a ban on prosecuting
children and madmen, to affirming a husband's right to cut off his
adulterous wife's nose. He divided the kingdom into three administrative areas, established central structures to supervise finance and
justice, and appointed delegates to govern the larger cities. The
strength of the kingdom appears also in the aggressive expansionist
policy pursued by the Norman kings, following in their ancestors'
footsteps: Roger II established control over a significant swath of the
North African coast—which his son lost by 1160—and the Normans
launched a number of expeditions to the Balkans.

The tight link between Norman authority in the South and papal support only became stronger with Roger's rise to kingly status. The medieval papacy claimed a general sovereignty over all Christian rulers, but this was officially far greater over the southern monarchy because papal recognition was the foundation of the Normans' ducal and royal titles. Several times in the late Middle Ages the papacy invoked its right to choose the ruler of Sicily and Naples, often succeeding at least in undermining the claims of those Rome opposed. The papacy remained a significant factor in the numerous changes in dynasty and control over the two areas well into the eighteenth century. Since the mid-eleventh century, it also controlled Benevento, inland from Naples. With brief exceptions, this old city, center of one of the richest and largest dioceses in Italy, remained a papal enclave within the kingdom until the nineteenth century, and offered refuge to bandits, exiles, and other opponents of whoever ruled the South.

On the other hand, the Normans were neither powerless nor unskilled in negotiating with Rome and in imposing their own will and needs. In particular, they were expert in exploiting the frequent crises in papal authority. In the eleventh and twelfth centuries, the struggles between Church reformers and their opponents, between rival aristocratic factions in Rome, and between the papacy and the German emperors who claimed dominion over all of Italy and superiority of their office to the pope's led to many disputed papal elections. The 1130 royal coronation was only the most brilliant example of how the Normans were able to extract concessions from the papacy at the time of one such disputed election.

Between 1139 and 1156 a series of agreements with the papacy gave Roger control of the border region of Abruzzo and settled the borders of the kingdom with the papal state, which then remained unchanged for seven centuries. Even earlier the Normans had been appointed papal legates: this privilege, granted in 1098, gave the Normans and their successors extensive powers of appointment to Church positions and control over Church affairs and revenues that were quite rare in medieval Europe. In 1156 the papacy managed to limit the legateship to the island of Sicily alone, but it remained a significant element of royal power throughout the existence of the kingdom.

Most of the time the relationship between the papacy and the Normans was mutually beneficial. The greatest service the monarchy offered the Roman Church was support of clerical efforts to reduce the status of Greek Christianity in the South, which accompanied the Normans' anti-Byzantine ambitions in the East. Roger I had favored his Greek subjects, and Greek rites, clergy, and monasteries prospered across the South. But the severing of southern political ties to Constantinople, the increasing theological divisions between Catholicism and Orthodoxy, and Rome's growing assertiveness led to a shift in policy. By the end of Roger II's reign, and especially under his successors, the Latin rites and clergy became dominant. Through the fourteenth century, monastic establishments formed the main element in Church life, since the parish and diocesan systems were not yet fully developed, and the quality of the priests was often quite low, especially in rural areas. After the 1130s, many Greek monasteries closed, and no new ones were founded. On the other hand, the kings sponsored new foundations of Benedictine and other Catholic monasteries, often emanating from the old houses at Montecassino and Cava, the richest and most prestigious Catholic monastic centers in the South.

Yet the Norman kings remained committed to the diverse heritage of their kingdom. The region was at least as multireligious, multicultural, and multilingual as the Iberian Peninsula before the Catholic Reconquest. Jews, Muslims, Catholics, and Orthodox Christian subjects of the Normans spoke Arabic, Latin, French, Greek, and Italian to each other. Numerous Jewish communities flourished. Sicilian Jews were central to Mediterranean trade networks between the ninth and the twelfth centuries. As early as 984 there was a synagogue in Naples. When in the 1160s the Spanish Jew Benjamin of Tudela traveled through Sicily and the South, he visited numerous large and prosperous Jewish communities near Naples, in Puglia, and in Sicily, where Palermo's fifteen hundred Jews formed probably the largest community in Italy at that time. Jews in the South participated in all economic activities and did not play the particular role in moneylending that Jews were constrained to undertake in other places and times.

Muslims lived mostly in Sicily, where the Arabic language flourished. Though most were farmers, many also worked in cities as craftsmen. However, new population trends caused strains. The arrival of settlers from the mainland, necessary for Sicilian agriculture

but less accustomed to coexistence with Muslims, led to a deteriora-
tion of the relationship between Muslims and Christians on the
island. There was increased pressure from Christian authorities,
clergy, and neighbors to convert and assimilate. The broader Mediterranean religious climate was also turning more mutually hostile in
this age of Crusades. Especially after the first decade or so of the new
kingdom, the Normans grew worried about the Muslim presence.
Roger II himself—claimed Bishop Romualdo—late in his reign
"made every effort to convert Jews and Muslims to the faith of Christ,
and gave many gifts and goods to converts."

The kings continued in any case to protect religious minorities
because they feared the consequences of ethnic conflict and population loss. Religious minorities also often provided workers skilled in
particular crafts, and they usually paid special tributes that strengthened royal finances. Like many medieval Christian kings in Iberia, the
Normans thus attempted to temper popular hostility to minority
groups. Muslims in particular were never as much in danger as when
royal power was weak. In 1162, for instance, at a time of upheaval and
anti-Muslim riots, William I (ruled 1154–66) "sent officers to help
the Muslims and ordered the killing to stop," albeit in vain. When
William I died, Falcandus, who loathed the king, noted the mourning rituals of women, "especially the Muslim ones, whose grief for the
king's death was not feigned."

The diversity of Sicilian government, society, and life under the
Normans appears in many other ways. Roger II, like his father, kept a
cosmopolitan court and government. Even Bishop Romualdo noted
with praise that Roger "called wise men of various ranks and from different parts of the world to participate in his council." About three-
quarters of royal documents under Roger II were issued in Greek. The
court employed Muslim eunuchs and Arab cooks. Roger modeled
many of the institutions and practices of his administration on those
of Egypt, with which Sicily maintained a friendly relationship. As late
as the 1180s, though aware of the worsening situation for Muslims,
the Arab traveler Ibn Jubair visited mosques in Palermo and other
cities in western Sicily and noted that "the groups of Christians we
met [on the road to Palermo] greeted us first and treated us with
friendship. We noted such politeness and such courteous manners on
their part towards Muslims that they could seduce the spirit of the

ignorant." Ibn Jubair also noted that William II (ruled 1166–89) was "extremely trusting of Muslims, and reliant upon them in his affairs and in the most important of his concerns." Though most of these officials "[hid] their faith," they "[clung] to the law of Islam."

Cultural diversity endured even as conversion, emigration, and assimilation slowly shrank the size of religious minorities. Many Sicilian Christians continued to speak Arabic into the twelfth century. Ibn Jubair offers a fascinating glimpse of cultural continuities in his somewhat excited account of the Christmas ceremonies he witnessed in Palermo in 1184: "[T]he Christian women's dress in [Palermo] is the dress of Muslims; they are eloquent speakers of Arabic and cover themselves with veils. They go out at [Christmas] clothed in golden silk, covered in shining wraps, colorful veils and with light gilded sandals. They appear at their churches bearing all the finery of Muslim women in their attire, henna and perfume."

The titles of officials in Roger II's service reflect the different sources of Norman administration: from the Arabic emir (admiral) or cadi (judge), to the Greek logothete (secretary) or strategos (governor), to the Norman seneschal (judge) or camerleng (chamberlain), as well as numerous officials with Latin titles. The diwan was the Arabic name for the central offices and treasury; it is the root of the Italian and French words for border customs. The monarchy minted coins dated to the Hegira (Mohammed's flight from Mecca, which marks the beginning of the Islamic era). One of Roger's gold coins bore inscriptions in both Greek ("Jesus Christ conquers") and Arabic ("By grace of God"). A famous 1148 funerary inscription in the Palermo cathedral gives another flavor of Sicily's layered culture. It adorns the tomb of Anna, the mother of a Norman cleric. As expected given its location and purpose, the text contains Christian messages, but they are presented in four scripts and three languages: Greek, Latin, Arabic, and Arabic written in Hebrew characters (each dated according to its own religious calendar).

Ancient, Byzantine, and Arabic models also inspired royal patronage of art and culture. The Norman kings supported scholars from across the Mediterranean and sponsored Latin translations of Greek texts, including works by Plato, Aristotle, and Ptolemy. Al-Idrisi, an Arab geographer employed by Roger II, produced the so-called *Book of Roger*, a compilation of available knowledge about the world;

Roger had a huge silver disc (now lost) built to represent this knowledge. The kings were also great builders. Al-Idrisi wrote that
"[Palermo]'s buildings dazzle the eyes." New royal palaces with gardens, fountains, menageries of fish and animals, and exotic plants
were built around Palermo. In 1132 Roger II founded the Palatine
Chapel in Palermo, next to the apartments he had established in a
ninth-century Arab palace. The chapel served not only a liturgical
function but also as a royal hall, with a beautiful throne for the king
dominating the entrance wall.

   French and Sicilian masons built the chapel, Byzantine artists decorated it with splendid mosaics, and Arab craftsmen added an elaborate wood ceiling with pictorial decorations. The ceiling depicts
secular subjects, such as musicians, dancers, women, chess players,
and a crowned ruler, sitting cross-legged and wearing a caftan, which
probably depicts Roger himself. The images are accompanied by
inscriptions in Arabic celebrating the king's qualities. The chapel's
mosaics have Christian themes (with inscriptions in both Latin and
Greek), but in the palace apartments one also finds ornamental
motifs and depictions of animals, flowers, and trees in Islamic style.
These works in Palermo are among the most beautiful examples of
Byzantine mosaics. The same mix of cultural traditions appears in
Roger's mantle, a silk garment depicting fights between lions and
camels. The mantle (today in a Vienna museum) was produced in
1134 for the king by a royal workshop, bears an Arabic inscription,
and is dated to the Hegira.

   The Palatine Chapel was one of many new buildings that celebrated the dynasty, its new kingdom, and the skills of its artists. In
1131, on a site where supposedly he had landed after a storm, Roger
founded the grand church in Cefalù, east of Palermo, with its enormous mosaic of Christ the Creator. The church also has a wooden
ceiling with painted secular images of drinkers, musicians, and
hunters. It was here that Roger desired to be buried, in a huge sar-
cophagus made of porphyry, a material regarded as imperial since
antiquity. In 1174 his grandson William II founded the Benedictine
church and monastery at Monreale, just outside Palermo. Monreale,
endowed by the king with enormous estates and ecclesiastical authority, displays the largest mosaic decoration in Italy, with complex
cycles of Old and New Testament images and countless representa-

tions of saints. Although the style of the Monreale mosaics is primarily Byzantine, the inscriptions are in Latin, indicating the advancing Latinization of religious life under the later Norman rulers. The cloister next door features French decorations.

The final mosaic masterpiece of Norman Sicily is not a royal foundation but the Greek Orthodox church of St. Mary of the Admiral (the "Martorana"), founded in 1143 by George of Antioch. George was born of Syrian-Greek parents and for a while served the emir of Tunis. In 1112 he came to Palermo, where he entered Roger's service and took part in the king's African wars. By 1126 he was an admiral and in 1132 became the head of Roger's naval forces. He died in 1151. The most famous image in the Martorana is of Roger's coronation. The king stands almost even with Christ, whom he resembles, and is identified by an inscription in Greek characters. Ibn Jubair called the Martorana "the most beautiful monument in the world."

Under the Normans the southern landscape acquired features that are still apparent. In much of northern Italy, because of sharecropping and other land contracts, farms and homes were scattered in the countryside. In the South, on the other hand, villages developed on hilltops or mountains, where they were better protected from attackers (pirates or soldiers) and the malaria that lurked in the plains. This pattern was greatly reinforced by the vast estates that grew with the introduction of the feudal system. Feudal castles often became the core of villages and towns. To this day much of the southern countryside is marked by rare scattered farms and by large, often hilly villages that are separated from each other by significant distances. Southern Italian mountain villages are considerably larger than anywhere else in the Mediterranean. Well into the twentieth century many southern peasants left their villages before dawn to reach their fields and returned home after dark. This labor and residential pattern became established in the first centuries of the southern kingdom.

Feudalism, as it developed at the end of the first millennium in parts of western Europe, was based on a pyramid of hereditary obligations, linking the king to his most powerful subjects, and the latter in turn to their own military retainers, and so on further down the social and power scale. This form of social, political, military, and

Christ Crowning Roger II King of Sicily,
mosaic from the church of the Martorana, Palermo

economic organization originated mainly in northern France, and the Normans brought it with them to the lands they conquered, England and Sicily. With it, knightly culture also came to Sicily, where it echoes to this day in the *pupi*, traditional colorful marionettes representing feudal knights.

The feudal system established under the Normans was primarily one of land distribution and military recruitment. The fundamental obligation of the vassal—guaranteed by an oath of loyalty—was to serve the king in arms. For each 20 *once* of landed revenue (an *oncia* was originally an actual ounce of gold and equaled six ducats), the vassal owed the service of a fully equipped knight. This, the main fighting unit in this era, consisted of a fully armored horseman and three retainers, themselves armed and on horseback. The use of feudal forces was arguably the main reason for the Normans' remarkable military successes from England to Sicily. The land granted was usually in the form of a village or group of villages. Villagers owed their barons—as feudal lords were usually called—dues, fees, and, initially, labor services. Soon barons also gained the right to levy special subsidies from their vassals (as subject peasants came to be called) for specific events: to ransom the baron if he was captured in war, when the baron's son became a knight, and when his daughter married.

Roger II and his successors until the late thirteenth century insisted that all power to tax and to dispense justice remained fully with the king and his officials. The most powerful barons sought early on to usurp royal authority and jurisdiction, but by and large they achieved little success on this front. Feudal possessions were not fully the property of the barons. Though fiefs quickly became hereditary, the king limited the scope of succession. Even in the allowed succession degrees, barons owed a succession tax. If there were no close heirs, fiefs reverted to the king. The monarchy also regulated the obligations of barons to their own families. Frederick II, for instance, set shares and payments that the heir to a fief would owe to his younger brothers—"so that those younger by age should not labor in misery"—and to his sisters—"so that women do not grow old at home, unable to marry."

Military service was the main element of the feudal system until the fifteenth century, but exceptions soon appeared. Women were granted the right to inherit fiefs, although the king held the right to choose a husband for any feudal heiress, to guarantee the military service. Whenever the fief-holder was unable to provide the required service, by reason of age or physical inability, he owed the king the *adoa*, a payment representing about half the fief's income. Over time, many barons paid the adoa rather than serving in the king's wars, and at the end of the thirteenth century barons obtained the right to charge their own vassals for half this tax. Even after its military function declined, feudalism continued to dominate southern society until well into the nineteenth century, and its effects have yet to disappear entirely from southern life.

The death of William II in 1189 opened a major crisis. Though the king had not been an especially skilled ruler, such was the chaos that soon the memory of William "the Good" bloomed. A later chronicler called him "flower of kings, crown of princes . . . in his kingdom everyone was happy with his lot." Dante (in *Paradiso* 20.62) wrote that Sicily "cried" for William. The law of succession was unclear. The closest heir was the king's aunt, Constance, born in 1154 shortly after the death of her father, Roger II, and married in 1186 to Henry of Swabia, eleven years her junior, the son of Emperor Frederick "Barbarossa" (Swabia, in southwestern Germany, was one of the largest German principalities). Many southerners feared German rule and sought to preserve the kingdom's autonomy. Prominent clerics and aristocrats joined to support Tancred, count of Lecce and an illegitimate member of the royal family, and he was crowned in Palermo in 1190.

The kingdom descended into confusion. As had happened at every succession, religious tensions increased, and "with fear of the king removed," Christians assaulted Jews and Muslims. The Christian loss of Jerusalem to Saladin in 1187 exacerbated Christian hostility. To add to the chaos, in 1190 the kings of England and France stopped in Sicily on their way to the Third Crusade, and the usual rowdy bands of Crusaders sacked Messina. Pirates took advantage of the crisis to raid the kingdom's coasts, and ships from the Genoese and Pisan republics took control of southern ports. Aristocratic factions struggled with each other. Warfare flared across the kingdom as Henry of Swabia made his way to the South to claim his wife's inheritance. After Tancred's death Henry easily advanced from Naples to Palermo, where he was crowned king on Christmas Day in 1194 and quickly dispatched Tancred's son. At the same time, his wife Constance scored her own success.

Traveling from Germany to rejoin her husband in Sicily, Constance was pregnant with her first child. She was forty years old, which was unusually late for a medieval woman to have a child, let alone her first child. Any suspicion about the legitimacy of the empress's off-spring would be a crucial weapon for the imperial couple's opponents. On reaching the town of Jesi in the Marches, Constance realized that she was about to give birth. She had a large tent erected in the main square. Under this tent, and in the presence of many of the town's women, on December 26, 1194, she gave birth to her only child, one day after the baby's father was crowned king of Sicily in Palermo. Neutral witnesses could attest that no sleight of hand had occurred and that the boy was in fact Constance's son. To mark his double inheritance the baby was baptized Frederick Roger, after his two grandfathers. Thus began the life of the man who would later be called "Wonder of the World"—and many less flattering names.

Before her marriage Constance had lived in a convent. An old prophecy stated that the anti-Christ would be born of an old nun. Thus, in later years Frederick's adversaries used his birth, however legitimate, as evidence that he was the greatest enemy of all Christians. But early on, the Church played a central role in ensuring Frederick's life and the survival of his realms. Neither Henry nor Constance lived long to enjoy their victory. Henry died of dysentery in 1197 and his wife died the next year. Their deaths renewed the Sicilian crisis: German warlords grabbed land, feudal factional strife flared, Muslims across Sicily rebelled against mistreatment. The dying Constance tried to save her son's inheritance by entrusting him to the care of Pope Innocent III (ruled 1198–1216), one of the most power-ful figures in the history of the papacy and forceful in the pursuit of papal authority. As Sicily's overlord, Innocent had a stake in the king-dom's survival; moreover, Frederick's hereditary rights and his status as an orphaned ward entitled him to papal assistance.

While papal delegates and German nobles slowly brought order back to Sicily, Frederick grew up in Palermo. We know little of his boyhood. A witness described him at thirteen as "alert, full of sharpness and doctrine, but inappropriate in demeanor." Constance had had her young son crowned king of Sicily in May of 1198. Though this would prove to be only the first of five coronations for Frederick (two more than his excommunications), his claim to his father's German lands, let alone to the imperial throne, was shaky. The pope's support was therefore essential both in and beyond Sicily. Innocent took care of the political and personal interests of his ward. He arranged Frederick's marriage, at age fourteen, to his first wife, Constance of Aragon, who was ten years older than the boy. This marked presumably the start of Frederick's lively sexual life. Over the next forty-odd years it included three wives, four legitimate children, at least eleven illegitimate ones (from at least eight different women), and numerous other dalliances.

Pope Innocent also championed Frederick's German rights, opposing other claimants to the empire, in the hope that his pupil would prove a malleable figure for papal concerns. Soon Frederick began to display significant political skills. In 1212 he traveled to Germany, where he achieved recognition as ruler of both his ancestral Swabian lands and the empire as a whole. Germans hailed him as "the kid from Puglia." In Mainz in December 1212 he was crowned king of Germany, and in Aachen in 1215 he added the crown of king of the Romans, which declared his claim to the imperial role. Frederick preserved papal goodwill by pledging to keep his Italian and German realms separate, in order to protect the Church's freedom from the political pressure an overpowerful emperor would exercise. To honor this promise he set up his oldest son Henry—aged only five—as ruler in Germany and returned to Italy. On November 22, 1220, Pope Honorius III (ruled 1216–27) crowned him Holy Roman emperor in St. Peter's.

After 1220 Frederick spent most of his life in Italy, especially in his southern kingdom, though he was constantly on the move and never established a settled resident court. He was the first king of Sicily to spend little time on the island, and he favored the development of Naples and other continental cities. To strengthen his papal alliance, Frederick pledged to Pope Honorius that he would pick up the crusading mantle of his paternal ancestors. Christians held parts of the Holy Land but they had lost Jerusalem in 1187. Frederick's grandfather

Barbarossa had died in 1190 in the Third Crusade, which had failed to recover the city. Frederick's second wife brought him a hereditary title to the Kingdom of Jerusalem and this furthered his crusading ambitions. Frederick's Crusade, part of the Fifth, proved the greatest Christian success since the First Crusade. Yet his slowness to embark on it and his proceedings once he arrived in the Levant increased the suspicions many had begun to develop about his lack of scruples and dubious religious orthodoxy.

As emperor, Frederick was the political leader of Christendom and the main defender of the Roman Church. But as king of Sicily he ruled over Christian, Muslim, and Jewish subjects. This tension may have been part of his reluctance to embark on the promised Crusade and of his relatively bloodless methods once he undertook it. Honorius III was very patient with Frederick's delays and pursued a conciliatory policy toward Frederick's many violations of his promises to the papacy and his continuing power in Germany. But Pope Gregory IX (ruled 1227–41), an ambitious and powerful personality committed to an assertive political role for the papacy, abruptly changed papal policy toward Frederick.

After another delay in the promised Crusade, Gregory issued the first excommunication of Frederick and did not revoke it even after the emperor finally left for the East in 1228. Frederick, in the peculiar position of an excommunicated Crusader, negotiated with the sultan of Egypt and obtained the return of Jerusalem, Bethlehem, and Nazareth to Christian control. Accompanied by his Muslim body-guards, he entered the Holy City. When no local cleric dared defy the excommunication by crowning him, on March 18, 1229, Frederick crowned himself king of Jerusalem in the Church of the Holy Sepulcher. Jerusalem remained under Christian rule until 1244.

His unusual Crusade amazed and troubled Frederick's contemporaries. The emperor fascinated Arabs. One Arab observer thought little of Frederick's appearance: "red-haired, bald, short-sighted: had he been a slave, he would not have been worth [much]." But many others were surprised by his knowledge of Arabic and Islam. Frederick, Arab writers reported, deplored the intolerant attitude of Christian priests in Jerusalem and complained when, out of respect for him, the call for prayer from the minarets was suspended. He also consulted Arab scholars on philosophical and scientific matters. An observer described him as "distinguished and learned, a friend of philosophy, logic, and medicine, and favorable to Muslims." Christians, on the other hand, especially those loyal to Pope Gregory, condemned Frederick's methods and views.

Frederick's admirers have often regarded his Crusade as the strongest evidence of his unusual tolerance and free-thinking temperament. Certainly his attitude stood against new trends in Latin Christendom. In the early thirteenth century a more aggressive papacy, strengthened by new religious orders, pursued a policy of Christianization and Latinization throughout Italy and the rest of Europe. Greek and Orthodox monasteries in Italy lost revenues and members, and Jews and Muslims were subjected to harsher measures. In 1215 the Fourth Lateran Council prohibited the building of new synagogues and banned Jews from owning slaves and holding office. The fight against heretics also became much more brutal, with the Crusade proclaimed by Innocent III against the Albigensians in southern France in the 1210s and 1220s, and the establishment of the Inquisition in the 1230s.

Frederick himself implemented stricter policies and we should not exaggerate his tolerance. Until about 1240, he encouraged the growth of the new Franciscan and Dominican orders in the South. He allowed harsh repression of heretical movements that advocated a radical return to Church poverty, which Frederick perceived as a threat also to state authority. He ordered the transfer of about fifteen thousand Sicilian Muslims to Lucera on the mainland, farther from their North African brethren, who had supported them in their revolt during Frederick's minority. But Frederick was also quite fond of the Lucera colony: he allowed the open practice of Islam there and built himself a palace with a harem and a stable of camels.

In an edict of 1221, Frederick required southern Jews to wear a distinctive orange sign, the same requirement (though not the same sign) the edict imposed on prostitutes. But he later removed the requirement, allowed new synagogues to be built, encouraged Jewish artisans, and favored the immigration into Sicily of Jewish farmers from North Africa to replace the Muslims transferred to Lucera. In 1231 he formally confirmed the royal protection to which minorities were entitled, allowing Jews and Muslims to bring lawsuits because "we do not wish them to be persecuted in their innocence simply because they are Jews or Saracens." In 1232 Frederick founded the town of Altamura in southern Puglia: though at its center stood a new Catholic cathedral, Frederick attracted Jews, Muslims, and Greeks to the town. Altamura housed synagogues and Orthodox churches. The town to this day preserves the *claustri*, peculiar courtyards-alleys that echo traditional Greek and Arab urban structures.

Frederick's tolerance applied beyond his diverse southern realm. While he was in Germany in 1236, Christians in Fulda accused the Jews in their city of ritual murder; the oft-repeated rumor that Jews killed Christian children to use their blood in rituals caused a slaughter of Jews there and in other cities. Frederick assembled from all over Europe a committee of jurists and Jewish converts—who would both be knowledgeable of their old religion and have no ground to lie to protect it—to examine and dismiss the accusation. He participated in the discussions, displaying his knowledge of the Talmud. Though Frederick was not the only ruler in his time to reject the ritual murder libel, his procedure exemplified his practical approach, intellectual curiosity, and concern for his own role as the source of fair justice.

Frederick's eclectic cultural interests reinforced his religious tolerance. He was interested in the natural world, in mathematics, and in technology, and he patronized scholars from across Europe. Leonardo Fibonacci (1170–1250), probably the scientist most responsible for introducing Arabic numerals to Europe, lived at Frederick's court. Like his Norman grandfather, Frederick sponsored translations into Latin of texts from the great Mediterranean intellectual traditions. In the eleventh through thirteenth centuries, in Sicily as in Spain, such translation activity did not simply transmit texts passively, but attempted to reconcile the celebrated accomplishments of ancient, Jewish, and Islamic culture with the world and ideas of western Christianity. Jewish scholars translated Arabic and Hebrew texts for Frederick, including Maimonides' *Guide for the Perplexed*, one of the most important works of medieval Jewish philosophy. The emperor also sponsored scholarly translations of the writings of Greek and Arabic philosophers.

Frederick was quite fond of poetry too. Troubadours from Provence, who formed then the leading poetical tradition in Christian Europe, frequented his court. He also patronized poets writing in the Italian vernacular. This so-called Sicilian school of poets adapted Provencal literary models and produced the earliest formal literature in Italian. In creating the sonnet, Frederick's Sicilian poets left a profound mark on world literature.

The emperor spoke German, Latin, Italian, and some Arabic; wrote poetry; and collected gems, antiques, coins, and manuscripts with illuminations in a new naturalistic style. His buildings include the grand gate at Capua, near Naples, and most famously Castel del Monte, in Puglia, an octagonal hunting lodge built in the 1240s; Castel del Monte is now on the back of the one-cent euro coins minted in Italy, the only southern monument or artwork on any of the Italian euro coins. Frederick also authored an elegant Latin essay, *On the Skill of Hunting with Falcons,* and he assembled an exotic menagerie through frequent exchanges with eastern traders and rulers. When in 1245 he visited Verona, he had with him an elephant, five leopards, and forty-four camels, which he temporarily housed in a local monastery.

His patronage of Michael Scot (died ca. 1236) illustrates Frederick's eclecticism and intellectual curiosity. Scot, one of the wandering cosmopolitan scholars typical of the medieval world, trained as a translator in Toledo, then one of the greatest intellectual centers of

Castel del Monte, Puglia, Frederick II's most famous hunting lodge

Christian Spain, and entered Frederick's service around 1220. For the emperor, Scot translated Aristotle's works on nature and animals, informing Frederick's own work on falcon hunting. He served as Frederick's alchemist, astrologer, and philosophical sparring partner. Various tales survive of Scot's necromancy and of his discussions with Frederick about the natural world. Though his fame as a magician later landed Scot in Dante's *Inferno*, he flourished at the Sicilian court.

Most of Frederick's cultural patronage took place in his southern kingdom. He was especially attached to his maternal legacy. When he visited the Holy Land, he supposedly remarked that God must never have seen the South of Italy, or He would not have so praised the promised land He offered the Jews. It was also in the Kingdom of Sicily that Frederick minted the *augustalis*, a new gold coin modeled on ancient examples and intended to reflect the ruler's power and his kingdom's wealth.

After returning to Europe from his Crusade, Frederick continued to fight on numerous fronts. When in 1235 his son joined a rebellion of German princes, Frederick traveled to Germany with his usual exotic retinue of camels and Arab slaves. He suppressed the revolt and jailed his son until the latter committed suicide in 1242. The struggle with the papacy—over appointments, revenues, and the political leadership of Christendom—proved the hardest. The pope relied on help from northern Italian cities, German princes, and all others who feared Frederick's power. Milan and other Italian cities, which were becoming wealthier as the northern Italian economy flourished, resisted imperial authority in northern Italy in order to enjoy greater political, fiscal, and military autonomy. The pope again excommunicated Frederick in 1239; this was followed by a siege of Rome by imperial forces, during which Gregory IX died. Innocent IV (ruled 1243–54) renewed the fight, excommunicated Frederick yet again, and in 1245, after declaring the emperor to be the anti-Christ, formally deposed him at the Council of Lyon and called for a Crusade against him.

Besides the various political reasons for this radical measure, the pope stressed Frederick's shocking friendliness with the infidel. The papal decree deposing Frederick listed examples of his perjury, sacrilege, heresy, and hostility toward the Church, and concluded with a litany of inflated and inflammatory claims:

[H]e is joined in odious friendship with the Saracens; several times he has sent envoys and gifts to them, and receives the like from them in return with expressions of honor and welcome; he embraces their rites; he openly keeps them with him in his daily services; and, following their customs, he does not blush to appoint as guards, for his wives descended from royal stock, eunuchs whom it is seriously said he has had castrated. And what is more loathsome, when he was in the territory overseas, after he had made an agreement, or rather had come to a wicked understanding with the Sultan, he allowed the name of Mahomet to be publicly proclaimed day and night in the Lord's temple.

Throughout these decades of struggle with opponents in Germany, northern Italy, and the Church, Frederick spent as much time as possible in his Italian realm. In 1235, when he traveled north to suppress his son's rebellion, Frederick issued new ordinances for Germany. But in legislation as in everything else, the Kingdom of Sicily was uppermost in his mind, and it is there that we find the best evidence of his ideas about government. He organized the seven Great Offices, which became the basis for the kingdom's administration until the Renaissance: the Justiciar, Admiral, Chancellor, Seneschal, Protonotary, Chamberlain, and Constable were in charge, respectively, of justice, navy, secretariat, royal household, archives, finances, and army. Frederick also organized the kingdom's provincial administration and strengthened central laws and tribunals. He permitted representatives of the cities to sit in Parliament—an assembly of barons, clerics, and others that had met occasionally since the reign of Roger II—though he was otherwise suspicious of communal autonomy.

Frederick saw law-giving and justice as essential to royal power: the king was "father and son, master and servant" of justice. In his legal texts he presented the king as the paternal protector of his subjects. One practical effect of this image was his requirement that all tribunals provide indigent defendants with a lawyer at the tribunal's expense. The constitutions issued at Melfi in 1231 asserted the primacy of royal justice and law and presented a coherent image of a lay, authoritarian monarchical rule that contrasted any feudal claim. Some barons were beginning to usurp jurisdiction over their vassals, but the constitutions firmly stated royal authority. All levels of justice in the kingdom emanated from the royal administration "as streams from one source." While Frederick, let alone his successors, was not always able to enforce this principle, its assertion marks a strong distinction from the later expansion of feudal powers.

The emperor's commitment to a strong central state and to its role as guarantor of justice also motivated his foundation of the University of Naples in 1224, the first in Europe created by a secular ruler. Naples was more convenient than Palermo to the Italian and European affairs that preoccupied Frederick, and he devoted much attention to the city. He expanded Castel dell'Ovo and Castel Capuano, the royal castles founded in Naples by William I.

The university expressed both a new conception of the state's needs and the emperor's devotion to learning. He intended the new university as a "source of science and seminary of doctrines," a motto that still appears on its diplomas. Frederick often declared his own passion for reading and study. In a letter to the University of Bologna he stated that "since our youth, before we assumed the burden of rule, we sought knowledge, loved its beauty, and breathed tirelessly the smell of its perfumes. After taking on the cares of our kingdom, even though the unceasing multitude of affairs often distracts us, whatever time we can spare from our habitual occupations we cannot bear to spend lazily; rather we freely spend all of it in the exercise of reading, so that the inclination of our soul to the acquiring of knowledge be stronger, without which the life of mortals is not conducted freely."

The University of Naples also served a clear, practical purpose: to train the legal personnel necessary to strengthen royal law and administration. The new university offered both a legal and a general curriculum, though medicine was reserved for the old school in Salerno that had been active since the tenth century. In the foundation edict, Frederick promised lodging and aid to needy students and extolled the beauty of Naples, to attract teachers and students: the city was rich, easy to reach by land and sea, and its air healthy. To avoid competition and prevent a brain drain, he also closed other schools that were teaching the same subjects, prohibited his southern subjects from studying elsewhere, and required those already at other universities to return to the kingdom.

The university—now officially named after Frederick—had a difficult life in its first centuries, but it also greatly advanced southern culture. Thomas Aquinas taught theology there in the 1260s. Naples scholars translated works of Aristotle and Galen from both Greek and Arabic. By the early fifteenth century, the Colleges of Law, Medicine, and Theology emerged, conducted examinations, and granted degrees. Above all, the university served well the practical needs that motivated its foundation, producing judges and notaries for service to the state. Naples became one of the major centers of legal studies in medieval Italy, and most royal bureaucrats earned their degrees there, as did the ever-growing numbers of lawyers that came to dominate the public life of the region in later centuries. The university provides an effective example of Frederick's approach to government: focused and practical, creative and innovative, eclectic, but also authoritarian and assertive of the ruler's ultimate power.

Overall, Frederick brought his Italian kingdom into an even broader European scene than had his Norman forefathers. He bestrode the continent and the Mediterranean world as the greatest figure of his century, and his influence and power were felt from England to Jerusalem. He arguably made the South the center of European life. Yet his reign also continued trends that damaged the southern economy. The spread of the feudal system in the countryside increased peasant subjection and dependence and reduced the chances for more innovative agriculture. The preference of the Normans and Frederick for royal control imposed royal monopolies on the production of salt, silk, wool, soap, and iron and heavy regulation of trade in grain and other goods. This eventually weakened southern commerce and manufacturing compared to the more flexible northern Italian cities. By the 1190s the South was already importing wool cloths from northern Italy and Flanders. By the mid-thirteenth century, Muslim flight or expulsion (after their revolt at the start of Frederick's reign), fiscal pressure for the emperor's wars, foreign control of much of southern trade, royal debts to northern Italian bankers, and weakness in craft production caused much harm to the southern economy.

The papal decree deposing Frederick did not produce any serious rival for the imperial throne, but after 1245 Frederick's forces and allies experienced a series of setbacks. On December 13, 1250, in one of his beloved castles in Puglia, Frederick died after requesting and receiving the customary Christian death rites. His death left the Swabian party severely weakened in both the empire and Italy.

Posterity has seen Frederick as a man far ahead of his time, a skeptical, modern, free spirit who brought a practical mind to his endeavors and achievements. This view is in part exaggerated. Frederick was deeply invested in the medieval notion of the emperor as the leader of Christian Europe and the supreme law-giver of his peoples, and in the dynastic mentality of his time. His Christian faith was likely sincere, though he certainly held the papacy in little trust or esteem. Some of his innovative policies reflect his study of the ancient and Arab worlds more than any radical novelty.

Yet his practical approach and his eclectic cultural interests were definitely unusual, and contemporaries already perceived Frederick as a man apart—for better and worse. A Franciscan chronicler who opposed Frederick provides a good summary of the prevailing and contradictory views of his contemporaries: "[Frederick] was an evil and accursed man, a schismatic, a heretic, and an epicurean. . . . [He] held the true faith to be worthless. He was a cunning, crafty man, avaricious, lecherous, and malicious, easily given to wrath." But on the other hand, the emperor "could be witty, charming, urbane, and industrious. He was adept at writing and singing, and was well-versed in the art of writing lyrics and songs. . . . He could speak many and varied languages."

When Frederick died, his illegitimate son Manfred wrote to his half-brother Conrad that "the world's sun has set." The emperor's death cheered his enemies. Innocent IV proclaimed to the Sicilians, "Let the heavens rejoice. Let the earth be filled with gladness. For the fall of the tyrant has changed the thunderbolts and tempests that God Almighty held over your heads into gentle zephyrs and fecund dews." The imperial party never fully recovered. The papacy began to search for a European prince willing to come to Italy with sufficient military forces to eliminate Swabian power from the peninsula and to claim the southern crown, which the papacy considered its own to bestow freely. Frederick's legitimate son, Conrad IV, duly claimed both the imperial and the Sicilian legacy, but he never managed to establish his rule in Italy. He died just four years later, leaving only a boy of two as his heir. Manfred, Frederick's son by his favorite mistress, governed the South unofficially and soon took the opportunity created by the lack of a strong legitimate heir to claim the kingdom for himself. Manfred gained the support of southern barons, and in August of 1258 he was crowned king of Sicily in Palermo.

Owing to divisions between German princes, no new emperor appeared for almost twenty years after Conrad's death. Therefore, Manfred continued to exercise influence in northern Italy, as head of the imperial, or Ghibelline, faction. This quickly soured his relationship with Rome, and in 1255 he was excommunicated, following in the family tradition. Successive popes depicted Manfred, like his father, as a despot and a friend of heretics and Muslims. It took a while, however, for Rome to find a suitable alternative to Manfred, especially after an offer to members of the English royal family—England being sufficiently distant from Sicily to assuage papal fears—failed to produce any effect.

In the meantime new powers appeared on the scene. Aragon emerged as a commercial and political power in the western Mediterranean. By the end of the twelfth century, as the Christian Reconquest of Spain from the Moors advanced, the inland kingdom of Aragon expanded to include maritime Catalonia. Over the course of the thirteenth century the kings of Aragon extended their power in southern France, the Balearic islands, and Valencia, farther south on the eastern coast of Spain. By the 1270s they ruled a network of lands that extended to coastal areas of North Africa, with prosperous cities and a diverse population. Their main capital was Barcelona, the most important mercantile and craft center in the western Mediterranean, with a dynamic textile sector and commercial links that extended to northern Europe, North Africa, Italy, and the eastern Mediterranean. The kings' political ambitions and the Barcelona merchants' commercial ones operated in tandem to expand Aragon's goals. Sicily was a worthy prize for those goals, and Manfred sought Aragonese support by marrying his daughter Constance to an Aragonese prince.

The other player in this international game was the French royal dynasty. Charles, count of Anjou and younger brother of King Louis IX (ruled 1226–70), acquired dominions in Provence and influence in northern Italy. He became the pope's champion against Manfred. Charles promised not only to respect the pope's eminent lordship over Sicily but also to follow his saintly brother's example and lead a Crusade. In 1265 Charles came into Italy with an army, and Pope

Clement IV (ruled 1264–68) crowned him king of Sicily in Rome. Charles and his army entered the southern kingdom, and on February 26, 1266, Manfred was defeated and killed at the battle of Benevento. In a beautiful passage of *Purgatorio* 3, Dante ascribes to Manfred a last-minute repentance and salvation, but politically Benevento marked the end for the descendants of Frederick II. The Swabians ended their Italian adventure and the Angevins gained a kingdom and a European role.

The Norman creation of the Kingdom of Sicily profoundly altered the history of the southern regions of Italy. Where fragmentation and ethnic diversity had prevailed, the strongest state in Italy emerged. The southern population benefited in many ways from the unified monarchy. Though local tolls and customs remained, the kingdom formed a more united market for trade and regional specialization in agriculture. Periods of strife persisted, but the monarchy brought order, stability, and military and judicial control. The new monarchy was a prominent player on the European and Mediterranean political scenes, and the kingdom gained influence, and at times power, over North Africa, the Balkans, and the Levant. The Norman and Swabian sovereigns sponsored remarkable artistic and intellectual activities and founded new institutions that made the South an important center of art, literature, and education. Palermo gained splendid monuments and mosaics, and Naples began its rise as a large center of population, education, art, and government.

The monarchy also had negative effects. The spread of the feudal system contributed greatly to the formation of a rigid and polarized society, especially in the countryside. As a system of government and power relationships, feudalism was probably the only option available to the Normans as they gathered their disparate conquests into one political entity. But its great expansion under the monarchy crystallized harsh conditions of exploitation that affected the great majority of the southern rural population.

By 1250 Sicily and the continental South were also much less diverse than they had been earlier. By the standards of their time, the Normans and Frederick were indeed far from intolerant. But, as happened also in Spain with the Christian Reconquest, once royal political centralization replaced political fragmentation, minority groups gradually emigrated, even when they were not harassed or expelled. The dominant religion, pushed by a nearby and powerful papacy, began to prevail over all other faiths.

The new southern monarchy also failed to aid the development of urban institutions and regarded with suspicion any growth in communal autonomy. The South became poorer and more rural. The decline in the political autonomy and economic vitality of southern cities represented a significant shift from the previous history of the South, and presaged later problems. In many areas of northern Italy the twelfth and thirteenth centuries saw the expansion of urban economies, the growth of civic institutions, and the increasing power of city interests over rural ones. At the same time, rural society in the South became more rigidly stratified, rural people became more dependent on their lords, and feudal interests prevailed over urban ones and dominated the kingdom's life.

✑ Chapter III ✑

Sicily Splits and Naples Rises
The South in the Late
Middle Ages

> We read in texts that are authentic and worthy of memory of the nobility and riches that once existed in the delightful country of the Amalfi coast. In the past, such things, and even greater ones, could with truth be said. Nonetheless, as to what we see now, not only the wealth and maritime trade have decreased and the great palaces are ruined, but the inhabitants can survive there only with the greatest difficulty.
>
> Masuccio Salernitano, *Il Novellino* (1470s), fifth story

On March 30, 1282, Easter Monday, a riot erupted at evening services outside a church in Palermo. An anonymous chronicle—not written by an eyewitness—claimed that "a Frenchman took a woman, touching her dishonestly with his hands, as they were used to doing. The woman cried because of this, and the men of Palermo ran to her, and began a fight." We lack reliable details, and it is in fact unclear whether the Frenchman's offense was in words or deeds, whether he was a soldier in the royal service, and whether the woman was noble or a bride, as some accounts claim. In any case, a struggle followed, and soon the whole city rose to the cry of "Death to the French." Rebels massacred the Palermo garrison, and the royal governor fled the city. About two thousand French people, including women and clerics, were killed. The rebels set up a communal government and raised the old flag of Frederick II.

Within days the revolt spread across the island and royal garrisons surrendered everywhere. The royal vicar for the island was in Messina, where part of the royal fleet was stationed. That city, closer in economic interests to the mainland, remained calm until April 28. Then rebels forced the royal vicar into the local castle and burned many ships. The entire island was soon lost to the Angevins.

Sicily and the Italian South were central to the network of connections that shaped the Mediterranean, from Iberia to the Holy Land, in late medieval times. The Sicilian revolt and ensuing war—later known as the Sicilian Vespers—therefore turned into the most significant episode in a protracted struggle between French, Iberian, Italian, papal, German, and Byzantine interests for control of the Mediterranean.

In 1282 Sicily was ruled by Charles of Anjou, who had gained the southern kingdom when he defeated King Manfred in 1266. In 1268 a military expedition into the kingdom by Conradin of Swabia, the sixteen-year-old grandson of Frederick II, ended in defeat and in the public decapitation of the ill-fated youth in Naples. Thus, Charles became the dominant power within Italy. He held land in southern France, northwestern Italy, Sardinia, Tunis, and the Balkans, continuing the Mediterranean ambitions of previous rulers of southern Italy. In the Balkans Charles confronted the rival interests of Venetians, Genoese, Greeks, and sundry local despots. In 1261 the Latin emperors installed in Constantinople by the Fourth Crusade of 1204 had been dethroned. A new Byzantine dynasty had returned Constantinople and the remnants of its empire to Greek and Orthodox control. Charles's Balkan ambitions thus also faced both the revived Byzantines and various claimants to the defeated Catholic Latin empire. His efforts extended beyond Constantinople. In 1277 he acquired the nominal right to the Kingdom of Jerusalem and sent forces to protect what little Christian territory remained in the Holy Land.

Charles's broad plans took his attention away from his southern dominions. Pope Martin IV (ruled 1281–85) leaned on Charles to support the Guelph (papal) faction across northern Italy, to ensure the papacy's control of its own lands, and to plan an invasion of the Greek empire. The papacy continued to fear German ambitions in Italy and saw in Charles its main ally. Martin IV also reversed earlier papal initiatives to reconcile the Catholic and Orthodox churches, and prodded Charles in his eastern plans. A fleet was set to depart for the East in the spring of 1282 when the Sicilian Vespers suddenly came to trouble the affairs of Christendom.

The causes of the revolt were varied, and many went back to the start of the thirteenth century, when the sovereigns of Sicily expanded their interests far from the island. Sicilians resented the growing fiscal and military demands of their ambitious rulers, whose ventures took them so far from the island and thus deprived local elites of access to royal patronage. Charles of Anjou barely visited the island that gave him his royal title. A new general tax to support the eastern expedition was being levied in the spring of 1282. Cities, barons, and peasants rebelled against Angevin fiscal pressure and military recruitment and clamored for greater autonomy and lower taxes, though it is not clear that Angevin taxation was heavier or more efficient than what Sicilians had endured under previous rulers. Some rebels supported those exiled because of earlier resistance to Charles. Many opposed the French landowners, administrators, and soldiers brought to power by the Angevins. Administrators from the mainland were unpopular. It is also possible that desire for autonomy had grown among the island's newer population of farmers and merchants from the mainland. They had, over the thirteenth century, replaced the Muslims expelled after their revolt under Frederick II and many of the Greeks whose numbers had been dwindling over a longer period as the kingdom became closer to Latin Christianity.

Medieval writers saw the Vespers as the result of a plan hatched by Sicilian exiles in complicity with the king of Aragon and the Byzantine emperor (who was eager to prevent Charles's expedition against his empire). It is unlikely that a real conspiracy lay behind the riot that began at the Palermo Vespers, but certainly after the revolt's early success many outside interests entered the picture. The pope refused to support the rebels and their plan for a federation of free cities under papal protection. In fact, on May 7 he excommunicated the rebels and anyone who aided them. The Palermo Parliament and the revolt's leaders turned to King Peter III of Aragon (ruled 1276–85), whose family had long eyed the island and whose marriage to King Manfred's daughter gave him a dynastic claim to the Sicilian throne. Aragon's rulers led a commercial and naval empire that stretched across the western Mediterranean, and they feared Angevin power in southern Italy. On August 30, 1282, after an Angevin blockade of Messina had failed, Peter landed in western Sicily with a large army. Rebel leaders who had sought a more autonomous government for the island fled or lost influence. Peter quickly reached Palermo and "the Palermitani made great celebration and great solemnity for his coming."

The war soon extended beyond Sicily. In June 1283 it even featured a rather absurd scheme for a duel between Charles and Peter III, to be fought in Bordeaux, then under neutral English rule. This plan came to naught, as the two kings showed up on the same day but at different times, accused the absent one of cowardice, and left the scene. More seriously, Peter III's forces attacked the mainland, and antipapal factions in northern Italian cities sided with Peter, while the king of France, with papal support, attacked Aragon. The pope excommunicated Peter and declared the war against him a Crusade. But Peter's control over Sicily was solid. In a naval battle in 1284 in the Bay of Naples the Aragonese scored a major victory and captured Charles "the Lame," son and heir to King Charles. Riots in Naples followed this defeat and showed Angevin weakness on the mainland. Peter III understood the need to satisfy the Sicilians' desire for a resident sovereign. When in 1283 he returned to Aragon to defend his ancestral kingdom against the French, he left his Sicilian wife behind as regent. He later agreed with the Sicilian Parliament to designate his second son as future king of Sicily, while the eldest son would inherit Aragon itself. When Charles of Anjou died, in January of 1285, he had made no progress in regaining the island.

In the same year Peter III also died. The war between Sicily and the Angevin rulers continued for two decades. Charles II (ruled 1285–1309) remained a prisoner of the Aragonese, so the mainland was governed by papal administrators. Pope Honorius IV (ruled 1285–88) alleviated fiscal pressure in the kingdom and gave concessions to the barons, to solidify Angevin rule, and negotiated Charles II's release. Charles returned to his mainland realm in 1289, but in losing Sicily, the Angevins had lost one of their main sources of income, the sale of Sicilian grain. The Naples monarchy, like the kings of England and France, turned for loans to northern Italian bankers, especially Florentines. Genoese and Catalan merchants profited from control of Sicily's trade networks. The separation of the two kingdoms thus added to the decline of the southern economy. The Strait of Messina, earlier a crucial link in an integrated economy, became an armed boundary.

Upon his return to Naples, Charles II launched a policy of moral and religious renewal aimed at securing divine protection for the Angevins and at pleasing his papal ally. This included the strengthening of the Inquisition in the kingdom, the forced conversion or expulsion of many Jews, and in 1300 the enslavement and sale of the Muslims settled by Frederick II in Lucera. With this last act, over nine thousand slaves were sold, probably the largest such event in Italy since antiquity.

Charles II, successive popes, the king of France, and even King James II of Aragon (ruled 1291–1327) sought a peace settlement that would return Sicily to the Angevins: Sardinia (which nobody truly controlled, but all felt free to offer to others) would go to Aragon, France would expand its southern borders, and Aragon would regain papal friendship. But James II's brother Frederick, who had been left in charge of the government of Sicily, obtained the endorsement of Sicilian barons and cities to resist this project and confirm the island's autonomy.

Early in 1296 Frederick was recognized as king of Sicily by a Sicilian assembly, and his court quickly became a magnet for antipapal and anti-French exiles from northern Italy. Like his father before him, Frederick was excommunicated, and Sicily placed under papal interdict. This strongest weapon in the papal arsenal prohibited the performance of all but the most essential Catholic rites. The Sicilians, however, resisted on land and at sea, and in 1302 the Peace of Caltabellotta acknowledged Frederick as king of Sicily, sanctioning the agreement by his marriage to Charles II's daughter. The treaty stipulated that at Frederick's death Sicily would revert to the Angevins, but in fact Frederick's successors managed to maintain their rule over the island after his death in 1337. To preserve Angevin dignity, in the peace treaty Frederick took the official title of king of Trinacria (an old name for the island), leaving the title of king of Sicily to Charles II. The title of king of Naples appeared informally in the mid-fourteenth century but did not come into general use until the sixteenth. Thus, with blithe disregard for reality, Charles II and his Angevin successors styled themselves kings of Sicily and Jerusalem, although they held neither.

The peace allowed Charles II to resume his father's aggressive policy in northern Italy, the Balkans, and the eastern Mediterranean. In 1291, Acre, the last Christian outpost in the Holy Land, fell to Muslim forces, giving renewed urgency to the eastern agenda of the Angevins. The Angevins also scored great successes in central Europe.

But Sicily would remain outside the Angevin empire in spite of numerous attacks and more decades of intermittent war. Since the papacy had chosen the Angevins as its champions, their defeat in Sicily also weakened the popes. Soon thereafter, the Avignon period (1309–77) and the Great Schism (1378–1415) marked the final failure of the hopes of late medieval popes for political dominion over western Christendom.

Sicily itself profited little from independence. Although the island's economy revived somewhat after the 1302 peace agreement, it was soon undermined by many factors: its kings' need to finance continuous warfare to defend their Crown; the severing of commercial links with the mainland; the rise of—and conflict between— powerful baronial factions that acquired or usurped royal lands; the accession to the throne of children and weak rulers; and the plague epidemic of 1347. The island went from about seven hundred thousand inhabitants in 1277 to about three hundred thousand in 1375. It did not surpass the earlier level of population until the mid-sixteenth century.

By 1350 Sicily's economy was dominated by merchants and bankers from Genoa and Barcelona. The island was almost exclusively a grain producer and exporter; the limited industrial sectors of earlier centuries—mining, silk, cotton—nearly disappeared after the disruption of the Vespers. Sicilian society also became more stratified and rigid. The feudal aristocracy extracted privileges from its weak rulers that made Sicilian barons virtual kings in their estates. The right of feudal succession was expanded: by 1300 Sicilian barons had ensured nearly unlimited succession and gained the right to trade feudal assets with almost no royal interference. Feudal barons in the mainland kingdom would vainly covet such rights for centuries, while the Sicilian barons enjoyed them until 1788.

The Vespers and succeeding wars also left a legacy of insularity and xenophobia in Sicilian life. There was no university in Sicily until 1445. Political isolation accelerated ongoing trends toward greater homogeneity. Sicilian society became increasingly Latin in religious rites and Italian in language. Greek monasteries declined in number (fewer than one in four remained by 1457) and often ceased using the Greek language. By the mid-fourteenth century, with the exception of the small southern island of Pantelleria, where a free Muslim community lived until about 1480, the only Muslims in Sicily were slaves. The Arabic language survived only in Jewish communities, which continued to use Arabic—written in Hebrew characters—in official texts, and in Malta, then part of Sicily's domains, where Arabic continued to be spoken even after Muslims were expelled in 1271. When the direct line of Frederick of Aragon's descendants died out at the end of the fourteenth century, royal authority almost disintegrated and Sicily again became the object of the conflicting ambitions of Angevin and Aragonese monarchs. By 1409 the island became part of a renewed Aragonese empire in the western Mediterranean. From then on, it was ruled by viceroys appointed elsewhere. It would never again have an autonomous, resident monarchy.

The separation of Naples and Sicily endured. Both kingdoms were weakened politically and economically, also by the hostility between their rulers, which continued until the 1430s, when the Angevin line in Naples died out. The two kingdoms were ruled by the same sovereigns for long periods of their subsequent history, but they maintained separate institutions, laws, and administrative and financial systems. They were reunited only in 1816, when the Bourbon kings centralized their power and formed a new entity, the Kingdom of the Two Sicilies.

The historical memory of the Vespers, idealized as a revolt against foreign domination, lived on. It was a prominent element of Italian patriotism in the nineteenth-century movement for national unification. Although northern patriots regarded their southern brethren with a somewhat jaundiced eye when they considered the latter's contribution to Italy's national regeneration, the Vespers remained an object of admiration. The "Inno di Mameli," the 1847 nationalistic song that is now the Italian national anthem, lists several heroic and patriotic episodes from the Italian past, and the Vespers is the only one that took place in the South. In 1855 Verdi used the Vespers as the subject of a rousing opera that premiered in Paris. The subject made an unedited Italian version unacceptable to the conservative governments of the peninsula, but after unification in 1861 the opera with its original plot was performed in Italy as well. In a later and entirely different context, the Vespers still made for an appealing, if slightly paradoxical, reference in 1992. After the murder of two prominent anti-mafia judges, the Italian government launched its largest postwar military operation by bringing armed forces to the island in the anti-mafia "Operazione Vespri Siciliani."

The Vespers isolated and impoverished Sicily, and the dire economic consequences were also felt in the mainland South. By the early thirteenth century, merchants, bankers, and entrepreneurs from northern Italian cities had begun to penetrate the southern economy. The disruptions caused by the Vespers, followed by prolonged warfare, heavy taxation, and soon the plague epidemic, accelerated the decline of southern trade and industry. The monarchy's needs for military aid and political support during the Vespers war forced it to accept the spread and growth of the feudal nobility in the South. As feudal power was based on control and exploitation of the rural world, its expansion further weakened urban society and interests. With the exception of Naples, which became the Angevins' new capital, the once dynamic cities of the mainland South lost economic vitality and political weight. One example may suffice.

The Italian navy's flag today consists of the national tricolor (red, white, and green) flag, plus a coat of arms in the middle. This middle decoration gathers together the symbols of four famous port cities: the lion of Venice and the crosses of Genoa, Pisa, and Amalfi. Today one may well wonder why Amalfi, a little tourist town on the peninsula that marks the northern end of the Bay of Salerno, would be placed side by side with the famous medieval maritime republics of northern Italy. Amalfi's glory was not long-lived, but at the turn of the second millennium its achievements were remarkable.

"The obscure town of Amalphi"—wrote Gibbon—"displayed the power and rewards of industry." In the 970s the Arab visitor Ibn Hawqal wrote that "Amalfi is the most prosperous city [in its region], the noblest, the most illustrious by its situation, the richest and most opulent." The Amalfitani to this day claim that one of them invented the compass. They certainly smuggled and traded slaves and many goods between the Byzantine, Muslim, and Latin worlds. Amalfi merchants, like their northern Italian peers, established trading bases across the eastern Mediterranean, and as late as 1254 they enjoyed legal and business protections in Constantinople and the Christian Levant.

Success in trade went hand in hand with agricultural growth. In spite of their ungenerous natural surroundings, where steep, rocky hills limit the extent of arable land, the Amalfitani produced grain, wine, oil, and fruits. From the eleventh to the thirteenth centuries much previously uncultivated land in the area was covered with vines and fruit trees. The Amalfitani invested capital gained through trade to build irrigation and canal systems that improved and expanded the production of agricultural goods, some of which were exported. They also built new mills to process grains. The town minted gold coins as early as the tenth century. At the end of the eleventh century the historian Guglielmo Apulo described Amalfi as "a wealthy and populous city, none richer in silver, gold and garments from innumerable places."

The entire society participated in this expansion. Many Amalfitani engaged in trade alongside their agricultural or other activities. The local Church was growing rich in positions and treasure as Latin Christianity expanded in the South and added to local wealth. By the eleventh century there were eight dioceses in the Amalfi peninsula. Local patricians occupied all episcopal offices and dominated the powerful cathedral chapters of each diocese. Numerous private churches and chapels reflected the affluence and devotion of the families that endowed them and helped maintain their status and influence. Many clerics were involved in economic activities. The splendor of the cathedral of St. Andrew, with its Moorish-style cloister, displays the wealth, taste, and eastern contacts of local elites.

There were, however, limits to what Amalfi could achieve even at the high point of its growth. Unlike Venice or Genoa, the city never held any foreign dominions, and its economy always faced structural obstacles. First of all, the local population was low in number. Much land, including precious land on the shore and in the few flat areas, belonged to the clergy and was not available for manufacturing concerns. The arsenal and harbor were small and constricted by the landscape, and local timber was limited, so the Amalfitani could never build the large ships the Venetians and Genoese built in their commodious arsenals.

Textile manufacturing, the strongest motor of medieval urban economies, in Amalfi never grew beyond the local market. This was due to both economic and cultural factors: the relative small scale of the population and economy generated limited capital for industrial enterprises. Moreover, even at its prime, Amalfi never had a group of citizens who clearly identified themselves as merchants or entrepreneurs. Elite Amalfitani engaged in trade, but they also owned land and served, usually at the same time, as judges, notaries, clerics, or doctors. Individuals from Amalfi became full-time merchants when they lived and worked elsewhere, from Cairo to Constantinople. But in the city itself, trade never reached the prestige it enjoyed in the maritime cities of northern Italy, where success in business often opened the path to political leadership as well. Amalfi never enjoyed great political autonomy, and nearby larger cities like Salerno and Naples attracted politically ambitious Amalfitani away from their city's trade economy. By the 1130s Amalfi was part of the new Kingdom of Sicily, and the spread of feudal estates and chivalric culture over the twelfth and thirteenth centuries created a more rigid noble culture that frowned upon business activities.

In the later thirteenth century Amalfi's fortunes began to decline sharply. Contacts with the East became ever rarer; the last evidence of eastern trade came in 1408. New buildings were still numerous in the early thirteenth century, but rare later. By the fourteenth century Amalfi's merchants traded almost exclusively within a limited coastal area, from the Bay of Naples to the Calabrian coast. Their vessels were small and there were few commercial or insurance companies in the town. Local elites sought in administration, the legal professions, usury, or royal service in Naples the wealth they had once drawn from Mediterranean trade. Amalfitani landowners could not maintain the investment levels that had earlier enriched local agriculture, and the town now needed to bring in grain from other regions. The poor, faced with shortages and unemployment, migrated to Naples and other cities. The dramatic and beautiful local landscape today brings to Amalfi wealthy tourists from across the world, but by the turn of the fifteenth century the area could not produce enough food even for a diminished population.

Nature also turned hostile. On November 25, 1343, a devastating storm hit the Naples and Salerno area. The poet Petrarch, then visiting Naples on a diplomatic mission, described its effects: "What rain, what winds, what lightning, what thunder in the sky, what tremor of the earth, what moans of the sea, what cries of people! . . . The entire shore was filled with corpses mutilated and still palpitating: from some flowed their brains, from others their bowels." The storm destroyed Amalfi's harbor. Soon after, the midcentury plague epidemic devastated Amalfi's population and economy. Prolonged warfare in the kingdom disrupted the remaining trade and agriculture and led to an increase in crime, especially banditry. Limited local manufacturing—textiles, paper—did not compensate for losses in agriculture and trade. Foreign merchants, in particular the Genoese, penetrated the economy of the kingdom: by 1297 there were forty Genoese merchants operating in Naples, and they soon controlled much of Amalfi's trade as well. Catalan merchant ships entered Amalfi from 1319 on.

Amalfi's economic boom was unusually strong for a small port town, but many other southern coastal cities enjoyed prosperous times in the eleventh to thirteenth centuries, as the beautiful Romanesque cathedrals of many Puglia towns show to this day. Amalfi's decline stands as a model of the general worsening of the southern urban sector in the later Middle Ages.

The city of Naples forms the exception to this bleak picture of the post-Vespers South. Now the new capital of the mainland South, Naples began at the end of the thirteenth century the remarkable rise that over two centuries would make it the largest city in Italy and a major cultural and intellectual center. In 1279–82, even before the Vespers, Charles I had built the city's third castle, the imposing Castel Nuovo, which Neapolitans still call the Angevin castle. Charles II cleared swamps, paved streets, and set sewers. King Robert "the Wise" (ruled 1309–43) attracted scholars and artists to his court from all over Italy. Petrarch, the greatest Italian poet after Dante, came to Robert's court, and in 1341 the king crowned him with the laurel crown that marked his achievements as a poet. Petrarch celebrated Robert as the "greatest king and greatest philosopher, no more illustrious for his rule than for his learning, the only king our age has seen to be a friend of both knowledge and virtue." The great Tuscan prose writer Boccaccio came to Naples as a young merchant and later set a few of the stories of his *Decameron* in the city. He described Naples as "happy, peaceful, prosperous, magnificent." Giotto worked in Naples, and Tuscan artists—then the greatest in Italy—produced the Angevin

Simone Martini, *St. Louis of Toulouse Crowning His Brother Robert of Anjou King of Naples,* from the Capodimonte Museum, Naples

tombs that grace the church of Santa Chiara. The Franciscan complexes of Santa Chiara and San Lorenzo, the cathedral, the charterhouse of San Martino, and many other churches and monasteries in the Gothic style date to the early Angevin reigns. So does the so-called Angevin portico—just off the old Roman forum—which to this day houses one of the oldest food markets anywhere in the world.

Robert expanded the urban walls and built the city's fourth castle, Sant'Elmo, which dominates from the hill above the old center. The city also acquired municipal institutions that lasted until the beginning of the nineteenth century. Six noble wards were formed around 1294 (two merged a half-century later). The Seggi were both administrative districts of the city and aristocratic clubs gathering the noble families of each district. Under Robert, representatives of the Seggi, the Eletti, formed the city government. Over time they came to be assisted by a number of committees charged with various tasks. The size of the city began to grow, as the presence and patronage of the monarchy drew people, business, and institutions to Naples: under King Robert, Naples had about fifty thousand inhabitants.

The early Angevins also set about fortifying their rule in their diminished kingdom, with mixed results. The Sicilian war weakened the Crown's resources. Feudal jurisdiction expanded. The Angevins were also especially beholden to the papacy for its support. Charles I returned the Benevento enclave to papal control and extended clerical exemptions. Church assets paid almost no taxes, clerics enjoyed personal fiscal and judicial privileges, and church buildings enjoyed sanctuary rights (anyone taking refuge in a church was safe from arrest). But the kings also strengthened the royal government. Charles I settled the organization of the kingdom into twelve provinces. Charles II established the Vicaria, a new central tribunal, and Robert founded the Sommaria, the kingdom's central financial structure. These remained crucial organs of the government until the eighteenth century. Although feudal military service remained the core of the kingdom's armed forces, the Angevins also employed paid troops, including foreign ones, and increased control of the kingdom's more than two hundred royal castles.

The dynasty's greatest political success extended beyond the South. In the generations after the Vespers, marriage policy helped the Naples Angevins pursue their international aims. The numerous offspring of Charles II were deployed in a veritable matrimonial offensive. Careful choices expanded the dynasty's territory in the Balkans, where Angevin princes ruled or claimed a number of principalities. Success in central Europe was even more spectacular. In 1308 Carobert of Anjou, grandson of Charles II of Naples, became king of Hungary. His son, Louis "the Great," was king of Hungary and Poland (and briefly of Naples too), ruling an enormous region that linked the Baltic, Adriatic, and Black seas. Throughout the century the Angevins were arguably the leading royal house in Europe.

The rise of Naples, and the Angevins' successes, ground to a halt in the 1340s. The political history of Naples and Sicily over the next one hundred years was dominated by the instability of the monarchy. The effects of dynastic mishaps and of the economic decline caused by the Vespers were compounded when the Black Death hit. This devastating epidemic of bubonic plague affected all of Europe between 1347 and 1350, killing about 40 percent of the continent's population. The contagion came from central Asia and its first appearance in the West was in Messina, where the disease arrived in October 1347 on Genoese ships from the Black Sea. The first wave was the deadliest, but the plague returned repeatedly to various areas of Europe over the following four centuries, disrupting economies and lives. Population recovery was slow and uneven. The Kingdom of Naples, which in 1268 had over 2,300 communities, had only 1,462 in 1505; many settlements, abandoned because of the plague or for other reasons, were never restarted. Since the demographic decline contributed to lower fiscal revenues, rulers tried to improve the situation by favoring the immigration of Albanians and Slavs from the Balkans. Similar problems confronted all European states.

Unpredictable survival rates, in an age when numerous epidemics increased an already quite high child mortality rate, endangered dynasties across the continent, though they also created opportunities, which the Angevins exploited in central Europe. Much of the instability of the southern kingdoms had to do with troubled royal successions. In this Naples and Sicily were not unusual in fourteenth- and fifteenth-century Europe. The Hundred Years' War in France, the Wars of the Roses in England, and the civil war in Castile all exemplify the inherent instability of monarchies in late medieval, feudal Europe. Neither the conception of monarchy nor its institutions were strong enough to withstand the problems caused by a weak sovereign or a dubious claim to succession. Economic decline and the resulting social tensions—including peasant revolts and banditry—compounded the difficulty.

When minors or women ruled, discontent and tension usually rose. Late medieval elites, steeped in feudal culture, perceived military leadership as the primary responsibility of the sovereign and were thus skeptical of any ruler who was unable to lead armed forces in battle. A weak sovereign was exposed to the ambitions of powerful relatives and aristocratic potentates. Across western Europe, it was only with the Humanist movement and legal studies of the sixteenth century that the principles of dynastic succession became firm and generally accepted. Even after that, rule by minors or women was often troubled. Aragonese Sicily and Angevin Naples offer repeated examples of crises under female rule. A chronicler lamented that after King Robert "the kingdom came into the hands of a woman." The reigns of Joanna I (ruled 1343–81) and Joanna II (ruled 1414–35) of Naples were marked by persistent fights between feudal and court factions and between royal favorites and husbands. Many feudal barons and powerful princes within the royal family kept large armies of their own. For nearly a century, soldiers from Provence, Catalonia, Hungary, and the Balkans roamed the kingdom nearly unchecked. After 1378 the politics of the Great Schism—when Europe and each country within it were divided between the claims of rival popes—caused further instability.

The role of a prince consort was not yet defined in law or practice. A weak royal husband was often useless, in that he failed to provide his wife with the military or political support she needed. A strong one, on the other hand, was a threat because of his own ambition to rule. The two Joannas between them collected six husbands, not all of whom left the scene from natural causes (neither did Joanna I). In spite of such an abundance of husbands, and of a few favorites who also met untimely demises, neither queen left any surviving children. Repeated civil war and at least six invasions added to the chaos and greatly damaged the kingdom's economy and international position.

The central state's powers were obviously affected by dynastic chaos. More and more feudal barons won the right to exercise criminal jurisdiction over their vassals, even in capital cases. The rulers elevated the prestige of the aristocracy to obtain its support. Joanna I bestowed the first ducal title outside the royal family, and King Ladislas (ruled 1386–1414) created the first marquis. The Crown allowed more and more communities in the kingdom to fall under feudal rule, which further reduced royal revenues and control. Over the decades of war the monarchy also surrendered its external holdings: by 1400 the rulers of Naples had lost old Angevin lands in both France and the eastern Mediterranean.

Joanna II's lack of heirs opened a new crisis. The queen adopted two men as her heirs, changing her mind four times between them. A new branch of the French royal family claimed the Angevin legacy, as did Alphonsus, king of Aragon and Sicily, one of Joanna's adopted sons. When in 1409 the Sicilian branch of the Aragonese dynasty died out, the island was joined to the main line, which ruled from Barcelona. Since 1416 Alphonsus "the Magnanimous" ruled Aragon and Sicily. When Joanna II died in 1435, war erupted in the Kingdom of Naples, ending in 1442 with Alphonsus's triumphal entry into Naples. He chose the city as his residence and from there ruled a revived Aragonese empire that stretched across the western Mediterranean. Alphonsus never returned to his Iberian domains, ruling them and Sicily through viceroys. He was the first ruler since 1282 to hold both Naples and Sicily, and he employed in his government his subjects from all his realms, but he ruled in each kingdom according to its own traditions and institutions.

Alphonsus proved as skilled a ruler in peacetime as he was successful in battle. His reign benefited from the economic and demographic revival that began to surmount the consequences of the Black Death. His victory also meant relative peace and new political stability. Like his contemporary, the great Cosimo de' Medici in Florence, Alphonsus was a clever state-builder who brought order to a country riven by instability: ruthless if needed, capable in compromise, engaged with all aspects of government, a man of action, but also a cultivated man, able to appreciate both the advantages and the enjoyment that could come from the new artistic and intellectual movements that were becoming prominent in fifteenth-century Italy. In short, Alphonsus was Naples's first—and greatest—Renaissance ruler.

Alphonsus's rule also concluded a long process of realignment for the Italian South. Between the late thirteenth and the early fifteenth century, Sicily and Naples became much less tied to the political and commercial fortunes of the eastern Mediterranean, and much more connected to developments in northern Italy and the rest of western Europe. The end of the Crusades and the decline of the Byzantine empire, the growing power of the more hostile Ottoman Turks in the Balkans, the connections of the Angevins in central Europe and France and of the Aragonese in Iberia, and the economic and political effects of the Vespers contributed to this change in the traditional orientation of southern Italy.

On coming to power in Naples, Alphonsus recognized the influence of the feudal barons and reached compromises with them that strengthened their grip on their vassal population at the local level. In 1443 the king granted all Neapolitan barons the *merum et mixtum imperium*, or full civil and criminal jurisdiction over their vassals, including most capital cases. The Angevins had granted this power to individual barons, usually for life, but Alphonsus made it into a hereditary right attached to most fiefs. This concession augmented the social and political uniformity the king sought throughout his policies, but it also gave barons a much more entrenched position at the local level and diminished the possibilities for intervention by the central state. Thus, the transformation of feudal barons from a warrior caste into a landowning aristocracy endowed with substantial local control was complete. The process was aided by the fact that when Alphonsus came to power, serfdom had virtually disappeared from the South. Villagers owed dues to their lords and were subject to the latter's growing jurisdictional authority, but they rarely owed labor services, they could sell their own land, and they could leave the village. Feudal lordship by the fifteenth century was jurisdictional and economic, but no longer applied to the persons of the vassals.

Alphonsus thus acknowledged the local power of the feudal barons, who ruled over 90 percent of the kingdom's communities, a higher percentage than even in Sicily. He countered it by developing nonfeudal central institutions staffed by a professional bureaucracy that directed finance and justice. The old feudal Great Offices continued to exist as hereditary titles for prominent families, but they lost most of their power. The new Sacred Royal Council, formed of jurists appointed by the king, served as a supreme appeals court for the entire kingdom. Record-keeping improved and royal archives expanded. Royal appointees were sent to the provinces as governors with appeals power over feudal courts and to supervise the collection of taxes.

Alphonsus also revived the kingdom's old parliament. Across medieval Europe, this institution comprised representatives of the clergy, nobility, and royal towns. The Naples Parliament was never strong. The Angevins rarely called it to session and allowed the nobility to dominate it. Alphonsus summoned parliament nine times during his reign and allowed delegates of royal towns again to participate in its meetings, to balance aristocratic power. Parliament's main function was fiscal. In 1443 it granted the king a permanent hearth tax, which became the cornerstone of the kingdom's fiscal system. In the same year Alphonsus also established the Dogana of Foggia. This royal agency, similar to its counterpart in Castile, regulated the interactions between landowners and sheep-owners and ensured the smooth working of one of the kingdom's most important economic activities, moving millions of sheep from winter to summer pastures. It also netted Alphonsus about a hundred thousand ducats a year. The Dogana continued to operate until 1806.

Drawing strength from his multiple kingdoms, Alphonsus pursued an aggressive international policy. In 1452 he gave visiting Emperor Frederick III a lavish welcome in Naples, where for the occasion wine poured out of public fountains and, wrote a chronicler, "horses' troughs were full of sweets." The king followed an antagonistic policy toward the papacy and reclaimed Benevento. Though he recognized traditional papal sovereignty over Naples and Sicily, Alphonsus negotiated the replacement of the annual tribute in gold with the gift of a white mare, the *chinea*. He enforced the Aragonese tradition of requiring royal approval of all papal appointments and bulls before they could be implemented in the kingdom.

Alphonsus also developed the armed forces of his new kingdom. The Naples arsenal produced ships and artillery. Several cities expanded or renovated their fortifications. Alphonsus wanted to free himself of dependence from feudal military service and curtail the private armies kept by prominent barons. He used revenues from the hearth tax to build a royal army and a militia, although neither became as large or settled as the king planned. Overall, Alphonsus— somewhat in advance of his peers in France, England, and Castile— laid in Naples the foundations of a modern state that did not depend on feudal institutions: a professional central administration, stable taxation, a royal army, and the assertion of royal power over the Church.

The king revived Naples as a major intellectual and artistic center and a worthy capital for his extended dominions. The city stagnated during the troubles of the late Angevins. Under Alphonsus Naples began growing again: it went from forty-five thousand inhabitants in 1400 to about one hundred thousand at the end of the century. In 1484 a new circuit of walls was started, with twenty-one towers and several grand gates decorated in Renaissance style. Alphonsus's triumphal arch for Castel Nuovo, with its frieze showing the king's entry into the city and celebrating his virtues, still stands as Naples's greatest Renaissance monument. Under Alphonsus and his successor Ferrante (ruled 1458–94; his name is an old version of Ferdinand), several churches were built or rebuilt in the new style that rejected Gothic principles in favor of classical models. The church of San Domenico housed the royal tombs. The Aragonese also built suburban gardens and villas and brought some of the greatest Renaissance musicians to Naples. This beautified city appears in the century's most famous image of Naples, the *Tavola Strozzi* of 1472.

Aragonese Naples thus came to share in the flourishing of the Italian Renaissance. By the mid-fifteenth century, Florence and other northern Italian cities were the theater of remarkable artistic and intellectual achievements. Scholars researched the world of antiquity and found, edited, and published ancient texts. Knowledge of ancient Greek spread among Italian intellectuals and gave them broader access to ancient culture. Artists, educators, philosophers, and poets found in antiquity models to emulate. Latin and Greek civilization inspired a more secular culture that celebrated worldly success, the achievements of strong individuals, and the ideal of civic involvement as the highest calling for talented men. An optimistic, lay, urban, cultured elite set aside Christian humility and disdain for secular accomplishment. This elite shared a new education based on

The Arch of Castel Nuovo, Naples, depicting the triumphal entry of
Alphonsus the Magnanimous into the city in 1442

immersion in ancient culture, rejecting the rigid focus on logic, law,
and theology of medieval universities. The Humanist advocates of
these new ideas instead studied history and politics.

Humanists helped build a stronger basis for state power. Their
study of Roman history and law led them to emphasize the authority

of the state in contrast to the more fragmented authority of medieval societies. In the urban republics of northern Italy, such as Florence and Venice, Humanism served as the theoretical foundation for an assertion of city autonomy and power over provincial and rural forces. Humanists also proved very effective as secretaries, administrators, and diplomats. They produced treaties, correspondence, edicts, and speeches in the formal language newly in demand. The invention of a movable-type printing press in the 1450s facilitated the spread of the scholarly and literary achievements of the Humanists and of their ideas, just as it aided the circulation of printed reproductions of works of art in the new classical style of the Renaissance.

Alphonsus recognized early on the usefulness of Humanism and of royal patronage of arts and letters to his rule. In 1434, even before conquering Naples, he hired Antonio Beccadelli (1394–1471), known as Panormita from his birth in Palermo (Panormos in Greek), as royal librarian. Panormita was one of the best-known Humanist writers in Italy. His 1425 collection of erotic poems in Latin, the

The so-called *Tavola Strozzi*, a 1472 view of Naples,
from the Museum of San Martino, Naples

Hermaphroditus, had brought him admiration pleasantly tinged with notoriety. He was court poet to the duke of Milan, taught rhetoric at Pavia, and in 1432 achieved a Humanist's greatest honor when he was crowned poet by Emperor Sigismund. Alphonsus showed great favor to Panormita, who enjoyed a series of highly paid sinecures while he served as royal secretary and historiographer. Panormita followed Alphonsus in the conquest of Naples and celebrated Alphonsus's glory and learning in orations and historical works. Panormita's services included prominent embassies to other powers. It was during one such trip to Padua that he acquired and brought to Naples one of the Roman historian Livy's arm bones, as a sort of Humanist relic to inspire others to emulate the accomplishments of learned antiquity.

In addition to his positions, literary productions, and skeletal purchases, Panormita served as a sort of minister of culture for the king. Alphonsus, however sincere his interest in learning and the arts, was very conscious of the propaganda value of making his lands centers of the new culture that was flourishing in Italy and beginning to be

admired across Europe. In 1445 he founded the University of Catania in Sicily, and in 1451 he reopened the University of Naples that
the war had closed. He founded a royal library in Naples. Panormita
dispensed most of the king's support for the numerous other
Humanists who gathered at the Naples court. In 1447 Panormita also
founded, in the king's library, an informal academy of reading and
conversation on the classics that grew into the Accademia Pontaniana
(named after Panormita's successor as its leader), the center of
Naples's Humanist life—and the repository of Livy's arm bone.

Humanists not only were decorative additions to the court that
proved the king's good taste and learning, but also served to celebrate
and implement a new model of government, based on the primacy
of royal law and the absolute nature claimed for royal power. King
Ferrante continued to sponsor poets and writers. Both Gioviano Pontano (ca. 1429–1503) and Jacopo Sannazaro (1458–1530), the greatest Humanist poets of the Italian Renaissance, worked for Ferrante
and spent most of their lives in Naples. Around 1473 printing began
in Naples, facilitating the circulation of literary, scholarly, and legal
texts.

Thanks to vernacular literature, another recipient of royal patronage, we begin to know more also about the daily life of the city. The
fifty short stories by Masuccio Salernitano (ca. 1410–75) in *Il Novellino* offer lively vignettes of the social and religious life of fifteenth-
century southerners, and show them to have been randy, sharp, and
skeptical of their clergy's virtue. The plots of the stories are often for-
mulaic and similar to those of Boccaccio's *Decameron* and other
Renaissance texts. But the details of Masuccio's stories illustrate the
social realities familiar to his audience. Not all the stories are set in
Naples, but those that are depict an active urban life, with craftsmen
interacting with merchants, jurists, clerics, and nobles. The famous
twenty-ninth story centers on the generous Viola, wife of a wood-
worker, who shares her favors during one busy night with a blacksmith, a merchant, and a friar. Merchants appear in nine of the
stories, but most of them—including Viola's lover, who hails from
Genoa—are not from the South, even if they operate there, reflecting
the domination of southern trade by foreign interests.

Masuccio also describes a society still deeply entangled with the
Muslim world, in both positive and dangerous ways. Southerners fre-

quently traded with Muslims, and many owned slaves or spent time as such. In earlier centuries slavery had been common in southern Italy, but many slaves then had come from the Greek or Tartar worlds. These slaves had been mostly white and often Christian, and southerners treated them with relative leniency. In 1310, for instance, King Frederick of Sicily decreed several protections for slaves, including prohibiting masters to prostitute their female slaves, out of concern for Christian slave women. He also urged the baptism of all children born to slaves. As Arab and African slaves became more common in the Mediterranean by the fifteenth century, the attitude to slaves grew more hateful. Europeans became more conscious of racial and religious differences, in part because of the growing threat posed by the Ottoman Turks. By the mid-fifteenth century the Ottomans ruled much of Anatolia, and in 1453 they conquered Constantinople, destroying the remnants of Christian power in the East. By 1517 they would hold most of the eastern Mediterranean. The Ottomans were more aggressive than previous Muslim states, and southern Italians found themselves at the frontier of Christian Europe.

In three of Masuccio's stories Christian women engage in sex with Moorish slaves, which Masuccio presents as the gravest proof of women's evil nature. In two of the stories, a white man witnesses the sexual act and assaults the woman in violently racial language for giving herself to "a black dog, an irrational animal," or to "a black crow, a fetid servant, a fiery mastiff." On the other hand, the sexual union and marriage of a Christian man with a Turkish woman forms a happy ending to another story.

Masuccio's thirty-ninth story presents the tale of Ioanni and Susanna, which runs the gamut of southern experience in the broader Mediterranean. Ioanni is a sailor in Gaeta, a port town north of Naples, and beloved of Susanna, a noble woman. In order to earn enough to marry her, Ioanni sails for Genoa but is taken by pirates and brought as a slave to Tunis. Susanna, dressed as a man, goes to Tunis on a Venetian ship carrying fruit from Naples. Once there, Susanna, aided by Genoese merchants, finds Ioanni, but her money is stolen. She sells herself to redeem her beloved and becomes a slave to the local king. Ioanni helps her escape, but their ship is met by a storm just off the Sicilian coast and forced to return to Tunis. Ioanni is hanged. When Susanna is stripped to be flogged, she is revealed to be a woman. In front of the king and numerous Moors and Christians, she tells her story, stabs herself, and dies. In this dramatic tale of the dangers of piracy and slavery, contacts between Muslim and Christian traders are routine, and the Neapolitan protagonists of the story find their economic fate beholden to Genoese and Venetian ships and traders, while their personal fate is in the hands of the Muslims.

Masuccio's traders, craftsmen, and sailors display some of the renewed vitality of southern society in the fifteenth century. The Aragonese kings supported not only cultural flourishing but also urban and commercial interests. Ferrante favored the wool and silk guilds in Naples. The number of fairs across the kingdom doubled to about 230 every year. In 1480 Ferrante decreed the weights and measures used in Naples the only legal ones in the kingdom, greatly aiding internal trade. The government welcomed Genoese merchants, Florentine bankers, and other foreign entrepreneurs to Naples. Foreign business communities had their own officially recognized consuls and built their own churches.

The Aragonese also resumed the tolerant policies of earlier southern rulers toward religious minorities, especially Jews, at a time when the situation of Jews was worsening elsewhere. They had been expelled from England and France in 1290 and 1306, respectively. By the end of the fourteenth century, their status in the Iberian Peninsula—where large Jewish communities had long prospered under both Muslim and Christian rule—was coming under attack. After enjoying favorable circumstances under the Norman and Swabian monarchs, southern Jews' situation worsened under the Angevins, whose alliance with the papacy pushed them to stricter policies. Conversions were urged, at times forced, and in 1307 Jews were required to wear distinctive signs.

The situation of Jews greatly improved under Alphonsus and Ferrante, who also recognized the economic advantages of the Jewish presence: in addition to their commercial and entrepreneurial experience, Jews paid special taxes to the monarchy, as was common in Christian kingdoms. Under the Aragonese, Jewish communities and neighborhoods flourished not only in Naples but also in many provincial centers. There were about thirty-five thousand Jews and at least fifty Jewish communities in Aragonese Sicily, where they formed over 5 percent of the population. One out of five Sicilian artisans was Jewish. The earliest dated book printed in Hebrew appeared in Reggio in 1475. Hebrew printing shops operated also in Naples and at least two other towns. Jewish merchants, bankers, and doctors acquired prominent positions in Naples, and Jews were active in all economic fields and throughout the South. They were free to travel, choose their work and residence, and establish synagogues and schools. They could own property and slaves, though not Christian ones. Ferrante even decreed that should Christians convert a slave owned by a Jew, the Jew—barred by law from owning a Christian slave—would be entitled to financial compensation for his lost property.

Ferrante also welcomed Jewish immigration from other parts of Europe. When in 1492 Jews were expelled from Spain, between ten and twenty thousand came to the kingdom. In the 1490s there were probably about fifty thousand Jews in the kingdom who had settled there earlier and over fifty thousand refugees, including most of those recently expelled from Sicily on Spanish orders. The French invasion of 1494 brought attacks on Jews and looting of their property. Many were forced to convert and thus fell under the control of Church authorities. Still, in 1497, under the restored rule of Ferrante's descendants, many Jews expelled from Portugal took refuge in Naples, and King Frederick (ruled 1496–1501) renewed royal protections. But when the Spaniards conquered the kingdom in 1503, Jews again came under attack. In 1506 those in Naples were required to wear a distinctive sign (a red circle), an imposition extended in 1509 to all Jews in the kingdom. In 1510 Jews were expelled from the kingdom, with the exception of two hundred wealthy families who were allowed to stay in Naples. In Sicily the Spanish Inquisition began operating around 1500. Sicilian Jews who had been forced to convert after 1492 came under its jurisdiction, and by 1550 about four hundred of them had been condemned to the stake. Complete expulsion from the Kingdom of Naples took place in 1541.

Alphonsus the Magnanimous accomplished much in his reign in Naples. From that city he ruled his three kingdoms, drawing power from each. Yet the inherent weaknesses of the southern monarchy endured, and emerged again after his death in 1458. No European king, however powerful, could alter the law of succession that barred illegitimate offspring. Alphonsus had no legitimate children, so his ancestral realms of Aragon and Sicily went to his brother John II. However, Alphonsus had acquired Naples by conquest and therefore claimed the right to bequeath that kingdom to his illegitimate son Ferrante. In order to ensure this succession, father and son sought the assent of the Neapolitan barons and parliament, which they obtained in 1443 (the king's grant of jurisdiction to feudal lords greased the way to this settlement). Nonetheless, Alphonsus's death in 1458 was followed by a war between Ferrante and supporters of the Angevin claim. Only in 1462 was Ferrante safe on his throne. But he now ruled a single kingdom that could not draw on the financial and military resources of Sicily and Aragon.

By the 1460s, Naples was no longer a prominent Mediterranean power. Even within Italy its forces were matched by those of the papacy, Venice, Milan, and Florence, and the five states lived by an uneasy agreement that acknowledged their balance of power. Ferrante was forced to give Benevento back to the papacy to ensure papal recognition of his rule. In 1463 he also gave to the papacy the small enclave of Pontecorvo, near the border. His illegitimate birth weakened the king's status in dealings with both the feudal aristocracy and foreign enemies. In 1480 Ottoman forces took the city of Otranto on the southeastern coast of the kingdom, killing thousands. This was a shocking setback for a kingdom that had long harbored expansionist eastern plans. If Mehmet II—the conqueror of Constantinople—had not died shortly thereafter, the entire southern kingdom might have been in trouble. Even with the Ottoman empire in a succession crisis it took royal forces over a year to reclaim Otranto.

Camillo Porzio, who in the 1560s wrote a history of Ferrante, identified the basic weakness of the Neapolitan state: "the Kings of Naples, whenever they did not possess any other state, were in such low and contemptible condition, that not only foreign powers, but any of their own barons were heartened to conspire against them and expel them." The Otranto crisis invigorated the feudal barons. In 1485 a general feudal revolt, supported by the papal government, erupted against the king and his unpopular son and heir. Even members of the business and bureaucratic elites, appointed and enriched by Ferrante, joined the rebels. The barons demanded virtually complete authority over their estates and the king's recognition of their right to maintain substantial military forces of their own, which Alphonsus had limited. Royal forces eventually suppressed the revolt, which ended with several gruesome executions and numerous exiles. Ferrante thus survived two major feudal revolts, but the power of the feudal barons both over their subjects in rural areas and as a political force in the state was considerable. The Neapolitan monarchy remained fundamentally unstable, as became evident after Ferrante's death in January 1494.

The political developments of the late fifteenth century baffled educated Italians. Theirs was the leading culture of the continent, and the superiority of their artistic and intellectual achievements to anything produced in the benighted lands to Italy's north or west was undisputed. Italian envoys and merchants were shocked when in northern Europe they had to eat and drink from pewter plates and wooden cups, while in Italy they were surrounded by the luxuries and comforts produced by skilled craftsmen. Italian language and customs—and the new education created by Italian Humanists—formed the model of elite behavior and identity across the continent, and even mediocre Italian scholars easily impressed northern Europeans with their learning and sophistication. The works of Italian artists were prized by Europe's kings and nobles.

But the political and economic picture was quite different. Italian states were caught in their rivalries and in the instability or illegitimacy of many of their regimes. They were also weakened by the continuous subversive efforts of the political exiles whom decades of civil wars had scattered around and outside the peninsula. Italy's traditional economic networks were declining, and cheap products from Flanders and elsewhere competed successfully with Italy's vaunted crafts and entered even the Italian market itself. Meanwhile, European monarchies—especially in France and Spain—developed stronger administrative, financial, and military institutions over the course of the fifteenth century. Unlike many petty Italian princes, foreign monarchies by then also relied on a more settled tradition of hereditary rule and authority and on royal control of Church resources and appointments.

Perceptive Italian observers worried about these developments, but little changed until the situation got much worse in 1494. In that year, old King Ferrante's death sparked the so-called Italian wars, a prolonged series of conflicts between 1494 and 1559 that set various European and Italian states against each other in a bewildering series of shifting alliances. Control of Naples became the central element in the Italian wars. The aim was hegemony over Italy, still one of the wealthiest parts of Europe, and through it hegemony over the continent. France and Spain became the most important players in the conflicts, which ended with the establishment of Spanish control over much of the peninsula. Spain's hegemony would last until the start of the eighteenth century. Renaissance Italians were shocked when these wars proved the weakness of their states and made even those that managed to maintain formal independence into satellites of foreign powers. It was galling to have to accept uncouth French or Spanish overlords, but it could not be avoided.

Between 1494 and 1503 Naples had seven different rulers and the kingdom was the theater of nearly continuous warfare. The starting point of the conflict was the claim by King Charles VIII of France (ruled 1483–98) to be the heir to the Angevin rulers of Naples. Neapolitan exiles egged him on. Exploiting the unpopularity of Ferrante's son, Alphonsus II, as well as political crises in other Italian states, Charles VIII led an expedition into Italy. He encountered almost no opposition until after he entered Naples on February 21, 1495. At his Naples coronation, Charles even practiced the miraculous healing traditionally attributed to French and English kings, by touching several who sufferred from scrofula.

Although ultimately quite brief, Charles's rule in Naples left an important legacy in the municipal government. The city's government consisted of the Eletti, representatives of the five aristocratic Seggi, which were becoming ever more exclusive in their admission policies. Charles added the Eletto del Popolo to represent nonnoble interests. This gave elite businessmen, professionals, and merchants an official voice in local affairs. The reform was maintained by Charles's successors. These years of turmoil saw the expansion of Naples's municipal government and of the privileges of both the city and its citizens. Neapolitans were exempted from many taxes, and they won the right to transfer any judicial case in which they were involved to the city's tribunals, where they could expect favorable treatment. In 1496 the Annona was established. This new agency of the local government guaranteed the city's provision of basic foodstuffs. The Annona licensed bakers, supervised the flow of grains and other food items into the city, and regulated retail trade. The establishment of the Annona reflected the challenges posed by the quickly increasing population of the city, as well as the more prominent role gained by its elites during a time of royal trouble. The Annona lasted until 1795.

Charles VIII never managed to solidify his rule in the South. His conquest shocked Italian princes into action. A coalition of Italian and European states formed to resist this expansion of French power. In May 1495 Charles left Naples, and by the end of the year he was back in France. The young King Ferdinand II (ruled 1495–96), old Ferrante's grandson, reentered Naples on July 7 to the great joy of a chronicler: "this day was so beautiful, that the stones in the streets jumped, and the stars in the sky sparkled, and the fish in the sea leapt, such was the happiness at this lord, who was well loved by everybody, including children." Ferdinand II remained popular through his short life. His death was preceded by an elaborate procession of the miraculous relics of San Gennaro and followed by great popular mourning. But the inherent weaknesses of the Italian states remained, and in 1501 King Louis XII of France (ruled 1498–1515) again invaded Italy, aiming for Naples. This time the French king had agreed with Ferdinand of Aragon to share the Kingdom of Naples between them. Ferdinand already ruled Sicily and Sardinia and would not tolerate French power so close to his possessions. He also had hereditary claims to Naples since he was the nephew of Alphonsus the Magnanimous. His marriage to Isabella of Castile in 1469 had brought together the two Iberian Crowns and greatly strengthened their monarchy. After the 1492 conquest of Granada, the last territory on the Spanish peninsula ruled by Muslims, Castilian energies and interests centered on the exploration and conquest of the New World across the Atlantic, but Ferdinand remained focused on the Italian interests of his Aragonese kingdom.

In 1501 both French and Spanish forces entered the kingdom and quickly dispatched those of the ruling King Frederick. An uneasy division began, and soon gave way to open conflict. It was then, on February 13, 1503, that the Challenge of Barletta took place, an episode that remains famous in Italian patriotic lore. After French knights in this Puglia town accused Italians of cowardice, thirteen Italian knights redeemed Italian honor by defeating thirteen French ones. More important, on April 28, 1503, Spanish forces under Gonzalo Fernández de Córdoba—the "Great Captain"—won a resounding victory at Cerignola in Puglia, and Spain's rule over Naples was settled. The battle at Cerignola also played a significant role in military history. It marked the first appearance of a mixed force consisting of light cavalry, foot soldiers carrying pikes, and infantrymen armed with individual firearms. Spain perfected this new type of fighting force. The Spanish army went on to dominate military events across Europe and remained undefeated until the 1643 battle of Rocroi in the Low Countries.

Thus ended the autonomous Aragonese monarchy in Naples. In 1266, when the Angevins had conquered it, the Kingdom of Sicily was the strongest state in Italy and a major player in European and Mediterranean affairs. By 1503 Naples and Sicily were under Spanish rule, and from that date to 1734 neither had a resident sovereign. The Vespers had severed the link between Sicily and the continental South, and the economy of both regions had become subordinate to the interests of northern Italian merchants and entrepreneurs. The southern clergy's privileges and wealth grew considerably. A powerful feudal aristocracy dominated society and politics. The losses inflicted by the Black Death and by a century or more of warfare and social and political turmoil had damaged all aspects of southern life. By the mid-sixteenth century, Italy was marginal to European politics, as colonial trade and expansion made Atlantic powers much more prominent within European life.

Yet not all the developments of the Angevin and Aragonese period were negative. By 1450 economic and demographic growth had resumed in the South. In fits and starts, the Neapolitan state had developed more effective central institutions. Naples had become the largest city in Italy and a dynamic cultural center. The Aragonese kings made it a central instrument of their rule. The capital became not only the king's residence but also the political, administrative, judicial, social, military, and cultural center of the kingdom, a role that grew further under Spain. Finally, the South came under Spain's rule as the golden age of Spanish power and culture was beginning to spread across the globe, so southerners found themselves participants in a world empire that posed problems but also offered opportunities.

✍ Chapter IV ✎

Subject to a Distant King
The South in the Spanish Empire

Now, as justice had been restored and put in its place, criminals were punished without fail; and, without attention to individuals, equality was maintained; and everyone, out of fear, lived properly, so that it really seemed a golden age: the good thus enjoyed a tranquil life, and the evil restrained themselves from acting badly. But the proud, unable to tolerate the yoke of justice given equally to nobles and plebeians, began to blame the viceroy, saying that everything he did was not the result of the virtue of justice, but of the vice of cruelty.

S. Miccio, *Vita di Don Pietro di Toledo* (1600)

On November 25, 1535, Charles V, Holy Roman emperor and king of Spain, Naples, Sicily, and Sardinia, made a triumphal entrance into the city of Naples. Charles had just led Spanish forces in the conquest of Tunis—part of the ongoing Mediterranean struggle between Christians and Ottomans—and now came to visit his southern Italian realms. It was the first time since 1506, when Charles's grandfather Ferdinand had come to Naples shortly after the Spanish conquest of the kingdom, that southerners beheld their sovereign, and Neapolitans pulled out all the stops to impress him. The visit produced a profusion of essays and verses. The Humanist poet Antonio Minturno, for instance, addressed his city:

> Mother of illustrious minds,
> of spirits always intent to the greatest honor,
> living and eternal source
> of feats glorious and known to the world,
> how happy will you be,
> when you will behold your king?

Charles approached from land—he had made similarly splendid visits to Palermo and Messina in the preceding weeks and was marching up the peninsula—and rode into the city through Porta Capuana, the eastern gate that the Aragonese kings had decorated in classical style. The city's government—the Eletti—welcomed Charles and escorted him into the city. The emperor wore dark velvet clothes adorned only with the emblem of the Golden Fleece, Europe's noblest chivalric order, of which Charles was master. He rode under a baldachin held by the Eletti, and led a long procession that stopped at the cathedral and at all the city's Seggi on its way to Castel Nuovo, where Charles lodged during the four months he spent in Naples.

The arrival brought a flood of lavish pageantry, which drew from classical and medieval models. At Porta Capuana three angels descended to give Charles his scepter and crown, and the keys to the city. Along the procession, trumpets blared; Latin inscriptions glorified Charles; allegorical, religious, and mythological statues saluted him; decorated arches compared him to Caesar, Alexander, and Scipio Africanus (the Roman general who defeated the Carthaginians, an apt reference for the conqueror of Tunis, which is near the site of Carthage) and celebrated "the most happy vanquisher of the Ottoman fury." In Piazza Selleria, center of the popular element of the city government, Charles found a huge mountain peopled by giants: on his arrival an eagle—symbol of empire—darted lightning that destroyed the mountain and the giants, evoking Jupiter's own victory over the giants. Pyrotechnics accompanied this impressive spectacle.

During Charles's stay in Naples, the city and its elites competed in entertaining him with banquets, theatrical performances, and bullfights (Charles himself killed a bull in one). The kingdom's parliament met in the emperor's presence. Delegates from all the Italian powers came to attend Charles, and Naples for a few months was almost the world's capital. But a fierce battle raged behind the entertainments. There were, of course, the usual struggles for precedence and rank that, in the hierarchical society of the time, pitted noble families, clerics, and prominent officeholders against each other whenever symbolic rituals were enacted. But there was more: since the Spanish conquest in 1503, when Neapolitans had lost their resident sovereign, the Neapolitan aristocracy had been trying to assert and expand its role in governing the kingdom. Naples was after all the largest city ruled by Spain, and local nobles still hoped to persuade Charles to settle his residence there. Speeches, treatises, and inscriptions during Charles's visit emphasized the contribution of the Naples nobles to the emperor's wars—especially to the conquest of Tunis—and their rank and authority. Neapolitan aristocrats recognized in the emperor's visit their best chance to react to the troubling developments of recent years, when they had felt their power waning. The main target of their ire was the viceroy Charles had appointed a few years before: Pedro de Toledo (1480–1553).

Pedro de Toledo's life linked the Spanish empire and its dominions and shows how public achievement and private advancement were intertwined in early modern politics. Toledo was the second son of the duke of Alba, of a family that had emerged as one of the leading ones in Castile after the civil wars of the mid-fifteenth century. Toledo's father reached the pinnacle of Spanish society and government under Ferdinand the Catholic and Charles V. Under his father, Toledo gained the military training and courtly experience customary of his class, though, as a second son, he had to find fortune outside of his family's patrimony. After serving as a page at the court of Ferdinand, Toledo in 1503 married Maria Osorio Pimentel, an heiress who brought her husband considerable estates and the title of marquis of Villafranca. After 1519, when Charles V became the Holy Roman emperor, Toledo was part of Charles's immediate circle, and he traveled in Italy and Germany with the emperor. In July of 1532 Charles appointed him viceroy of Naples.

The appointment marked a transition. For the first few decades after the 1503 conquest, the guiding principle of Spanish rule was continuity with the past. Although Naples was a conquered kingdom, Ferdinand preferred to stress his ancestral right to the kingdom and to treat it as a hereditary possession. This—in the tradition-based mentality of the period—entailed the recognition of the kingdom's laws, privileges, and institutions. Ferdinand saw Naples in parallel to Sicily and Sardinia, his other Italian possessions, as separate entities within the federal system of the Crown of Aragon. The very figure of the viceroy, which was new to Naples, came from the Aragonese federal tradition and had been first deployed in Aragon itself, which was formally divided into three separate entities (Aragon, Catalonia, and Valencia). The viceroy was the sovereign's representative in a kingdom in which the sovereign did not reside. He was the head of the military and the government and could legislate. He also embodied sovereignty in its symbolic aspects and was therefore surrounded by royal protocol. In Spanish Italy most viceroys were Spanish aristocrats, though Italians occasionally served in an interim capacity. About forty-five viceroys served in Spanish Naples (1503–1707) and about eighty in Spanish Sicily (1412–1713).

After Ferdinand's death the continuing wars with France for hegemony over Italy advised against antagonizing the southern elites by attempting to diminish their power or status. Royal revenues and royal control in the kingdom were fragile, and wars took viceroys away from Naples. But in 1528–29 a French invasion and siege of Naples failed and many pro-French Neapolitan aristocrats lost their lives and estates. In 1530 Charles was crowned emperor in Bologna by Pope Clement VII (the last time a pope crowned an emperor). The papacy and France now acknowledged Spain's rule over Naples. Charles could therefore more aggressively assert royal power in the southern kingdoms. The Naples viceroy became the head of the Spanish power system in Italy. In later generations, the viceroyalty of Naples was often the reward for successful service as viceroy in Sicily or Sardinia, governor of Milan, or ambassador to Rome.

The viceroy's position had inherent weaknesses, especially his short tenure and his status as a foreigner. It often took months to learn about each kingdom's administration, and communications with the royal court were slow. The more powerful viceroys became and the more they enjoyed the trappings of royalty, the more potential there was for mistrust on the part of the king. Local elites exploited these circumstances. In each kingdom, the aristocracy, the capital city, and the parliament preserved the right to petition the sovereign directly, bypassing viceroyal authority. Moreover, the monarchy periodically appointed "visitors," officials charged with gathering information for the king, proposing reforms, and mediating between different interests. These visits (there were seven in Spanish Naples) also formed the occasion for elite griping about the viceroy and the bureaucracy.

In his first years, Toledo concentrated on learning Naples's administration and on forming ties with the feudal aristocracy, the city's nobles, and the higher officials of government. His interest in local matters surprised observers, one of whom noted that "[Toledo] was curious to see and understand all the actions of past Kings, and the Statutes, Articles, Privileges, and Laws" of Naples and the kingdom, "to examine in detail the approach and actions of viceroys," in order to be "well instructed and informed of everything." This, and Toledo's general assertiveness, troubled the Naples aristocrats. But their attempt to convince Charles to dismiss Toledo failed. At the end of his visit, Charles officially praised Toledo's "prudence, vigilance, and solicitude" and the "peace, quiet, and justice" he had brought to the kingdom. He confirmed Toledo in office with expanded powers: for example, Charles greatly increased the number of offices the viceroy could bestow without royal input.

Now Toledo's rule became much bolder. He purged the administration, placing his creatures, clients, and allies in positions of power in all central institutions. He exploited the rivalry between the old aristocracy and the rising administrative elite to diminish the power of the former. He reformed all central tribunals and organs of government and brought them together in one location—the fortress of Castel Capuano, where many tribunals in Naples still meet. He also increased judges' salaries to limit corruption. By 1550 statutes regulated how many, and in some cases which, officials had to be citizens of the kingdom (the balance between Spaniards and locals was a constant source of tension in all Spanish possessions) and which positions could not be sold (usually those charged with the administration of justice). In the 1540s, as fears of Protestantism grew, Toledo targeted intellectual freedoms: prepublication censorship was established for theological books in 1544 and extended to all books in 1550; the chair of humanities at the university was abolished in 1541; and the government-controlled university's monopoly over the city's intellectual life was strengthened by forcing private intellectual gatherings to disband. By all these activities Toledo earned his nickname as the "Iron Viceroy," whose "austere and terrible nature" troubled Neapolitans.

Toledo's energy and concerns were boundless. He legislated on matters ranging from the sublime to the faintly ridiculous, mostly affecting the capital city: he passed measures against the false wit-

nesses who infested the Naples tribunals, and against usurers; prohibited duels and nocturnal serenades; confined prostitutes to specific areas of the city; curtailed the right to bear arms; forbade, under
penalty of death, the carrying of ladders at night (to limit burglaries
and elopements); ordered the draining of swamps near Naples; and
aided in the rebuilding of Pozzuoli after the seismic events of 1538
(when a new hill, the Monte Nuovo, emerged). Although he monitored intellectual life, Toledo also understood the advantages of
being a patron of arts, letters, and entertainment. He enjoyed bullfights (he was wounded in his leg in one) and sponsored feasts,

A seventeenth-century print depicting the castle Castel Capuano,
in Naples, where Pedro de Toledo gathered all the Naples tribunals

dances, and masquerades. He started a new palace for the viceroy, built fountains, paved streets, and supported poets and artists. He also supported charitable institutions and founded the church and hospital of San Giacomo degli Spagnoli, which served the Spanish community of Naples. A funeral monument to Toledo and his first wife is there (to some scandal, the widower Toledo lived openly for years with the widowed sister of one of his sons-in-law and only married her shortly before his death).

Combating crime was a particular concern of Toledo's, and generally of Spanish government in both Naples and Sicily. There were, for instance, forty homicides in the city of Naples in May of 1531, shortly before Toledo's appointment. Smuggling was a constant threat to tax collection. In the 1530s the new inquisitorial system of justice, which limited the rights of defendants and established secret, written procedures for criminal trials, was implemented in all Spanish dominions and soon became the norm across Europe. It replaced the medieval procedure, based on oral, open accusations, under which it had been harder to obtain convictions.

Giovanni da Nola, *Tomb of Don Pedro de Toledo and His First Wife*, in the church of San Giacomo degli Spagnoli, Naples

Toledo brought about a much stricter control of crime, at least in Naples itself, and expanded the number of capital crimes. He stated to a Florentine agent that as many as eighteen thousand criminals had been executed in Naples under his government. Even if Toledo exaggerated, his rule was no doubt harsh compared to what followed: probably fewer than four thousand executions occurred between 1556 and the late eighteenth century (with a yearly average that fell from thirty-two in the late sixteenth century to three in the eighteenth). This decline in executions occurred even though successive viceroys continued to increase the number of capital crimes—in 1563 even to include those who forcibly kissed married women in public, which the law defined as "an enormous and detestable crime."

Rural crime was much harder to control. Bandits attacked travelers, pillaged castles and villages, and exacted protective payments from the population. These organized armed groups emerged from the widespread poverty and discontent of the rural population and at times received the support of local people. Many nobles also entertained profitable relationships with bandit groups, while the Spanish government struggled to control them. Banditry increased in times of heightened economic crisis, famine, or especially harsh taxation. The papal enclave of Benevento with its porous borders was often a haven for bandits. The problem was not seriously limited until aggressive operations under Viceroy Carpio in the 1680s.

Viceroys cooperated with numerous other government organs. Administrative complexity characterized the Naples monarchy like all governments of the time. As in most European countries, Sicily and Naples had traditional parliaments that consisted of representatives of the privileged groups in each kingdom and met when summoned by the sovereign. The Sicilian Parliament included delegates of the three traditional orders: feudal lords, clergy, and royal towns. In Naples after 1504 only the lords and towns participated, and the parliament's power dwindled. Since 1505 the main organ of government was the Collaterale Council, which supervised all administration and governed whenever a viceroy died in office. Next in authority was the Sacred Royal Council, which was the final court of appeals for the entire kingdom. The Vicaria was the intermediate criminal appeals court for all provincial courts and the primary court for the city of Naples and its immediate region. The Sommaria was the highest

financial organ. All these institutions exercised jurisdiction over matters specific to their field of operation and over their personnel. Thus,
for instance, the Sommaria adjudicated all tax disputes.

Given the judicial nature of these institutions, their personnel
came overwhelmingly from the legal elites of the kingdom. By 1542
Toledo excluded nobles without legal training from most Collaterale
business. In Naples the legally trained elite, whose power and prestige grew over the early modern period, were called the *togati*, or
robed ones. Their numbers grew as the government established new
offices. The University of Naples produced about nine hundred law
graduates between 1400 and 1600, but several thousands in the seventeenth century. Many aristocrats resented the power of these officials, although many nobles also gained law degrees and entered state
service. Stronger royal institutions meant the decline of aristocratic
privileges and were bitterly resented by members of the traditional
elites. In the 1550s an aristocratic essayist deplored that "one prison,
one penalty, one rigor of justice and one procedure serve to punish
the good and the bad, the noble and the ignoble." In the 1580s
another noble critic stressed the old distinction between robe elites
and warrior nobles: "not all those who govern and wear long robes
are apt to judge what is suitable to the honor of those who have
crossed mountains, rivers, or oceans, in full armor, loyally serving
their king with valor."

Over time, however, the togati formed tight links with many aristocratic families. This gradual blending of elites was customary across
early modern Europe. At the end of the Spanish period, the jurist
Francesco D'Andrea (1625–98) recommended to his nephews a legal
career as the best avenue in Naples for social ascent: "there is no city
in the world in which talent is better rewarded, and where a man
without other qualities than his own merit can rise to great charges
and immense wealth, to supreme offices that govern the commonwealth, without needing either birth or money."

In addition to the organs of the central government, the capital
had its own institutions. Naples's government consisted of five Eletti
elected by the noble Seggi plus the Eletto del Popolo, added in the
1490s to represent the "People" of Naples. The noble Seggi became
increasingly exclusive, and the Crown took a keen interest in their
membership: in 1559 the king prohibited any admissions without

royal permission. Around 1600 about 150 families belonged to the noble Seggi. The Popolo consisted of the higher ranks of professionals, merchants, and artisans of the city. The city itself was divided into twenty-nine *ottine*, or neighborhoods. Each *ottina* had a captain whose responsibilities included local order and safety. Since 1498 the king chose the captains, the crucial links between the city's masses and the government. The ottine chose six men from whom the Eletto del Popolo was elected and later selected by lot. Toledo gained the power of appointing the Eletto del Popolo, who henceforth became the viceroy's agent in the city government. The city government was further weakened in 1560 when the viceroy created a new official to supervise the city's provisioning, until then the responsibility of the Eletti.

The kingdom was divided into twelve provinces, each governed by a *preside* (governor) who commanded local military forces and who, if he had a law degree, directed the provincial *udienza*, or tribunal. The territory of each province was divided into *università*, or communities, each based in a city or village. These were the basic units of the tax and justice systems. Most università were fiefs of the aristocracy, which meant that local justice was exercised in feudal courts by agents of the barons. Appeal to the udienza was possible but costly. There were about fifteen hundred università in the kingdom around 1500, and close to two thousand around 1600, as the population grew. Only about seventy—larger or more strategic ones—were not under feudal rule, fewer than under the Aragonese. This meant that about three-quarters of the kingdom's population had no immediate access to royal justice.

Toledo left his mark on all these institutions, though his power, as that of any government of the time, diminished the farther one went from the capital. His long tenure also allowed him to reap substantial personal advantages. The viceroy received a salary insufficient to the princely lifestyle expected of one who represented the king of Spain, but his power was substantial and so was his ability to influence the workings of justice and the tax system. Such power and influence brought financial rewards. Toledo also exploited his position as the leader of Charles V's forces in Italy to promote his family. His greatest personal achievement was the marriage in 1539 of his youngest daughter, Eleonora, to the new duke of Florence, Cosimo de' Medici (ruled 1537–74).

The Medici were latecomers to the ranks of European sovereigns, and Cosimo, son of a mercenary captain and first in his line of the family to gain power, was perhaps not the grandest of matches. But the marriage joined Eleonora to the sovereign of a real principality, one closely linked to the emperor and to Spain. Cosimo's ducal predecessor had married a daughter (albeit illegitimate) of Charles V himself. Cosimo proved to be one of the most clever rulers of his time, and by their deaths he and Eleonora, as grand-dukes of Tuscany, enjoyed the highest rank among Italian sovereign princes. The marriage enhanced the status of Toledo's family among Italy's elites. Toledo died at his daughter's court in Florence in 1553. The marriages of two other children with members of Neapolitan aristocratic families also rooted Toledo's family in its new context.

Toledo acquired property in and around Naples, including a city palace and two suburban villas. Two of his sons joined the noble Seggi of Naples; one, Garcia, was later viceroy of Catalonia and Sicily before retiring to Naples. Toledo's nephew, the duke of Alba, himself viceroy of Naples in 1556–58, was later sent to repress the Dutch revolt against Spain and became arguably the most important figure in the monarchy of Philip II. Toledo's brother Juan was bishop of Burgos in 1537, cardinal in 1538, almost pope in 1549, and archbishop of Santiago in 1550, a rich see he never visited because he remained a prominent figure at the papal court until his death in 1557. In later generations, other members of the family served as governor of Milan, viceroy of Sicily, and again as viceroy of Naples. The family owned property in Naples until the 1760s. In the 1540s and 1550s Toledo, his brother the cardinal, his son-in-law Cosimo, and his nephew the duke formed a tightly knit network at the center of the Spanish monarchy's power system, linking familial fortunes, private wealth, public service, and advancement of the state.

The establishment of Spanish power enhanced the position of southern rulers in the old struggles against Mediterranean threats. Charles V and his successors, in their self-declared role as champions of Christendom, poured resources into the struggle against the Ottoman Turks. In 1522 the Ottomans expelled from the Greek island of Rhodes the Knights of St. John, the old crusading military order. In

1530 Charles V gave Malta to the Knights—who thus gained the name by which their order is still known—in exchange for a symbolic payment of six (presumably Maltese) falcons a year to the Sicilian Crown. The Ottoman threat to Italy remained formidable until 1571, when Christian allies, including about thirty Neapolitan galleys, defeated the Ottoman fleet at Lepanto, off the western coast of Greece. After that, naval warfare in the central Mediterranean decreased, to the obvious benefit of the southern kingdoms.

Yet decline in open warfare did not eliminate all danger from the East. Pirate raids were features of southern life into the eighteenth century, though they declined in intensity over time. Muslims and Christians had raided each other's coasts since the Middle Ages. Pirates and privateers came from the Ottoman East and from North Africa, where the Barbary states developed under indirect Ottoman authority. After the defeat at Lepanto, the Barbary states probably became more dangerous, as Ottoman ability to control them diminished.

Raids affected the entire South. For example, Pozzuoli and Castellammare, in the Bay of Naples, were attacked in 1548, as was the island of Ischia—just opposite the capital—in 1544; Reggio, in Calabria, was sacked in 1594 and its cathedral destroyed; Vieste, Vasto, and Manfredonia, on the Adriatic coast, were sacked in 1554, 1566, and 1620, respectively. In each case hundreds of people were killed or taken prisoner. Coastal fortifications often proved insufficient and small villages were rarely defended at all. There were also countless attacks on ships in the waters of both kingdoms. "Li Turchi," the Turks, were still playfully mentioned as a scarecrow for unruly children in my childhood in the 1960s.

Captivity was thus an ever-present fear for southerners. Many southern institutions allocated funds for the ransom of those captured by the infidel. In 1548 the Neapolitan confraternity for the Redemption of Captives was founded, the first such institution in Italy. In the 1580s the confraternity established agents in Palermo and Messina, and in 1596 a parallel confraternity was founded in Palermo. Members donated and collected alms and arranged trips to ransom captives, giving priority to children, clerics, women, and the old.

Captured nobles or clerics could expect to be ransomed quickly, but the majority of captives lived for many years in slavery, in Constantinople or the North African cities, or as rowers on the galleys (the warships of the era) of their captors. Around 1600 there were over thirty thousand Christian slaves in the Barbary cities, at least two-thirds of them captured from southern Italy. There were still about five thousand such slaves in Algiers and Tunis in 1721. Many slaves converted to Islam, and some converts (renegades in Christian eyes) ascended to prominent positions in the Muslim world: Uluj Ali (d. 1587)—who ruled Algiers, fought at Lepanto, took Tunis from the Spaniards, and rose to high office in Constantinople, where he endowed a mosque—was a Calabrian renegade; Scipione Cicala of Messina (1545–1605) became, as Sinan Bassà, a pirate chief and led raids on the very coasts where he had grown up. Christian authorities were especially concerned with renegades and attempted to gain them back. The Inquisition in Naples between 1563 and 1686 accepted 190 of them back into the Catholic fold.

Southern Italians also encountered slavery in their own society. Until the eighteenth century, Muslim slaves were common in the region, from elite households in the capital to feudal castles in remote villages. This slavery was different from its medieval precedent. Large-scale slave trading had greatly declined by the early sixteenth century, and few slaves came from the Tartar or Slavic East. Most slaves in Italy were now the victims of piracy and warfare and came from the Muslim world; sub-Saharan Africans were also common. The majority of male slaves served as rowers on galleys, side by side with convicts and a few others whose misery pushed them to seek this desperate employment. In the seventeenth century, slaves formed between 20 and 30 percent of the crews of southern galleys. Women—and a few men—were used as domestic servants. Slavery as a form of rural labor was extremely rare. At the end of the sixteenth century about 1 percent of Sicily's population consisted of slaves, concentrated in large cities. In Naples there may have been as many as ten thousand in the late seventeenth century (about 3 percent of the city's residents).

Slaves were purchased and included in legacies, gifts, and exchanges. A Sicilian proverb warned against buying elderly slaves because they "work little, and drink a lot." In the mid-sixteenth century a good slave could fetch the equivalent of about ten tons of wheat. Many slaves converted to Christianity, and preaching to Muslim slaves was a prominent Christian good deed. The most famous southern converted slave was Benedetto "the Moor," the son of baptized slaves whose master freed Benedetto when he was eighteen years old. First a hermit, and given to mystical experiences, the illiterate Benedetto later joined the Franciscans and lived a simple, saintly life in Palermo until his death in 1589. In 1652, well before his 1743 beatification, he was declared a patron of Palermo by local authorities. He was long popular among slaves in Latin America. Canonized in 1807, Benedetto is today an official patron saint of African-Americans.

Conversion, however, did not emancipate a slave or necessarily change his or her daily life. By the eighteenth century, conditions improved and raids diminished, but the children of slaves remained enslaved, so slavery did not disappear. Almost four hundred slaves worked in the construction of the new royal palace in Caserta in the 1760s and 1770s. The last law case in Palermo concerning the legality of a man's enslaved status took place in 1812.

Though the threat of piracy remained prominent, after 1529 the South did not experience military attacks by land. Overall, the area was less affected by warfare than other regions of Italy or Europe. Toledo's major contribution to defense matters was his expansion of the walls of Naples, made necessary by both the growth of the city and the French siege of 1529. Beginning in 1537 a broader circuit with thirty-six towers was built; it nearly doubled the enclosed area and connected the old city to outlying castles. Toledo also developed new neighborhoods where Spanish troops lodged (still called the Spanish quarters) and opened up a wide street—today named after him—that connected one of the new gates to the royal castle and became an elegant new center of the city's life. Toledo and his successors also attended to coastal fortifications. By the 1560s there were over three hundred towers guarding the Neapolitan coasts.

The Spanish government attempted to centralize the administration of defense. The monarchy feared feudal forces and encouraged barons to pay their way out of their traditional military obligations. In 1563 the government instituted the Battaglione, a local militia. For every hundred households, localities were required to support five men in arms. But soon, as the Ottoman danger receded, the Battaglione suffered from neglect, the poverty of local communities, and bureaucratic inefficiency. An inspection in 1616 showed its ranks to include numerous old, disabled, and even dead men. Its only call to action came in 1707, when Austrian forces invaded the kingdom and the Battaglione proved useless to oppose them. A parallel militia of light cavalry was equally ineffective.

Spain also kept its own soldiers in the South: in this age most policing was done by military forces, so soldiers helped to keep internal order. There were usually about three to five thousand Spanish infantrymen in the Kingdom of Naples, plus a few hundred cavalrymen, and generally about one thousand armed men in Sicily. Soldiers were concentrated in the border fortresses of Gaeta and Capua, the fortresses in Naples and Palermo, and a few coastal and strategic towns. There were thirty-one fortresses in the Kingdom of Naples, but most were guarded by minimal forces. Usually at least one-third of the Spanish forces in the Kingdom of Naples was stationed in the Stato dei Presidii, a small territory on the Tuscan coast that Spain claimed in 1557 when the Medici, with Spanish aid, annexed to their duchy the old republic of Siena. The Presidii administratively belonged to Naples. The heavy military presence in the Presidii shows how Spain saw the main danger to its southern possessions as coming from its traditional adversary, France.

Therefore, by the end of the sixteenth century there were about three to four thousand Spanish soldiers in the entire South of Italy (not counting the distant Presidii). Since they were concentrated in major cities and fortresses, most of the rural population rarely encountered them. Given the dreadful reputation and behavior of early modern soldiers everywhere, this scarcity of troops must be counted as a blessing, even though the southern people paid heavily in taxes and recruitment to buttress their imperial overlords. Neapolitans and Sicilians continued to serve in the armies of the king of Spain, but they were sent to the many fronts in northern Italy and Europe where Spain fought its wars. If needed, the Genoese fleet, a constant ally of Spain, and Spanish naval and land forces could reach the South quickly in times of crisis.

Until 1547 Toledo and his government prospered. In that year an attempt to introduce the Spanish Inquisition in the kingdom proved a rare setback for the viceroy. The Inquisition already existed in the kingdom but in its Roman form, which operated through the bishops. The Spanish version—whatever its reputation from Elizabethan England to Mel Brooks movies—differed not so much in its cruelty but in its dependence on the royal government. It was introduced in Sicily and Sardinia around 1500, shortly after it started operating in Spain itself. Introducing it in Naples would further strengthen the monarchy. Ferdinand's government tried in 1510, but gave up after the Naples nobility objected. Now the mounting threat of Protestantism, and Charles V's 1546 victory against Protestant princes in Germany, motivated another attempt.

By spring of 1547 it became clear that Toledo was considering innovations in how heresy was prosecuted in the kingdom. By mid-May city leaders were organizing opposition to the viceroy's plan. The city government—dominated by the old nobility—elected two noblemen as envoys to Charles V to seek confirmation of the status quo. As protests and violence spread in the city, Toledo ordered the execution of three young noblemen, guilty of interfering with guards during an arrest. That evening, May 26, Toledo defiantly rode through the city accompanied by infantry and cavalry, while city leaders urged the tense crowds to remain quiet. Toledo then began strengthening the defenses of various royal buildings, as armed groups across the city engaged in street fighting.

Several days of bombardments and struggle ensued, during which up to two thousand Spanish soldiers and Neapolitans died. Elite families fled the city, as reported by Toledo's sympathetic biographer: "it was a lamentable thing, to see the city emptied of its nobles and of honest citizens, filled with arrogant plebs and numerous bandits, without religion, without justice and without trade." An uneasy truce followed, as the viceroy and city leaders awaited the emperor's response. In early August the envoys returned. Charles ordered the city to surrender all weapons to the viceroy, offered clemency for the unrest, and promised not to introduce any changes in the matter of the Inquisition. Ultimately the episode was a rare failure for the viceroy: elite opposition proved strong and the danger of urban riots forced the government's retreat.

Thus began the final phase of Toledo's career, which was characterized by much tenser relationships with the Neapolitan aristocracy.

Toledo punished the 1547 rebels—many noblemen fled to exile and some even went on to serve Spain's enemy, France—and strengthened political and intellectual control. Noble critics began to call him a "new Nero"; a French historian described Toledo as "a man of high and vehement spirit, heavy to the nobility with his excessive severity." Giovan Antonio Summonte, a historian writing at the end of the sixteenth century, offered a balanced portrait of the man and his rule: "[c]areful in government affairs, of acute mind, severe and circumspect in matters of justice; outside of government affairs he was affable, cheerful, and amenable, and in all things the perfect courtier; but on the other hand were some flaws, for he was very inclined to gambling, to the point of consuming in it entire nights and large sums of money; stubborn and vindictive in his hatreds . . . he was given, more than would be appropriate to his age and rank, to the love of women . . . [overall] among all of the emperor's ministers, in whatever kingdom or dominion, he was always regarded as the first."

Toledo's government set the parameters for Spanish rule in Naples. His successors had to accept the practical limits of royal authority: viceroys could not afford to alienate the aristocracy, they had to accommodate Church interests, Neapolitan masses had to be both pampered and monitored, and in the provinces royal policies could not be enforced efficiently with the limited financial means available to the central government. Toledo's rule was followed shortly by the last significant change in the position of the southern kingdoms within the Spanish imperial system: the creation in 1558 in Madrid of the Council of Italy. Until then the Italian domains had been governed by the Council of Aragon. Members of this council, which was part of the innovative administrative structure Ferdinand and Isabella had given their dominions, had to be Aragonese. Philip II (ruled 1556–98) was less tied than his ancestors to the Aragonese traditions of the monarchy and did not wish to be limited in his appointments. The new Council of Italy, staffed by Spaniards and Italians, supervised the administration of Naples, Sicily, Sardinia, and Milan (which Spain acquired in 1535) and served as appeals court for most cases decided in those territories. Thus, by the 1550s Spanish administration in Italy was settled. When war with France finally ended in 1559, Spain's hegemony over Italy was solid, though not unlimited.

The following hundred years brought a gradual decline in Spanish power and effectiveness. Philip II's traditionalist approach and the delays caused by the mounting detail of his bureaucratic administration slowly atrophied Spanish government. Once the agenda was no longer state building but preservation of existing balances and procedures, powerful groups and institutions (the aristocracy, the bureaucratic elites, the clergy) could appeal to the Crown and exploit the king's suspicions of innovation and of his own agents. By the 1590s the Italian economy began a general decline, just as Spain's renewed military commitments in the Netherlands and France exhausted its own resources and forced it to increase the burden on its Italian domains, which already gave the Crown more money than any of its European dominions outside of Castile.

The economic and international difficulties of the last decades of the sixteenth century were among the causes of the most severe threat to Spanish rule in the South in that century: the unrest of 1585 in Naples. In the spring of that year a grain shortage and the resulting hunger riots—relatively common occurrences in early modern cities—coincided with political discontent among more settled and prosperous groups of the city population, resulting in a dramatic and violent challenge to Spanish power.

The immediate cause of the crisis was the decision by the Eletti to raise the price of bread shortly after the same Eletti had authorized large exports of grain to Spain. Popular demonstrations followed. The Eletto del Popolo, supposedly the representative of the people's interests, was Giovan Vincenzo Starace, the son of a silk merchant. Like many rich members of the urban elites, Starace—in the words of the historian Summonte—"lived very nobly," and he had been the Eletto twice before. He was closely linked to the grain merchants who stood to profit from the Eletti's recent decisions. Starace's pride, arrogance, and lack of political savvy did not help the situation: on May 8, as tumultuous crowds gathered, he apparently threatened them with retribution and said he would have them eat bread made of dirt.

The next day, a planned assembly met in the church of Santa Maria la Nova, supposedly under Starace's leadership. But the crowd, much larger than what any of the neighborhood leaders expected, forced the transfer of Starace to Sant'Agostino, the traditional location of the popular government. He was placed on his chair and carried, facing backward and his head uncovered. This sort of reversed triumph mocked traditional signs of deference, symbolically denying Starace's authority, and mimicked the rituals surrounding execution, when the condemned were paraded through the city. As the crowd marched, people shouted insults, shopkeepers shut their stores, weapons appeared. Once at Sant'Agostino, the furious crowd lynched Starace.

The "bitter and cruel" death of Starace was not random, but a ritualized, symbolic murder. The naked corpse was dragged through the streets, mutilated and castrated, and the crowd tore pieces of Starace's flesh. Threats of cannibalism and the dragging of the corpse face down in the dirt mirrored Starace's actions and comments regarding the bread supply. The corpse was dragged first through the poorest areas of the city, then in the principal streets, and eventually in front of the viceroyal palace. Afterward, his relatives were able to find and bury only fragments of Starace's body. The crowd "having cut his nose and his pudenda, tore out his heart and guts, cut one of his arms and one of his legs, and then carried all these body parts skewered on the tops of their swords and on their sticks, like trophies, and in their hands they kept bits of his brains and pieces of his guts, telling observers that they wanted to eat [these fragments], roasted or boiled." Starace's house was threatened with fire, though ultimately only sacked. In a symbolic gesture that accused the deceased himself of robbery, the rebels did not simply loot Starace's property but they distributed it to city convents, "to prove that they were led not by desire of gain, but of vengeance." Other prominent merchants were hunted down and forced to flee the city while their homes were attacked.

The large participation of urban masses—including established artisans, professionals, and shopkeepers—in this behavior horrified contemporary observers, and the violence of the events resounded in reports across Europe. The treatment of the body appeared almost inconceivable. The historian Summonte, though critical of Starace's arrogance, remembered that in 1563 the crowd had allowed the burial of a Turk killed during a pirate raid, whose body had also been dragged through the city. Instead, "this was not done with the corpse of the unhappy Starace, who was born a Christian, and had grown up among us, and we are all children of the same Father God, and of the same Mother Church, baptized in the same sacrament of baptism, washed and purged by the same blood of our Lord Jesus Christ, citizens of the same heavenly city."

The original organizers of the assembly of protest included neighborhood leaders. A contemporary diarist blamed not only the "vilest plebs" but also "the disgusting dregs of the People," acknowledging the participation of settled urban elements in the riot. Some of the popular demands (for lower taxes, for justice, for more balance between aristocracy and people in the city government) that appeared after Starace's murder also indicate that the troubles involved groups extending beyond the poorest citizens. There were even a few anti-Spanish comments, and the contemporary Dutch revolt was explicitly invoked as an inspiration for the Naples rebels. The viceroy managed to calm down the turmoil by importing grain and selling it cheaply. In July, after forty Spanish galleys came to Naples, a vast repression was unleashed. About 800 people were tried, 270 tortured, 430 jailed, while up to 12,000 residents of Naples found it wise to flee the city. Thirty-one people were condemned to death, 71 to the galleys, and 300 exiled from the kingdom. The executions were especially ferocious: the condemned were carted through the city, their right hands were cut off at Sant'Agostino, their left hands were cut off in front of the main criminal tribunal, and they were finally hanged and quartered in the market square, the traditional place for executions in Naples.

The roster of the condemned again shows the broad appeal of the revolt: craftsmen, a clothing merchant, and four scribes of various tribunals were among the executed. The December amnesty excluded thirty-three people—deemed undeserving of forgiveness—and these included a cleric and a pharmacist, Giovan Leonardo Pisano, who was identified as the revolt's main leader and by then had fled to Venice. Two months later, Pisano's house was razed and in its place rose a monument that held the hands and heads of the executed. It remained in place until June 1586.

An angry crowd was a clear danger to the government, and the revolt of 1585 exposed some of the problems of Spanish rule in Naples. The Eletti's decisions regarding the price of bread and the export of grain came at a time of increasing lag between the rise in prices and that in wages, and of weak harvests, as decades of economic and demographic expansion turned to stagnation and decline. Since the midcentury, moreover, the office of the Eletto del Popolo had come increasingly under the control of the highest layers of the city's merchant, banking, and professional groups. Royal actions had favored this trend. In 1548, taking advantage of the failed unrest of 1547, Toledo had forbidden the direct election of the Eletto del Popolo and instead ordered that the Popolo nominate six men, among whom the viceroy would select the Eletto. The Eletto del Popolo had also lost his traditional veto power over the city's decisions, though he could appeal them to the viceroy. These moves had weakened the Eletto del Popolo, loosened his ties with the urban population at large, and accelerated the process by which nonnoble elites tried to assimilate themselves to the aristocracy. This movement of urban governments toward more oligarchic forms was occurring in many other cities of the kingdom, usually with royal encouragement. In Naples one result was that artisans, shopkeepers, and lower professionals—and, even more so, the fluid and unorganized mass of the poorest citizens—felt ever more detached from urban authorities.

During the first decades of Spanish rule, any aspirations to independence from Spain exhibited by Neapolitans came from the aristocracy. The troubles of 1547 had as their primary target the government's attempt to introduce the Spanish Inquisition into the kingdom, and members of the aristocracy led the agitation, worried that the government's move would diminish elite autonomy and privileges. In 1585, the Spanish empire had been fighting a popular rebellion in the Netherlands for about twenty years, and Dutch events were echoed in popular cries in Naples. This larger international context, and the broader social bases of the 1585 unrest, did not bode well for the future.

Finally, the 1585 revolt contributed to a trend toward greater intellectual openness in Naples. At the end of the sixteenth century the issue of potential conflict between political loyalties and religious loyalties was paramount in France, England, and the Netherlands, and this was leading to new conceptions of the proper scope of government and of the nature and powers of monarchy. While religious division was not a significant factor in the South, or anywhere in Italy, Neapolitan authors began to address larger political issues. Summonte's history of the city and Kingdom of Naples, the first two volumes of which appeared in 1601 and concluded with a discussion of the tumult of 1585, called for the monarchical government to raise popular elements to more equality with aristocratic interests. Summonte's ideas about the proper government of the city and kingdom led to his imprisonment, and the later sections of his work did not appear until long after his death. In the same decades, Neapolitan scholars interested in the natural world began to develop new ideas that challenged dominant orthodoxies, as we will see in another chapter.

The economic troubles of the late sixteenth century only grew in the following decades. By 1620, as the supply of American silver that had fueled Spanish power ran low, the monarchy had to make do with diminishing resources. Spanish intervention in the Thirty Years' War (1618–48) led to fighting in northern Italy, the Netherlands, and Germany. A tone of disillusionment began to pervade Spanish culture— in 1616, to give the most famous example, Cervantes finished *Don Quijote*—and Spain's economy and population declined. Dynamic personalities still existed among Spain's agents in Italy in the seventeenth century, but overall their level of competence and commitment fell. As the financial crisis deepened and popular discontent grew, it became ever more difficult to continue the struggles Toledo had pursued. Urban disorder, rural crime, and aristocratic violence resisted repression and became almost endemic in southern life. Duels among noblemen—which jeopardized public order in the pursuit of private honor and as such were prohibited by most European monarchs—were common in Naples throughout the seventeenth century in spite of oft-repeated bans. Domestic violence in elite circles also caused scandal but little surprise. The general situation worsened significantly by the 1640s, as the monarchy's financial needs spiraled out of control.

Bartolomeo d'Aquino built his career on service to Spain's financial exigencies. After a start in trade, d'Aquino became the main organizer of loans to the cash-starved government. Between 1636 and 1644 he obtained about 16 million ducats for the monarchy and greatly enriched himself in the process. An aristocratic historian described d'Aquino as "a great spirit, greater than a merchant's,

though his appearance was emaciated, ugly, and suitable to his birth
. . . prudent in business, of quick and sharp mind, and heavily
favored by fortune. But he was on the other hand full of dirty and
deplorable defects, of shameful life, he cared little for God and the
saints, and was tainted by other horrible evils."

Taxation in Naples and Sicily came first in the form of direct taxes,
which weighed on the kingdoms' communities and were apportioned
on the basis of the latest census. Both clerics as individuals and ecclesiastic property were exempted from most direct taxation. Feudal
property followed a separate fiscal regime. Direct taxes expanded
greatly under Toledo but soon became insufficient to meet the mounting royal needs. They were complemented, as was customary across
Europe, by three other sources of income: borrowing in return for
interest-bearing, long-term bonds; the sale of royal land, titles, and
offices; and indirect taxes. Over time, little in the South went untaxed:
one paid to export or import goods, to buy most foodstuffs and products, to obtain all sorts of licenses and permits, to travel from one
province to the next. The government lacked the means to collect indirect taxes, known as *gabelle*, and so farmed them out under agreements
called *arrendamenti* to entrepreneurs who bought the right to collect a
specific *gabella* in a specific area and then tried to maximize their
income. The Crown often also granted to its lenders the direct taxes
from specific communities over specific periods of time or even in per-
petuity. By the eighteenth century these practices resulted in the alienation to private hands of much of the state's fiscal revenue.

Taxing exports and internal trade hurt the kingdom's productive
sectors. Until the 1590s, however, the situation was not tragic, as the
kingdom gained in population. But with the 1590s came a downturn
of the economic and demographic cycles. Major plague epidemics
affected Sicily in 1624 and Naples in 1656. Between 1617 and 1622
the Kingdom of Naples went through repeated devaluations that hurt
trade, exchange rates, and public loans. Starting in the 1620s Spanish
demands for soldiers, goods, and money increased dramatically, just
as the kingdom's economy worsened. Viceroys pursued desperate
means: lands and titles were sold, producing a boom in the number
of titled landowners; all available sources of royal income were sold
to the highest bidder; nonessential towns in the royal domain were
sold as fiefs; and even the *casali* of Naples—communities outside the

walls that in theory formed part of the capital city—were sold to new and old barons.

D'Aquino worked at the center of this increasingly frayed system. Speculative loans, tax farming, and government bonds were the basis of his fortune. New gabelle were created solely to pay him off. In 1640 d'Aquino, by then the wealthiest man in Naples, decided to turn his financial success into social affirmation. He planned to marry Anna Acquaviva, sister of the count of Conversano, of one of the noblest families in the kingdom. The viceroy supported this plan because of his debts to d'Aquino and—wrote an aristocratic historian—"to give such scorn to the count of Conversano, making him the brother-in-law of a vile merchant."

With the consent of another of her brothers, Anna moved from the convent of San Marcellino to the palace of a friendly noblewoman. Recognizing the awkwardness of the situation, D'Aquino revised the usual custom in which the bride's family provides the dowry: he himself granted her forty thousand ducats as her dowry so that she would be able to marry again were she widowed. But the count, incensed by the shameful prospect of a mercantile marriage in his family, gathered noble supporters in San Lorenzo, the location of the city government. An embassy sent to d'Aquino to express the count's opposition to the marriage failed. Several dozen noblemen with up to eight hundred armed followers marched through the city to the palace where Anna stayed. They quickly overwhelmed soldiers and officials sent by the viceroy and forcefully entered the palace. Prominent aristocrats escorted Anna to Benevento (which Spanish troops could not enter), where she was again confined to a convent.

The public humiliation of d'Aquino was clearly intended as a rebuff to the position he had reached with government support, and the armed assault defied royal authority. At a meeting of the Collaterale, the viceroy sought severe punishments for the culprits. But the counselors, many of whom were noble and closely allied to the Seggi families, opposed all punitive measures. The viceroy was obliged to accept the result of the confrontation. D'Aquino continued to bring loans to the monarchy, in 1641 he became the prince of Caramanico, and he later married a noble lady from Milan. Anna Acquaviva married a minor nobleman from a Seggio family, with a dowry of nine thousand ducats, rather low for her rank.

If d'Aquino had married Anna Acquaviva, their union would not have been the only example of lopsided alliances in seventeenth-century Naples, though it may have been one of the most extreme. Many aristocratic families were deeply indebted by the start of the century, and many noblemen sought wives of inferior birth but solid purse to strengthen their battered patrimonies. However, since aristocratic culture across Europe accorded wives the rank of their husbands, it was usually the men who married down. D'Aquino's case was thus especially distasteful for his intended bride's family.

The episode also shows how by the early seventeenth century the old distinction between the noble families of the capital city and the feudal barons had evaporated. These two groups intermarried, they all owned feudal estates, and they all spent part of the year in their Naples residences. Many families of elite judges, lawyers, and officials also joined the Seggi, acquired feudal estates and titles, and married into the traditional nobility. Francesco D'Andrea noted, "[A]s the Kingdom is filled with lawsuits . . . one can say that lawyers in Naples govern it. . . . [The nobles] treat lawyers with great respect . . . and recognize them not only as equals but as their own superiors. . . . [Lawyers] are their own masters . . . and they fear no one, since they need no one." Even families from the world of trade—whom noble culture regarded as inferior to lawyers and officials—rose to mingle with the old nobility. Southern nobles famously shunned business. The Tuscan Humanist Poggio Bracciolini noted that Neapolitan nobles "abhor trade as a most low and shameful thing." The Neapolitan noble Humanist Tristano Caracciolo countered by accusing Florentines of greed and usury and arguing that "no one should be blamed for the customs of one's country." In 1594 the Tuscan agent in Naples still remarked that "the nobles live very grandly, regarding the care of business, even as pertains to their households, as disgraceful." But the nobility could not always avoid entering alliances with wealthy merchant families.

Feudal estates and titles had become much easier to acquire, and this made social divisions harder to maintain for the old nobility. In the sixteenth century, feudal barons petitioned the monarchy for the extension of the allowed degrees of feudal succession, so uncles, cousins, nephews, or female relatives could inherit fiefs that otherwise would revert to the Crown in the absence of direct male heirs. In

1655 the king granted the right of feudal succession to the fourth degree (in 1720 it reached the fifth). But the Crown also began to realize the financial advantages it could reap from making the trade in fiefs easier and from selling more feudal rights and powers. It was necessary to obtain royal assent to the sale of anything held in fief, but such assent was easily granted to those able to pay for it. The result was that a fief became almost like any other property, of which owners could dispose at will. Moreover, the Crown gave away as feudal property separate items within each fief. Thus, one lord could own the land while another held feudal jurisdiction over the people living in that fief. Feudal jurisdiction itself could be fragmented in numerous components, each of which could be sold to a different owner. Though this was rare, one could envision a feudal village whose residents would pay feudal rents to one lord, be subject to the criminal jurisdiction exercised by another, pay the feudal monopolies to a third, and so on.

The feudal system had thus become a bonanza for lawyers, but this had not made it any less burdensome on the kingdom's population. A few old families still held large estates with numerous vassals over whom they exercised all feudal powers. In 1557, for instance, six families (each with numerous branches) ruled over almost half a million vassals (about one-third of the vassal population in the entire kingdom). But by the seventeenth century, patrimonies of this size existed side by side with feudal fragmentation. Thus, more and more people—coming to wealth from different paths—entered feudal ranks. The possession of feudal assets became more a sign of wealth than of noble status. The situation made it possible for an upstart like d'Aquino quickly to reach not only great wealth but also the highest feudal rank, and the count of Conversano found it easy to persuade his peers that this posed an unacceptable threat to their own status.

In the long run, the aristocracy's struggle was a losing one, and d'Aquino met opposition only because of the speed and arrogance of his ascent. Many old Seggi families were impoverished beyond repair and many went extinct. Economic crisis made investment in feudal assets—which gave modest but safe revenues and granted status—all the more appealing to the wealthy. The distant, needy Crown was only too eager to sell not only feudal assets but titles as well. Aristocrats found alliances with the newly wealthy necessary, although they preferred jurists to merchants. But in the first half of the seventeenth century the tensions that accompanied these trends were especially severe, and they explain the drama of the d'Aquino affair.

In the 1640s the crisis of Spanish rule extended well beyond Italy. Spain's forces fought Protestants and French across Europe and northern Italy, and Portuguese and Catalan rebels on the Iberian Peninsula. Financial demands on the Italian possessions mounted each year. Viceroys could not meet Madrid's desperate appeals for men, goods, and money. The government sold everything it could. Direct taxes increased and gabelle were imposed on most goods. Naples was exempted from most of the former, but the latter hurt the urban population. In 1646 the state debt, which had been 30 million ducats in 1626, stood at 80 million. Naples and other communities of the kingdom were themselves in debt for at least another 60 million ducats. Merchants and financiers went bankrupt and corruption reached new heights. The hapless Viceroy Arcos arrived in 1646 to a desolate kingdom. That fall French forces occupied some of the Tuscan Presidii, adding a new threat to the kingdom's woes. New gabelle on flour and fruit were especially galling to the people of Naples. News of a revolt in Palermo in the late spring of 1647 raised tensions and fears in Naples.

On July 7, 1647, riots began in the main market square of Naples, in the middle of the poorest neighborhoods. A young fish seller from Amalfi named Tommaso Aniello, nicknamed Masaniello, took the lead in these riots, which targeted the most unpopular gabelle. The first day of the revolt was fairly peaceful and ended with a nearly bloodless occupation of the royal palace and several prisons. The viceroy moved to Castel Nuovo, where he remained under a sort of siege as rebels controlled the flow of provisions into the castle. Immediately, the rebels displayed their unhappiness about their powerlessness in urban affairs: on the first day of the revolt, the Eletto del Popolo was pelted with fruit, the object of the most resented new gabella.

On July 8 the revolt spread to more settled artisan neighborhoods. The houses of prominent ministers and rich bankers were assaulted, as often happened in urban hunger riots. Cardinal Ascanio Filomarino, the archbishop, intervened to save some of the targets of popular fury. Armed men, women, and children roamed the city. On July 9 the crowds occupied the city government offices, symbolically reclaiming the city, and replaced the Eletto. At the same time the crowds' basic attachment to the Spanish monarchy remained strong. The Vicaria, the main tribunal and prison in the city, was not attacked in the first days of the rebellion. Rebel groups paraded around the city holding the coat of arms and a portrait of Charles V, extolling his supposedly benevolent rule.

As events unfolded, Masaniello's rise was meteoric: soon he was hailed as the Captain General of the People and feted by nobles and officials. He dispensed justice in the market square as if he were a king. From early on he had at his side Giulio Genoino, a lawyer who had been the Eletto del Popolo in 1620, at the time of a murky episode in which the viceroy had vainly tried to strengthen the Popolo against the nobles within the city government. Genoino had spent the years 1622–40 in jail, and, now eighty years old, still hoped to effect a more balanced government for the city that gave more power to the professional and mercantile groups to which he belonged.

On July 10 bandits in the pay of prominent aristocrats failed in an attempt to kill Masaniello. This infuriated the masses and intensified violence in the city, as crowds turned brutal and summarily killed several bandits. Many aristocrats kept armed retainers and employed them to enforce their will both in the city and in their lands. This time the crowds took revenge and the killings were vicious. The notoriously violent nobleman Giuseppe Carafa was killed and his body mutilated and dragged through the streets. Many aristocrats fled the city after that, and attacks on noble palaces intensified.

In the midst of increasing violence, with the cardinal's input, Genoino drafted an agreement, which the viceroy accepted on July 13: it abolished all gabelle and granted the Popolo more power within the city government. Genoino hoped to unite the viceroy and the moderate popular elites against aristocratic power. The viceroy swore his acceptance of this agreement in a ceremony in the Naples cathedral. Masaniello attended the ceremony dressed in a magnificent silver suit he had received from the archbishop and the viceroy. However, during the ceremony Masaniello began to exhibit signs of mental imbalance: he fainted, ranted, and tore his rich clothes. The agreement proved the beginning of Masaniello's fall. By accepting it, he alienated his own most radical and poor supporters. On July 14 and 15, in part because of sleep deprivation and heavy drinking, his behavior became violent. On July 16, at the instigation of moderate leaders, Masaniello was killed in the church of the Carmine, in the midst of the market area, during the celebrations for the feast day of the popular Madonna del Carmine.

The crowds subjected Masaniello's corpse to vilification and abuse. These gruesome, morbid actions followed clear models. The dragging of bodies (as was done with Giuseppe Carafa and Masaniello) reversed or reflected traditional rituals, such as those accompanying triumphal entries or the processions that led criminals to the place of execution. Even looting and lynching fit patterns: goods taken from sacked palaces were usually distributed to the poor, and the display of heads and body parts mirrored what was done to those guilty of nefarious crimes. As in 1585, popular justice thus appropriated the practices of official justice.

Soon after Masaniello's murder, the government, misreading its hold on the situation, reduced the weight of bread: bread, the main food item for the poor, was sold at a fixed price for a standard loaf, the weight of which was set by the government. This hasty action sparked new turmoil. The masses' mood swung back: Masaniello's mutilated body was recomposed, and on July 18 he received a funeral fit for a hero and a saint, with Church services attended by four hundred priests and one hundred orphans, and military honors offered by Spanish soldiers in front of the royal palace. Masaniello—wrote an observer—was "honored by the people like a king, killed like a criminal, adored like a saint." Another chronicler reported:

> It is not easy to express the great sentiment that the People showed at the moment of burying Tomaso Anello; one could see in the faces of the passionate crowd a sorrow mixed with anger; this was also expressed by the words they uttered, which were mixed of the same feelings. There were many who said that Tomaso Anello had returned to life: and anyone who by misfortune had contradicted this would have been in clear danger for his life: others said that [Masaniello] had already moved his hands, and taken a crown, which he held tight in his right hand. Many women tore his hair

and kept them in their bosoms, as if they were relics. The blind who were at the door of the Carmine church cried loudly, "To whom do we address the prayer of Blessed Masaniello?"

The rituals that marked Masaniello's death and apotheosis strengthened unity among the various rebel constituencies. Afterward, it proved much harder to maintain unity.

Many different forces shaped later events: the crowds in Naples and their discontent with taxes; each group within the working population with its specific complaints; the Popolo elites seeking a more balanced power structure; the aristocracy keen on protecting its position; the Spanish authorities desperate to reestablish order and resume Naples's contributions to the war effort; and the provinces. Unlike 1585, when the revolt had not spread beyond Naples, in 1647 provincial and rural tensions exploded as the Naples events became known. Revolts began in many provincial towns, often led by local notables seeking more access to entrenched governing oligarchies. People in the provinces were also ferociously against taxes: in Potenza in August rebels drank the blood of a tax farmer. As authority broke down throughout the kingdom, rural areas exploded in antifeudal rebellion: peasants sacked castles, attacked feudal agents, looted feudal property, and gruesomely killed a few nobles. In Naples Genoino proved unable to balance the various elements of the revolt, quickly lost power, and died shortly thereafter. Gennaro Annese, an arms maker who had been the captain of one of the poorest neighborhoods, emerged over the summer as the rebel leader and took the title of Generalissimo.

In the meantime Madrid had recognized the seriousness of the situation and sent reinforcements. On October 1 Arcos officially asked for the barons' aid to defend the king. Soon thereafter a Spanish fleet under Don Juan of Austria (an illegitimate son of Philip IV) arrived in the bay and began military operations by bombarding the city. An army levied by aristocratic leaders joined Don Juan's forces and took control of much of the area around Naples. This marked a sharp shift for the rebels. Rebel leaders always claimed to wish for nothing but the return to the benevolent rule the city had enjoyed under Charles V and his predecessors. No republican ideas were expressed by or under Masaniello. But after the Spanish fleet bombarded the city, a republican movement began among the rebels. On October 17 rebel leaders declared the end of Spanish rule and five days later a republic under Annese's leadership.

In the meantime anarchy reigned across the kingdom. Rebel armies operated in various regions and antifeudal rebellion spread. By this point, the strength of the link between the government and the aristocracy was clear. The feudal aristocracy had gained in power in the decades preceding the revolt. The state had nearly abdicated its traditional role as corrector of feudal abuses: in the 1630s and 1640s many barons had imposed with virtual impunity new extortions on their vassals and violently suppressed any local resistance. The barons were simply too necessary to the maintenance of Spanish rule to alienate them by judicially limiting their power over their vassals. Newer barons were often even greedier and more demanding than old ones. The aristocracy's power had grown also at the center. No parliament was called after 1642, and the Seggi of Naples—dominated by the aristocracy and its allies in the high bureaucracy—had become responsible for approving all taxes and demands of the government. That the city nobles, exempted from most taxes, should make fiscal policy for the entire kingdom was another sign of how much the government was willing to grant to them to ensure continuing support. The revolt thus found noble elites strongly committed to the defense of both the monarchy and their own local and central power.

The struggles outside of the capital proved especially brutal, after decades of mounting hatreds between nobles and the rural and provincial masses. That many local notables and professionals joined in antifeudal actions shows how far the situation in the provinces had deteriorated by 1647. But the Naples rebels failed to establish any alliance with provincial forces. Life for the city people was quite separate from that of the rest of the kingdom's population, which Naples dominated and exploited. The privileges and provisioning of the city and its role as the instrument and center of monarchical rule left it isolated. This inability to link the urban rebellion with the demands of provincial upheavals proved disastrous for both.

The Naples rebels' search for foreign assistance also yielded little. Some rebels hoped to emulate the Dutch model of republican independence from Spain. But the duke of Guise, with an unclear mandate from the French government, came to Naples on November 15. Soon the rebel leadership was divided between French supporters and opponents, weakening any republican prospects. On December 23 Guise removed Annese and claimed full powers over a vaguely defined Most Serene Royal Republic under French protection. He tried to attract aristocratic support, and this further alienated many rebels. A brief visit by the French fleet did not change the military situation. Fortunately for Spain, the economic, military, and religious tensions of the 1640s were sowing rebellion across Europe, not just in the Spanish dominions. What little French military support came to the Neapolitan rebels dried up as the Fronde revolts began in France early in 1648.

At the end of January 1648, Arcos left, Don Juan became viceroy, and Spain promised an amnesty and a general reduction of gabelle. By then a ferocious repression was under way in the provinces, where armies led by feudal barons looted, burned, and killed rebels and peasants. The Naples rebels encountered problems in provisioning the city since the usual roads of access were under attack by enemy forces. Food shortages and rising prices weakened the revolt. In March 1648 Madrid named the ambassador to Rome, the count of Oñate, as the new viceroy. He entered a mostly peaceful Naples on April 6 and soon issued a partial amnesty and lightened the fiscal burden on the kingdom. He also shaped a political compromise between different elites. After Oñate brought together the aristocracy and the nonnoble elites, it proved fairly easy to obtain the return of the urban masses' allegiance to Spanish rule. In provincial towns too, new settlements opened up local oligarchic governments. The main losers were the peasant rebels who saw their feudal masters return to their previous powers. Prominent rebel leaders like Annese and the provincial chieftains were executed over the following months. In the summer of 1650 Oñate led a reconquest of the Presidii occupied by the French.

The revolt of Masaniello, as the events are still known, was the most dramatic crisis during the period of Spanish hegemony in southern Italy and shows the weaknesses and strengths of Spain's position: there were relatively few troops in Naples, the viceroy was nearly powerless when faced with an angry mob, and Spain's relentless fiscal demands were causing deep discontent. But, as was true of other European countries in this period, the monarchy had military forces it could call upon when needed. More important, it could rely, when its rule became endangered, both on the support of the aristocracy and on the fundamental loyalty of the general population.

People in England and the Netherlands—in the 1640s undergoing their own political upheavals—were fascinated by the Naples revolt. They read eyewitness accounts, bought medals minted to commemorate the revolt, and attended dramas about the events. While Dutch and English accounts tended to be anti-Spanish and anti-Catholic, they frowned on the violence of the Naples events. English monarchists regarded Masaniello as the epitome of a plebeian turned tyrant and used reports from Naples to criticize Cromwell's role in England. Interest in the revolt did not fade: two plays and an opera about it were produced in Germany between 1682 and 1714. By the Romantic period Masaniello had become an idealized hero, and as such he appeared in an 1825 English play, an 1828 French opera, and *Undine*, an 1845 painting by J. M. W. Turner. The opera, Auber's *La Muette de Portici*, centers on Masaniello's sister, who is mute—a rare disability in an opera—and dances her part; at the end she commits suicide by throwing herself into erupting Vesuvius. A performance in Brussels in 1830 sparked the revolution that led to Belgian independence.

After 1648 the southern kingdoms, like much of the Spanish empire, entered a period of stagnation. Fiscal and military demands diminished, though not enough to soothe the weak economy of the area. Compromise between dominant social groups brought more stability. Spain lost its European hegemony by the 1650s, but its dominant position within Italy remained unchallenged. Old problems persisted: bandits roamed mountainous areas, foreign merchants controlled the South's trade, pirate raids and malaria afflicted the coasts. The catastrophe of the plague of 1656, which killed hundreds of thousands across the South, further debilitated the economy. After 1665 a regent ruled Spain for the child Charles II (ruled 1665–1700), and the resulting factional strife blocked any coherent policy toward the Italian dominions and their problems. During yet another war with France in the 1670s, Spain's forces proved so thinly stretched that it took them four years to tame a revolt in Messina (1674–78).

The government attempted no significant reform of institutions or finances. Spain remained in control of Italy mainly because it asked less of its subjects, in terms both of taxes and of displays of obedience. At the end of the century, as the childless and sickly Charles II aged, a sort of holding pattern prevailed while all of Europe awaited the resolution of Spain's impending succession crisis.

How then to assess Spain's rule in the South? In the nineteenth century, as Spain receded from the ranks of Europe's great powers, it became customary among European historians to regard Spanish power with contempt. Here was everything modernity rejected: a tyrannical government, a backward economy, censorship, the Inquisition, and ethnic and religious intolerance. Italian historians in particular blamed many of the flaws of Italian society, and especially southern backwardness, on Spanish influence and misrule. As late as 1952, the historian Gabriele Pepe attacked Spanish greed, dishonesty, and incompetence and wrote that even the peace and security some attributed to Spain's rule in the South "were those of an animal held in the stable to be milked and butchered."

Certainly the Spanish government altered some southern traditions. The harsh treatment of ethnic and religious minorities, when compared to the Aragonese kings' protection of southern Jews, is the most obvious example. The Spanish government's unwillingness significantly to limit the Church's wealth and influence or the feudal lords' local power shaped southern society in ways that still affect social relations and popular beliefs. Castilians occupied many offices in Spain's Italian realms. Misguided trade and financial policies—aimed at maximizing short-term fiscal gains even as they hurt long-term prospects—increased the South's dependence on foreign capital and shipping and failed to support what manufacturing potential existed in the southern economy. But virtually all these policies had parallels in other early modern states, and the southern economy was far from prosperous even before Spain's rule.

On the other side of the ledger are the advantages of Spanish empire: cultural and economic contacts across a global system; the foundations for modern administration and justice, however gradual their impact; the end of the civil warfare of the late medieval period;

the support given by the monarchy to new social groups, such as financiers and especially the learned togati, who became the leading intellectual class in the South; and the southern elites' access to a broad, cosmopolitan network of patronage and employment. Most important perhaps was the defense of the kingdoms. No foreign invasions came to Sicily for about three centuries and to Naples for almost two. Rural violence, pirate raids, and brief periods of revolt occurred, but no large-scale war was fought in the South under Spanish rule, a rare and blessed fate in early modern Europe.

Spain's rule in southern Italy illustrates the strengths and limits of early modern absolutism. The increase in state organization brought by the Spanish did not mean unfettered power. The Crown remained committed to traditional institutions and laws, and—after 1547—it never tried to assert in Naples the broader powers it enjoyed in Castile or Sicily. Feudal dominance in the rural world continued, many feudal rights expanded, and feudal succession was enlarged. The complexity of early modern institutions itself limited state power: in Naples around 1610 there were, for example, forty tribunals, each with competence over specific categories of actions or individuals (such as university graduates, soldiers, prostitutes). Many of these were emanations of the Crown's authority, but at least six were under ecclesiastic authorities, seven under autonomous corporate entities, and five under the city government. Such remarkable confusion of jurisdictions—and jurisdiction was the main expression of power in early modern Europe—undermines any confident assertion of the strengths of royal absolutism. Ultimately, in southern Italy, as elsewhere in early modern Europe, absolutism was founded upon—and limited by—necessary compromises with feudal elites, Church institutions, local powers, and urban masses.

Within these limits, the Spanish Crown effected a remarkable expansion in the institutions and powers of the state. The aristocracy lost its political independence and the ability to be king makers. The Church gained much in wealth but became more subservient to the Crown. Fiscal, judicial, and military structures were strengthened, and administrative centralization advanced. Southern Italians developed a fundamental loyalty to the Spanish monarchy. Charles V himself told his son after the 1547 revolt that "overall, the situation of the kingdom is what suits good subjects."

✍ Chapter V ✍

The Indies over Here
Church and Religion in the
Early Modern South

These mountains of Sicily and Calabria could be novitiates
to test those who wish to go to the Indies.

A Messina Jesuit to his superior, 1575

*I*n October 1675 an odd case came to the notice of the Inquisition
office of the archbishop of Naples. In a poor neighborhood of the
city, sick people flocked to the home of a five-year-old boy called
Francesco Belli, the son of a fisherman, who allegedly healed them by
making the sign of the cross. Church authorities across seventeenth-
century Europe often confronted situations in which laypeople—
often poor or ignorant—regarded a living person as a saint and
miracle worker, and the Church responded with skepticism and
severity to what it considered simulated sanctity, if not even demonic
possession. But a boy of five presented a peculiar challenge, as conscious simulation was unlikely in one so young. When the Inquisition called in Francesco's mother for questioning, things became
even stranger.

Ursola Ciaccia declared that her little boy had always been special.
Her pregnancy had been unusually easy. A priest had prophesied the
hour and day of Francesco's birth and his saintly character. When she
was almost due, a man to whom her husband Antonio owed money
had had Antonio jailed for debts; Ursola visited the creditor to ask for
mercy and he, on observing her belly, not only agreed to obtain her
husband's freedom but also asked to be the boy's godfather. Nurses

and midwives were eager to help with the infant Francesco, because of the bliss they experienced in holding him. Almost from birth, Francesco refused to nurse on Fridays, just as later he refused to eat meat. From a tender age, he always wanted to wear the simple habit of a Franciscan, to go barefoot, and to sleep on straw. He built himself and cared for a little altar around a statuette of St. Francis. There Francesco practiced his wonders: he cured seven people (mostly neighborhood women afflicted by pregnancy problems), exorcized his own mother and grandmother when they were bothered by demons, and miraculously increased his family's stock of flour, straw, and oil (the latter to light the lamp on his little altar). He also gave alms and engaged in fervent devotions, having learned numerous prayers at a very young age. The Franciscans of a nearby monastery gave him some instruction and strongly supported him and his family throughout the Inquisition proceedings, as did several neighbors.

The archbishop, in consultation with Roman authorities, had Francesco removed from his family and entrusted him to a Dominican monastery. The Dominicans—perhaps especially disturbed that Francesco stubbornly refused to exchange his Franciscan habit for their own—subjected the boy to eight rounds of exorcism, to no avail. No demon left the child and he answered wisely all questions he was asked. When his father complained about the "slaps, punches, kicks, stick and rope" used on his son, the archbishop finally took Francesco away from the Dominicans and entrusted him to a monastery of a small order, the Pious Workers, where his mother was only allowed to visit him twice a month. Church authorities soon prohibited visits altogether. We know nothing more about Francesco or his family.

We see in this episode many features of the religious life of Neapolitans: rivalries between religious orders, which flourished and competed in an atmosphere of intense religious impulses; the effort of Church authorities to control all aspects of religious life and their struggle to assess all evidence of sacred or supernatural occurrences; how popular views of saints as primarily miracle workers troubled Church authorities; and the eagerness of Neapolitans to search for and believe in prodigies and prophecies. The religious attitudes and experiences of these times shape southern religion to this day.

Between the sixteenth and eighteenth centuries the South partook of the great spiritual, intellectual, and political currents that shaped early modern Catholicism: from the reform movements that began in the late fifteenth century to the crisis of the Protestant Reformation in the sixteenth; from the spiritual fervor and institutional strength that pervaded Counter-Reformation Catholicism in the late sixteenth and seventeenth centuries to the religious, intellectual, and political conflicts of the eighteenth century. At the same time, throughout this period southern religious life exhibited particular traits, shared by elites and masses: an intense desire for direct contact with the sacred, expressed in fervent devotion to the saints, ardent belief in miracles, and an eager search for relics; a powerful wish to remain connected with the dead through mutual obligations and solidarity; and a strong taste for the dramatic, emotional elements of religious practice.

The Catholic Church was first and foremost a powerful institution whose strength was, above all, a matter of resources and organization. As happened in much of Catholic Europe, over the fifteenth and early sixteenth centuries the secular clergy—those engaged in the care of souls and living in the *saeculum,* or world, such as deacons, priests, and bishops—became better organized and took on a leading role in the religious life of the laity. At the same time, the regular clergy—the communities of monks, friars, and nuns that lived under each order's *regula,* or rule—remained strong and numerous, especially in the mendicant orders (the many branches of the Franciscans and Dominicans), which enjoyed great popularity across the South since their start in the thirteenth century.

The Spanish monarchy, deeply committed to the Catholic cause, did not greatly object to Church wealth and privileges. Both clerics and Church assets enjoyed extensive exemptions, and assets and clerical numbers grew substantially. The South, like all of Italy, was characterized by a proliferation of Church structures. There were about 315 dioceses in Italy around 1600, of which almost half were in Naples and Sicily, while there were only 113 in France and 55 in Spain (there are 195 in the United States today). The high number of dioceses created opportunities for clerical careers but also some poorer prelates, since the revenues of some of these dioceses were quite low. Bishops enjoyed income from diocesan land and property, tithes, and various Church fees, but they also had to send contributions to Rome. Moreover, the southern dioceses were burdened with numerous pensions levied on their income and paid off to royal and papal favorites. The amount of Church revenue that left the South because of these pensions was a source of tension between the government and the papacy.

The Council of Trent (1545–63), the most significant institutional element of the Counter-Reformation, reformed the Catholic Church with the goal of making it better prepared to fight Protestantism. It strengthened the powers of bishops in their dioceses and aimed to ensure their conformity with papal policies. But numerous obstacles to the assertion of episcopal power endured. Some of these obstacles were common across the Catholic world: many bishops preferred a life of comfort or intrigue in Rome or Naples to tedious residence in their dioceses; the clerics who formed each diocese's cathedral chapter defended their traditional rights; lay donors had the power to appoint the holders of significant Church positions (the numerous ones endowed by lay patronage); confraternities and other lay initiatives of a spiritual or charitable nature proliferated (in 1623 there were 180 in the city of Naples alone); rural people resisted Church rules; many priests, especially in rural areas, were ignorant or indifferent; holding synods and opening seminaries to train better priests—as Rome required—was costly and difficult; and religious orders escaped episcopal authority altogether. This last factor was especially pronounced in the southern kingdoms, where monastic foundations were numerous and wealthy, and where old and new orders built new houses and accumulated estates. Around 1650 Naples and Sicily were home to almost half the regular houses (monasteries and convents) in Italy, although their overall population was at most one-third of the peninsula's total.

One final obstacle to episcopal power was peculiar to the Kingdom of Naples: the *ricettizia* church. In this form of parish structure, all local clerics owned local Church property collectively and shared its revenues. Only local natives could serve as priests. The bishop received a share of the tithes but had virtually no administrative control and limited spiritual jurisdiction over the priests. The ricettizia system affected about one-third of the kingdom's parishes, and lasted, though weakened, until the 1860s. In certain provinces (especially Basilicata and Terra d'Otranto) up to 80 percent of parishes followed this model. Thus, many rural priests remained very close in outlook and background to their fellow villagers; the Counter-Reformation model of educated priests separate from the views and practices of their parishioners did not penetrate much of the South until the nineteenth century.

Clerical numbers also represented a problem, both for bishops and for secular authorities. Anyone who had taken minor orders could claim clerical status with its attendant fiscal and judicial exemptions, including some married men, who exploited this legal status to obtain tax advantages for themselves and their families. The *diaconi selvaggi* (wild deacons), tonsured dependents who performed minor duties for churches, were also entitled to exemptions. Clerics in minor orders, married clerics, and wild deacons formed about half the southern clergy in the mid-seventeenth century.

The relationship between monarchy and Church was also not without its problems. The peculiar relationship of the southern kingdoms with the papacy posed difficulties for the viceroys. Formally, the kingdoms were papal fiefs, so the papacy had to be handled delicately in diplomatic affairs. On the other hand, Spanish power greatly strengthened the monarchy's hand compared to earlier periods, and Charles V used his Italian victories to force successive popes to be more compliant to his wishes. Pope Paul IV (ruled 1555–59) fought a brief war against Naples, which amply demonstrated papal weakness and Spain's unchallenged military superiority. The papal enclaves of Benevento and Pontecorvo were occasionally sources of friction, and Spanish troops occupied them when tensions got out of hand. Overall, however, their common struggle against the Ottomans and the Protestants led the two powers to cooperate more than conflict.

The main area of trouble in the relationship was the extent of papal jurisdiction over the Church in the kingdoms. In 1529 with the Treaty of Barcelona, Charles V had gained the power of appointment to eight archbishoprics and sixteen bishoprics in the Kingdom of Naples—generally the most important sees—but this still left about 120 dioceses in the kingdom to papal appointees. For all his devotion to the Catholic cause, Philip II defended royal power even more fiercely than his father. Following the tradition of the Aragonese kings, he and his successors required all papal appointments and bulls to be formally approved by the government in order to be valid. The Church's sanctuary right, which guaranteed anyone on Church property freedom from arrest, was the object of frequent disputes. In 1573, for instance, the viceroy ordered the extraction of a thief from the Naples archbishop's residence, and the prelate excommunicated both the guards who conducted the arrest and the viceroy until negotiations led to a compromise. Conflicts over ecclesiastic jurisdiction increased in frequency and intensity over the seventeenth century. In the next century criticism of ecclesiastic privilege played a crucial role in the early development of the southern Enlightenment.

The royal government had a freer hand in Church affairs in Sicily than in Naples. In Sicily, as in Spain and its American colonies, the Crown appointed virtually all bishops. It also claimed jurisdictional control over the Sicilian Church. This privilege, based on the apostolic legateship conferred by the pope on the Normans, led to the establishment of a tribunal known as the Monarchia Sicula, staffed with lawyers appointed by the king. The Monarchia Sicula, which operated until the 1860s, served as an appeals court for all cases from the episcopal courts, and greatly added to the powers of the Sicilian viceroys. In Sicily, finally, the government-controlled Spanish Inquisition operated, while in the Kingdom of Naples this tribunal remained under episcopal and thus ultimately papal control. The Sicilian Inquisition, however, clashed with the Spanish viceroys just as often as happened in Naples. Since in Sicily both the viceroy and the Inquisition answered to the king back in Spain, both could appeal to royal authority in their frequent disputes, producing tensions and delays. This was particularly the case with the privileges claimed by the Inquisition's dependents, who by the 1550s numbered above twenty thousand and were notorious for their abuse of their tax and judicial status.

The issue on which the papacy and the royal government achieved the highest level of cooperation was their policy toward religious minorities. At the start of Spanish rule, the Kingdom of Naples in particular was home to several religious and ethnic minorities. All were small but reasonably vibrant and rooted in society. Jews had flourished under the protection of the Aragonese kings. Albanian communities had settled in rural areas in Puglia and other provinces, mainly in the fifteenth century. Small groups of gypsies lived in the kingdom. Greek liturgical and linguistic traditions persisted in several mountain regions and in Naples itself. The papacy recognized the legitimacy of Greek traditions and communities and of Greek Catholic (not Orthodox) services, though it called for them to be monitored by Latin Catholic bishops. Married priests who celebrated mass in Greek continued to operate peacefully among villagers who often spoke dialects with substantial Greek elements. Finally, communities of Waldensians survived in Calabria and elsewhere. These groups, descended from medieval heretical movements, migrated from northwestern Italy to the kingdom in the thirteenth century and led relatively undisturbed lives in poor, remote areas.

By the mid-sixteenth century, as state and Church anxiety about Protestantism grew, all these groups came under attack. Religious conformity—and often ethnic homogeneousness—became a high priority for both Church and state, mirroring similar processes elsewhere in western Europe. In addition to the expulsion of Jews from the kingdom ordered by Viceroy Toledo in 1541, viceroys also issued repeated edicts expelling gypsies from the kingdom, especially in the 1550s and 1560s. Many gypsies were, however, settled and relatively integrated in local society and managed to remain; in the early seventeenth century a community of gypsies lived just outside the Naples walls, where they received the attentions of Jesuit and other missionaries.

The cruelest fate befell the Waldensians. They had lived for generations in a handful of villages in Calabria. By the 1540s they began to be confused with Protestants and were therefore treated as both heretics and rebels against the king. In February 1561 papal orders required the Waldensians of Calabria to attend mass every day; prohibited large gatherings and the use of their old language, a form of medieval southern French; and required marriage outside of their communities, to force integration into the larger Catholic population. In June 1561, after the orders were disobeyed and several villagers began to flee to the woods, the provincial governor, under royal orders and with seven hundred armed men, launched a military campaign to destroy these communities. Up to a few thousand people— of both sexes and all ages—were killed, dismembered, or tortured, and their fields and houses burned. The archbishop of Reggio reported on June 21 that eighty-six of the worst offenders "had their throats cut in a tremendous and exemplary punishment, and then were cut in half, and hanged on the road from Murano to Cosenza, along 46 miles, to make a frightening spectacle to all who pass by." Hundreds were arrested and trials continued into the 1570s.

Finally, between the 1590s and the 1620s zealous bishops in Calabria and Puglia attempted to suppress the Greek rites in their dioceses. They investigated the competence of Greek priests, objected to their married state, and were troubled by their dubious books. Most Greek-rite priests were removed, whereas some unmarried ones adopted the Latin rites. This also occurred in Albanian communities, which generally followed the Greek rites. The Greek rites were, however, most common in the countryside, and rural populations always had a way of resisting passively by relying on the bishops' distance and inefficiency. Therefore, there were traces of the Greek rites in remote regions into the eighteenth century, and dialects linked to Greek and Albanian continued to be spoken in a few villages into the twentieth century. But by and large, the cultural and ritual heritage of centuries of Greek history in the South lost its vitality by the start of the seventeenth century. With the exception of Arab and African slaves, the kingdom had become religiously and ethnically homogeneous.

The Church as an institution was only one component of religious life. Europeans' experience of Christianity underwent profound changes in the early modern period. The Protestant movement was rooted in impulses of spiritual renewal and concerns about clerical misconduct that already affected much of western Christendom in the fifteenth century. The Catholic Counter-Reformation itself drew much of its strength from this earlier spiritual dynamism. The two sides became bitterly divided by the late sixteenth century, and mutual hostility and repression marked their relationship for over a century after that. But both Catholicism and Protestantism derived much of their energy from the same spiritual fervor, intellectual vigor, and concern for reform that marked late medieval Christianity, especially in the urban world.

Well before the Protestant movement came into being, efforts to renew religious life appeared in southern Italy. Francis of Paola

(1416–1507), a hermit from Calabria, founded the Minims, a strict Franciscan branch that went on to enjoy great success across the Catholic world. Francis advocated spiritual improvement, strict adherence to the rule of poverty, and intense prayer and devotion. The papacy recognized his new order in 1474 and approved its statutes, or rule, in 1493. Francis's fame as a spiritual mentor expanded beyond the South, and in 1483 he was called to France to aid the ailing King Louis XI in preparing for death. Francis remained in France, where he founded many communities of his followers. He was canonized in 1519.

Many Catholic reformers shared Francis's more intense and engaged religiosity. The new initiatives they nurtured revived Catholicism just as the Protestant Reformation began its own movement for change. Neapolitans, or at least elite circles in Naples, actively took part in this spiritual movement. In the early sixteenth century, clerics and laypeople, men and women, poured their energies into the reform of religious life, and especially into more active and effective service to their fellow human beings. This ferment produced new institutions devoted to the welfare of the city's growing, needy masses. In 1519 Maria Longo (1463–1539), a noble widow originally from Catalonia, founded the Incurabili, the first permanent hospital in Naples. It soon specialized in the care of patients suffering from the new scourge of syphilis and by 1535 housed six hundred patients. The hospital's name—the "incurables"—reflects the threat of syphilis and the prevailing early modern attitude to hospitals. The general expectation was that the infirm would receive care at home, and hospitals were regarded as places where one awaited death while in the gravest stages of disease. Still, the spiritual and material care offered at the Incurabili provided support and solace previously unavailable to sick Neapolitans. Longo went on to gather a community of like-minded women, dedicated to the service of others, and in 1538 formed a new convent, Santa Maria in Gerusalemme, that was the basis for a new order of nuns, known later as the Capuchinesses.

Longo was at the center of a group of men and women who shared her commitment to active charity to those in need. Maria de Ayerbe, the duchess of Termoli and a close friend of Longo's, addressed another urban problem with her foundation of a convent for repented prostitutes, the Convertite. The Company of the Bianchi di

Giustizia (the White People of Justice, from the color of the robes they wore in processions) was also founded in 1519, by the notary Ettore Vernazza, another friend of Longo's, and housed for some time in the Incurabili. Members of this confraternity helped those condemned to death in practical matters, like writing a will, and in spiritual ones. They urged them to repent and seek absolution for their sins, and to report accomplices, and they offered spiritual comfort at executions. The need for these services increased with Toledo's aggressive approach to justice and the growth in Naples's size. Similar institutions existed in other cities. The Bianchi had a sister confraternity in Palermo. Other initiatives of these decades include the Monte di Pietà, founded in 1539, which offered loans to the poor at low or no interest in exchange for pawned goods, to alleviate the widespread problem of usury. The confraternity for the Redemption of Captives also originated from practical concerns, in its case to aid those enslaved by pirates.

These institutions were begun by laypeople who sought an active expression for their faith. These people were also close to currents of spiritual renewal brought to Naples by preachers and members of new orders. The founders of the Theatines, Gaetano da Thiene (1480–1547) and Giovan Pietro Carafa (1476–1559); the Humanist writer Juan de Valdés (ca. 1498–1541); the Augustinian preacher Pietro Martire Vermigli (1500–1562); and the Capuchin Vicar General Bernardino Ochino (1487–1564) were all active in Naples in the 1520s and 1530s, showing the strength of local interest in spiritual revival. A historian reported that in 1536 even Charles V "had much pleasure in hearing [Ochino, who preached] with great spirit and devotion, causing stones to weep."

Inspired by the ideas of Erasmus of Rotterdam, the greatest European Humanist and a committed religious reformer, preachers and theologians advocated a new way of living one's faith that was more spiritual but also simpler and gentler in its focus on individuals and their needs rather than on the ceremonies and rituals of the Church. Their views on inner renewal and commitment encouraged the charitable activities and spiritual readings and reflections of Longo, Ayerbe, Vernazza, and their friends in the Naples elites. At the same time, these ideas implied a lesser role for the clergy in guiding the faithful and stressed the individual's capacity for spiritual contact with God. For these reasons, and because these views spread beyond a narrow educated elite, Church authorities became concerned. Such was the interest in religious issues in the 1530s that a chronicler reported that "even some workers at the market tannery feel free to talk and discuss the Epistles of St. Paul and their difficult passages."

By the 1540s this focus on inner spirituality and emphasis on lay initiative was quite alarming to the authorities, as the break between Catholics and Protestants became more definitive. Books by suspected Lutherans were discovered to have entered Naples through its busy port. Ochino's flight to Geneva in 1542, where he embraced Calvinism, and Vermigli's own apostasy soon thereafter, brought swift repression of these spiritual and charitable movements. In 1551 Galeazzo Caracciolo, a member of one of the noblest families of the kingdom and the son of a close confidant of Toledo, fled to Geneva, where he converted and joined Calvin's consistory. Viceroy Toledo regarded with deep suspicion any group that met to discuss spiritual issues. Carafa became archbishop of Naples (and in 1555 Pope Paul IV) and furthered a climate of repression. From 1543 on, Church and state organized several burnings of forbidden books and tried and fined booksellers for stocking works by Lutherans or Humanists. Heresy trials continued into the 1560s in Naples and other cities, when they also took place in Castile. The Palermo Inquisition held nineteen autos-da-fé (the ceremonial group punishment of those sentenced by the Inquisition) between 1537 and 1572, condemning 660 people and burning 22 at the stake; the victims included heretics, relapsed Muslims, bigamists, and sorcerers. This change in atmosphere probably explains why Longo's charitable activities were largely forgotten in the decades after her death: her beatification trial did not begin until 1880 and has not advanced very far.

The same climate of suspicion affected Neapolitan intellectual life, at a time when spiritual and intellectual trends were closely linked. In 1542, after suspicions of heresy fell on its leader, Toledo shut down the Humanist Accademia Pontaniana, the last remaining link to the intellectual dynamism of Aragonese Naples. In 1546–47 he also closed all aristocratic academies, or informal cultural gatherings. Surviving charitable initiatives begun by laypeople, including the Incurabili and the Bianchi, were brought under the control of the Church hierarchy. The Inquisition became more active. The Jesuits, soon to be the order most closely connected with papal authority, arrived in Naples in 1539 at Toledo's urging, and in 1552 they established their Neapolitan province (or district) and founded their first school in the city. This was shortly after the 1548 opening of the very first Jesuit school, in Messina. Naples's size and needs continued to foster the growth of welfare institutions, but by the 1550s in Naples, as in most of Italy, religious life lost much of its independent spiritual momentum and stressed conformity with Church dictates and practices.

The suppression of autonomous lay initiatives did not, however, mean the end of all spiritual fervor. Thoughtful Church leaders realized that repression had to be accompanied with spiritual renewal and Church reform. In the early phase of the Counter-Reformation many bishops were active pastors: for instance, thirty-eight seminaries were founded between 1564 and 1594 in the Kingdom of Naples, though most did not last long. The new religious orders that formed a major element of the Counter-Reformation also fostered and guided charitable and spiritual activities. The Jesuits and Theatines established numerous communities in the South and encouraged lay participation in their endeavors. The Jesuits targeted both the urban and the rural world for mission work designed to improve the quality of the laity's religious life and to address the social and moral evils that resulted from urban crowding and from rural poverty and ignorance. Prostitutes, prisoners, slaves, and other suffering groups were the focus of urban missions. Jesuits and other priests preached to these groups and offered them easier access to the sacraments. The Jesuit Francesco de Geronimo (1642–1716) converted many by his agitated preaching. He especially pursued prisoners and prostitutes, at times running after the latter to hit them with his rosary beads— though he also helped them find housing if they renounced their ways. Jesuits also favored the creation of lay congregations under clerical guidance to minister to downtrodden urban groups. Naples's parish structures remained insufficient for the city's growth until 1598, when Archbishop Gesualdo doubled the number of parishes to thirty-seven and achieved a more even distribution of the population among them (the number grew to forty by 1792).

Missions to the rural population faced graver problems. Groups of priests visited remote areas to offer confessions, sermons, and masses. The rural population stunned the Jesuits: at the start of the seventeenth century a missionary reported that here were Christians "not having anything worthy of this name except baptism." A missionary to shepherd communities near Eboli wrote that the people he had visited were not too "different from the very beasts they guarded." The image of the southern countryside as "the Indies over here," in need of as much conversion effort as the New World that was posing such challenges and opportunities to Christian missionaries, quickly became a cliché applied to many remote European regions. Rural missions included dramatic preaching, theatrically staged group conversions, reconciliations of long-standing local feuds, elaborate processions, and mass confessions. Missions also served to spread the new emotional devotions of the Counter-Reformation, such as the Guardian Angel or the Rosary prayer.

The fervor of these generations did not last. The valiant efforts of the new regular orders and the engaged activism of many bishops withered by about 1620 as, under a new generation, the Counter-Reformation entered a less intense phase. This slacking off of spiritual energy combined with the climate of political, intellectual, and religious censorship that had grown since the 1550s. Religion in Naples became increasingly formalistic. Clerical privileges also attracted to the clergy many whose vocation was tepid at best. Although the southern population stagnated, clerical numbers expanded and stayed high well into the eighteenth century. Estimates for the mid-seventeenth century number the secular clergy at about 60,000, or some 3 percent of the population in the Kingdom of Naples; the regular clergy probably accounted for almost as many. In 1734, when the population had likely grown somewhat, there were about 112,000 clerics in the kingdom, again divided about evenly between seculars and regulars.

The quality of this numerous clergy was, of course, variable. Many were learned and pious men. All archbishops of Naples came from the aristocracy until the late nineteenth century, as the jurist Francesco D'Andrea recognized when he advised his nephews that southern cardinals never came "from our sphere." Many prelates were seriously engaged in the spiritual life of their people. Two archbishops of Naples became pope (Paul IV in 1555 and Innocent XII in 1691). The clergy in the larger cities, where the regular houses also concentrated, was probably adequately educated and committed to

its tasks. About 80 percent of the Naples clergy died in the plague epidemic of 1656, indicating that although many fled or sought rich
bequests from the dying laity, many more suffered among their flock.
On the other hand, many dioceses did not open a seminary until well
into the eighteenth century, and the quality of rural priests and services remained very low. In 1699 the bishop of Bisceglie in Puglia still
had to order his priests "not to go around singing and playing," not
to carry forbidden weapons, and not to be involved in "masks,
dances, and carnival games." An inquiry near Benevento in the early
eighteenth century found that four-fifths of the local priests could not
properly conduct the mass.

The Counter-Reformation enormously expanded the physical presence of the Church in the city and kingdom. Religion pervaded early
modern life, and in Naples religious architecture invaded urban
space. Physical expansion prevailed over spiritual growth. Large numbers of new religious institutions and buildings cropped up in Spanish Naples, and the growth intensified in the seventeenth century,
even as the city's growth slowed down. Already in the 1580s there
were at least 70 male religious houses and 22 female ones in the city,
home to 1,995 men and 1,774 women. In 1634, one of several
seventeenth-century writers to describe the city listed 97 religious
houses, plus 27 conservatories (or hospices, 15 for girls, 11 for
women, 1 for old men), and 12 hospitals (all run by the Church), in
addition to the city's 37 parishes and at least 70 chapels. By the late
seventeenth century there were in Naples about 300 churches and
120 monasteries and convents. The city was then home to about
twelve thousand clerics (about 3 to 4 percent of its population).

Throughout the South the clergy—and its real estate—expanded
dramatically. In 1733, for instance, the diocese of Catania in Sicily
was home to 69 regular houses. Sicily as a whole had 784 regular
houses in 1737. The city of Lecce, in southern Puglia, is perhaps the
best example of a Baroque sacred city. Lecce, with about twenty-five
thousand residents in 1600, was the second largest city in the Kingdom of Naples. The city expanded its walls to manage the population
growth of the sixteenth century. Yet the numbers of both its Church
institutions and its clergy increased much faster and for a longer time
than the city's lay population or walled center. In the 1560s Lecce was
already home to 80 churches and chapels and to 8 monasteries and

convents. By 1600 there were also 27 confraternities. The Jesuits and Theatines bought and built profusely in Lecce. The city lost population after 1600, but it had 150 priests in four parishes in 1624. In the 1680s Lecce was home to about thirteen thousand people, whose spiritual needs were served by an army of 148 priests and 365 other secular clerics; the city also housed up to one thousand monks, nuns, and friars, living in 27 communities. Thus, the clergy formed over 10 percent of Lecce's population. This clerical abundance made Lecce a major center of Baroque architecture. Especially under Bishop Luigi Pappacoda (served 1639–70) and his architect Giuseppe Zimbalo (ca. 1620–1710), Lecce acquired new church buildings in an exuberantly ornate style that used light, pliable local materials. The result is one of the most distinctive urban landscapes in Italy.

The expansion of the Counter-Reformation in the urban world—in the South as elsewhere in Catholic Europe—included the growth of convents and a substantial increase in the number of nuns. This reflected not only more encouragement to devotion but also a changing social and economic context. Mediterranean culture always regarded with concern the sexuality of young women. Elite families in particular needed a safe haven for their daughters who could not obtain a suitable husband. As new families from the worlds of trade or offices rose in standing, and as elite patrimonies struggled to withstand sixteenth-century inflationary pressures and increased demands for a lavish lifestyle, the cloistering of excess daughters became an attractive alternative to the payment of dowries. The spread of the practices of primogeniture and entail, which ensured the survival of noble estates by limiting the rights of daughters and younger sons, made the destiny of daughters all the more problematic. Numerous convents in Naples and other cities became repositories for more or less recalcitrant elite nuns.

Convents fulfilled the needs of elite families and were rewarded by rich endowments and donations, which in turn made possible further expansion. But the Counter-Reformation concern for the purity of religious life increased Church demands for severity in the conditions of cloistering and posed problems for elite families and their conventual offspring. In 1554, for instance, the abbess and nuns of San Festo in Naples pelted with stones the soldiers sent by the viceroy to enforce stricter cloistering rules. In 1566 a papal bull prohibited

Façade of the Church of the Rosario in Lecce

most visits to convents, forbade gifts to and from nuns, and banned nuns from activities such as embroidering and preparing sweets for sale to outsiders. A 1589 bull imposed the use of grills in churches and convents to make nuns invisible even to allowed visitors, ordered all correspondence to pass through the abbess's hands, and forbade nuns from keeping pets and servants.

Though adherence was often lax, especially in older convents, these rules caused consternation among nuns, particularly those of noble birth who were unused to and unprepared for such strictness. After the 1566 bull, many noble nuns sought to leave Naples convents, some arguing that they had never agreed to such strict cloistering but simply formed "a congregation of ladies." A nun from San Gregorio Armeno—an elite Benedictine convent—wrote that "when among ourselves we considered . . . that we had to abandon the many things we had purchased, without being able to be mistresses of any money . . . our sorrow grew so much that we could do nothing but bitterly weep." When in 1577 the archbishop sent an inspector to the convent of Sant'Arcangelo a Bajano, the abbess proudly displayed her splendid rooms: she owned paintings depicting mythological love scenes; objects in ebony, ivory, and marble; crystal vases; a guitar; a Persian rug; and beautiful linens and silks. When the inspector berated her for her worldly possessions, this aristocratic nun burst out, "I, born of the most illustrious blood on this earth, deprived of my freedom and of my rights, cannot even enjoy these innocent objects?" Though the source for this episode is possibly apocryphal, luxurious accommodations were certainly common in Neapolitan elite convents.

The concern with the sexuality and religious status of women extended beyond the aristocracy. All sorts of institutions provided either dowries or a refuge for women who—because of age, poverty, or other reasons—could not acquire a husband. One peculiar southern tradition was the *bizzoche,* or house nuns. These women lived with relatives, but in sworn chastity, and devoted themselves to good works and prayer. Although they usually could not afford the entry fees convents required, they were associated with religious orders and often wore the habit and hair of a tertiary (or lay sister). Church leaders were very concerned about the bizzoche, who escaped a clear system of control, and bishops tried to regularize their identity and status: bizzoche had to be at least forty years old and have a minimum income, to guar-

antee against dangers to their virtue; they received at least some clerical privileges; and they were banned from any religious teaching,
though in fact many engaged in it. In Naples in the late seventeenth
century an episcopal survey recorded about eight hundred bizzoche,
though there were probably many more unofficial ones who enjoyed
at least some status in their neighborhoods.*

The life of Giulia De Marco further shows how women were one of
the central preoccupations of the Counter-Reformation. Giulia was
the daughter of a peasant from Molise and of a woman whose own
mother was a Turkish slave. From these inauspicious beginnings, Giulia launched a career as a mystic and spiritual guide. She began to
acquire fame as a Franciscan tertiary because of her visions and
ecstasies. After a first contact with the Inquisition, which was always
concerned about unregulated female spiritual experiences, Giulia
came to Naples in 1612 as a protégée of the Jesuits. She took the city
by storm: by 1614 she was hailed as the spiritual "mother" of prelates,
almost two hundred nuns (most of them noblewomen), and numerous laypeople from the upper echelons of the government and nobility, including the viceroy and his wife. Giulia claimed to have special
illumination that allowed her to see the secrets of her followers'
hearts and the destiny of souls. She minimized the importance of
confession and emphasized the complete abandonment of the soul
to God's omnipotence. Her views veered perilously close to those of
earlier condemned Spanish mystics and even of some Protestants.

It is remarkable that as late as the 1610s a woman of dubious social
origins, who was not a full member of any religious order, should
have enjoyed much social success thanks to her mystical fervor. Giulia was doubtless a charismatic figure. But eventually she became the
victim of rivalries between religious orders and of increased Church
concerns about affected sanctity, especially on the part of women.
The Theatines, archrivals to the Jesuits, supported another Neapolitan
female mystic—the much more sedate and obedient Orsola Benincasa (1547–1618), who, after her own troubles with the Inquisition

---

*Since 1970 the papacy has again given some recognition to women who live in chastity
in the secular world as "consecrated virgins"; as with the bizzoche, bishops set a minimum
age, usually in the thirties. There are several such women in the United States today; they
have an association and a Web site.

in the 1580s, lived in a hermitage and enjoyed great fame as a seer (Orsola founded the female Theatines and is now a venerable). A later admirer wrote that Orsola "was swept into ecstasy each time that she received the bread of life."

After her sole, chilly meeting with the more sociable Giulia, Orsola called her rival a "most notorious hypocrite." The Theatines accused Giulia of heresy and immorality, and a trial began. The viceroy threatened to expel the Theatines from the kingdom, but Rome promised immunity for Giulia's followers, and the trial moved to Inquisition headquarters in Rome. In December 1615, after interrogations and torture, Giulia, her spiritual director, and a lawyer friend confessed to heretical views and promiscuous sexual behavior. Giulia acknowledged that she had claimed to be exempt from sin and that even St. Catherine of Siena "would have envied Giulia's soul, as holier and more favored by God." The three abjured their views and were jailed for life.

Giulia's career and its end illustrate the extreme competition between religious orders at a time when the success of religious figures translated into power and wealth, and religious and political authority were inextricably intertwined. Giulia's low rank, both socially and as a tertiary nun, in the long run weakened her claim to sanctity. The Church in this period monitored and punished numerous cases, in Italy and elsewhere, of dubious holiness: women—or children like Francesco Belli—were especially suspect. The fact that Giulia, on the basis of her mystical union with God, offered guidance to members of the clergy was especially problematic because it placed a woman in a position of religious authority. The fact that her teaching focused on theologically delicate issues of grace, salvation, and the sacraments exposed her even more to retribution. Giulia's case shows the desire many Catholics felt for some form of spiritual intensity and contact with the divine. At the same time, her fate reveals how by the early seventeenth century both the Church's worries about these spiritual agitations and its ability to suppress their unregulated expression had increased.

The presence of religion in Baroque Naples went well beyond the architectural and institutional. The entire population of the city participated in frequent religious ceremonies, to mark the regular events

of the Christian calendar and to respond to the special moments of
celebration or danger that were typical of early modern life. With the
Counter-Reformation came new celebrations, rich in pomp and ceremony, such as the Forty Hours: starting in 1568, elaborate stages were
built in churches for this prolonged adoration of the Eucharist.
Church authorities devoted much effort to implementing in the kingdom the policies of the Counter-Reformation: more rigor in the
clergy's preparation and spirituality; stricter rules for the laity's moral
and sexual life; more centralized control of all devotional practices;
institutional coordination from the parish to the diocese; careful censorship of dubious opinions or publications; and, when needed,
more repression. But the religious experiences of Neapolitans continued to include elements that had characterized medieval Christianity
across Europe, such as strongly relying on the magical and the supernatural; mixing Christian and pre-Christian practices; searching for
divine forces through people and rituals not sanctioned by the official Church; and understanding religion as primarily a practical
exchange between worship and protection.

These continuities and the slowness of Counter-Reformation reforms
were common across the Catholic world, particularly in rural areas.
What was peculiarly pronounced in Spanish Naples was that an intense
relationship with the supernatural grew in strength over the period
and shaped the beliefs and experiences of all elements of the population. Aristocrats, lawyers, and ecclesiastics venerated Giulia De
Marco just as uneducated Neapolitans may have fallen under the
sway of neighborhood healers or sorcerers. Giulia's lay followers
found through her a reassurance and protection similar to what the
city's masses craved in their rituals and devotions. Everyone sought a
similar connection with the sacred. In the seventeenth century these
practices and beliefs acquired an increasingly dramatic form, in keeping with the theatrical culture of Baroque Naples. To this day, southern popular beliefs reflect this intense search for the protection and
help of divine forces.

Church tribunals, acting on Roman directives, tried to control what
official doctrine now regarded as superstitious practices. Between 1590
and 1710 the Naples Inquisition conducted over six hundred trials
against various popular practices, though, like its Spanish counterpart,
it remained skeptical and mild in its dealings with accusations of

witchcraft. Inquisition records document the reliance of many Neapolitans on incantations, potions, amulets, magic formulas, and a whole array of other methods to bring supernatural forces to bear on daily life. Devotion to the dead and the belief that they could intervene both positively and negatively in the life of the living were (and are) especially prominent among Neapolitans. All this troubled Church leaders. But educated elites participated so actively in many of these practices that any repression was only halfhearted.

A clear example of this intense search for supernatural protection was the growing number of official patron saints across the South. Secular and ecclesiastical leaders of Naples and other cities responded to the numerous crises of the century by adding to this well-staffed roster. At the end of the sixteenth century Naples made do with seven patrons, mostly its early martyred bishops, some of them likely apocryphal figures. Twenty-five more were added over the seventeenth century, beginning with St. Thomas Aquinas in 1605. Aquinas, who died in 1274, came from a Neapolitan noble family, which he shocked when he entered the Dominican order, then regarded as an upstart group of lowly born clerics. Aquinas went on to study in Paris, teach in Naples, and become the most influential theologian in the history of Catholicism. It was in San Domenico, the main Dominican church in the old center of Naples, that Aquinas heard the crucifix speak surely the most welcome review a theologian ever received: "You wrote well about me, Thomas." The crucifix is still there.

Four more patrons were added in 1625–26 alone, including St. Patricia, the city's first female patron (a niece of Emperor Constantine, she supposedly died in Naples and left behind a nail of the Cross, which turned bloody every year on Good Friday). Another burst of additions came between 1689 and 1692, soon after an earthquake, when seven more patrons were added. Three more were added between 1700 and 1731, for a total of thirty-five. These were officially sanctioned saints, several only recently canonized by Rome. The people of Naples also worshiped many unofficial saints, men and women (plus the occasional child) of holy disposition and life who lived in the city and to whom miracles were attributed.

This search for patrons was typical of southern devotions: 225 southern communities added 410 patron saints to the ranks of their heavenly advocates (the actual number of saints was only 130, as many worked in more than one town) between 1630 and 1750. The distribution of these choices was uneven. Over one-third of the additions took place in Terra di Bari and Terra d'Otranto, provinces that became veritable pantheons. Lecce added 19 patrons between 1654 and 1703, and Altamura added 21 between 1637 and 1741. Though the phenomenon slowed down in Naples after the 1690s, in the provinces it continued strong until 1750. This interest in saints appears also in an abundant production of books about them: 279 books about saints were published in Naples between 1500 and 1750, representing close to 10 percent of all published titles; two-thirds of these books appeared in the seventeenth century. The period witnessed an unrivaled flourishing of southern sanctity: over one hundred men and women who lived in the kingdom between 1540 and 1750 have received over time some formal recognition of their holiness from the papacy.

The same search for saintly patrons and their miraculous powers occurred in Sicily, where the plague of 1624 in particular brought new devotions and new patrons: the Madonna of the Letter in Messina (the letter the Virgin had written to the city sadly survived only in later translations), St. Agatha in Catania, and St. Rosalia in Palermo. The bones of Rosalia, a local virgin hermit of the twelfth century, were found after a female plague sufferer had a vision of their location, and the saint quickly became the city's main patron. Her fame as a miracle worker reverberated across the Iberian empires, and by the eighteenth century there were churches in her honor in Goa, South America, and California. Palermo added 18 more patrons between 1630 and 1700. The intensity of southern devotion to the saints is little abated today. In 2002 the pope canonized Pio of Pietrelcina, a Capuchin healer who died in 1968 and enjoyed, in life and in death, an enormous following in the South. It is difficult across the South today to find a shop or cab window—let alone a church—that does not display an image of the bearded "Padre Pio." His sanctuary in northern Puglia recently inaugurated a magnificent new church, designed by Renzo Piano and topped by the largest dome in Italy after St. Peter's.

The constant search for celestial protection explains also the central role of relics in southern religious life. Relics were venerated throughout the Catholic world, but in the South this worship reached unusual heights. A mid-seventeenth-century catalogue compiled by a city Dominican lists thousands of relics in Naples churches, including 367 complete bodies, 54 heads, 28 arms, and 18 ribs. The teeth, bones, hair, and skulls of countless saints were preserved, periodically displayed, and brought out in processions. Nails of the Cross, fragments of the clothes of Christ and the Virgin, the latter's milk, the blood of numerous saints, a feather of the archangel Gabriel, and even the grease of St. Lawrence (who had died on a grill, from which presumably a provident witness had gathered the holy fat) added variety to this pantheon. The city also housed at least five pieces of the Cross and eleven thorns from Christ's crown.

This collection grew after the 1570s, when early Christian catacombs were discovered at San Gaudioso on the outskirts of the old center. There, the Dominicans soon built the huge church of Santa Maria della Sanità, one of Naples's greatest Baroque temples and a repository of neighborhood relics. Numerous relics were preserved also in many other towns in the South: the bodies of the apostles Andrew in Amalfi, Matthew in Salerno, Bartholomew in Benevento, and Thomas in Ortona were just the cream of this heavenly crop. Scattered relics also gained fame: Catania, for instance, had many relics of St. Agatha, but pieces of her arms were in Palermo, Messina, and Salerno; her jaw, in Galatina; and one of her breasts, in Gallipoli (Agatha's martyrdom was the cutting off of her breasts, and the one in Gallipoli once miraculously gave milk to a hungry girl).

People coveted relics and sought new ones as soon as they became available. The deaths of saintly individuals were attended by such seekers. For instance, in 1608, when the godly Theatine Andrea Avellino died, two noble ladies fought off other claimants and took home his hat and some of his hair. This proved a wise move, as in 1625 Andrea joined Naples's official patrons. The behavior of the body of the reputed saint after death was crucial to establish the holiness of the life just ended and hence the value of the relics. Doctors often performed autopsies, seeking in the body of mystics traces of the divine fire that had inspired them. Orsola Benincasa's body, for instance, remained warm long after her death, furthering her fame. One touching example of saintly modesty was given in 1686 by the body of the Sicilian Capuchin Giuseppe d'Avola: as his brethren undressed the body to wash it, "the dead man, almost as if still alive, covered his pudenda with his hands."

Collectively, the presence and power of saints' relics offered guarantees to the faithful of the special status of their city, of its privileged relationship with the divine. Christ and Mary were, from this perspective, just like all other saints: powerful figures whose remains were to be sought and treasured for the practical aid they would bring (since Christ and Mary ascended into heaven, in fact ordinary saints were much likelier sources of relics). Relics were surrounded and matched by ex-voto objects, the signs of the gratitude of the devout to their intercessors. An ex-voto is a votive offering, usually a picture commemorating an episode of saintly aid or an object donated to a saint's image or chapel in acknowledgment of what Neapolitans still call a "grace," that is, a favor requested by the faithful and rendered by the saint. Between 1613 and 1619, for instance, 2,158 ex-votos were left at the tomb of Andrea Avellino. Still today in many southern churches (and, more rarely, elsewhere in Italy) one sees such pictures, or little silver lungs, hearts, or legs that give thanks for the healing of that particular body part. The best example of this practice in Naples today is the chapel (in the Gesù Nuovo church) dedicated to St. Giuseppe Moscati, a doctor who died in 1927 and was canonized in 1987: the walls are covered with silver body parts and the names of the healed.

Southern religion was thus almost a form of shamanism: saints and relics effected prodigies. The southern hunger for miracles was often satisfied. From the early sixteenth to the mid-eighteenth century, churches and religious orders in the kingdom kept track of well over three thousand cases of miracles attributed to saints or their relics, about half of which occurred in Naples itself. In the canonization trials for Andrea Avellino and Bernardino Realino (a Jesuit from Lecce), 516 people testified to having received a miracle by the candidate saint's intercession. At the trial for the canonization of Benedetto "the Moor" in Palermo, witnesses reported 90 miraculous cures effected by Benedetto or through his relics, spanning from paralysis to hemorrhoids. Nobles, clerics, peasants, and everyone in between solicited and received heavenly aid for a variety of problems, from illnesses to accidents, from demonic encounters to natural calamities. The great majority of these miracles occurred in the trou-

Ex-voto image depicting salvation from the 1631 eruption of Vesuvius,
dedicated to the sanctuary of the Madonna dell'Arco outside of Naples

bled middle decades of the seventeenth century, and they were often
connected to the search for effective patron saints. The cause of St.
Gaetano, for instance, whose relics were in Naples, was pushed by the
Theatines, the order he had founded. In 1649–57 at least 217 miracles were attributed to Gaetano, mostly in Naples, and he was added
to the city's patrons after the plague epidemic. The Theatines and the
Jesuits, the two largest new orders in the South, were often at odds
over the relative merits of their respective saints, as they were over the
mystics the two orders protected.

This intense contact with the saintly—and in Naples the saintly
was the main if not the only manifestation of the sacred—is nowhere
more obvious than in the rituals and beliefs surrounding the blood
of San Gennaro, which was kept in his splendid chapel in the cathedral. Gennaro, a mythical fourth-century martyred bishop, was one
of the earliest patrons of the city, and his head and blood were
paraded in processions since the late fourteenth century. But his worship then was irregular and no prophetic significance was yet attributed to the supernatural liquefaction of his hardened blood that

Ex-voto image depicting salvation from the 1656 plague epidemic,
dedicated to the sanctuary of the Madonna dell'Arco outside of Naples

occurred occasionally over the fifteenth and early sixteenth century.
Gennaro's prominence increased by the mid-sixteenth century, and
his chapel in the cathedral was the fulfillment of a city vow of thanksgiving for his aid in a plague epidemic in 1527. But Gennaro's true
moment of glory, when he acquired the status he has yet to surrender
to any other patron of the city, only came with the devastating eruption of Vesuvius in 1631. He then earned the tribute Neapolitans
from Naples to Brooklyn still give him.

On December 16 of that year, the lava arrived at the eastern boundaries of the city. This eruption killed over three thousand people and
was the volcano's worst since the one that destroyed Pompeii in AD 79.
Great panic ensued in Naples, with mass confessions and repentance,
processions, and chaos. The next day, the archbishop brought Gennaro's blood and head outside the cathedral, and the blood was found
to have liquefied. Camillo Tutini described what happened next:

The air was dark and full of ash, and there was a great rain; on the appearance of the sacred relics at the main door of the Duomo suddenly a ray of sun appeared so clear and shining, eliminating that obscurity, that the people there gathered, full of joy, started crying to the heavens: "miracle, mercy." And there is a rumor that at the same moment many people worthy of trust saw the glorious San Gennaro in his episcopal habit at the window of that church blessing the people, as if to assure them of the grace that he had obtained from God to have preserved the city of Naples from the fire. . . . The procession having reached the outside of Porta Capuana, at the sight of the burning mountain the most eminent archbishop took the sacred vials of the blood and with them he made the sign of the cross, so that those proud clouds full of burning matter, in the presence of the blood of he who other times had humiliated and extinguished them, began to dissipate and take another route, and from then on began to disappear.

Another witness reported that Gennaro "ordered the devils to go back, the abyss to stop vomiting flames, and the fire ended and the sky cleared."

From then on, the miracle of San Gennaro's blood became the main event of the saintly year in Naples. It still routinely occurs twice a year (on Gennaro's feast day, September 19, and on the first Sunday in May, which commemorates the transport of Gennaro's body to Naples), and its occasional failure is feared to portend great evils for the city. During the seventeenth century the miracle often took place on December 16 as well, when a solemn mass and procession were held in honor of the saint's intercession against the lava. The miracle also occurred on many special occasions, such as great dangers for the city (eight times between 1631 and 1692), special celebrations, and visits by prominent people. In the late seventeenth century the saint proved especially obliging toward famous visitors: while the liquefaction greeted only six of them before 1650, it welcomed forty-two illustrious visitors between 1656 and 1696, plus two more in 1702. In 1663 Rome declared Gennaro the principal patron of both the city and the kingdom.

Further evidence of the centrality of Gennaro's miracle to Neapolitans' sense of the sacred is the tribute of imitation the relics of other saints paid to Gennaro: the blood of John the Baptist, that of St. Patri-

Onofrio Palumbo, *San Gennaro Intercedes to Protect Naples* (ca. 1652),
from the confraternity of the Trinità dei Pellegrini, Naples

cia, and that of other saints began to liquefy regularly, and so did the milk of the Virgin, which melted on the feast of the Assumption (I have found no mention of changes in the condition of the grease of St. Lawrence). These miraculous fluids complemented the twelve images of the Virgin and six crucifixes in the city that at various times spoke, moved, or engaged in other extraordinary behavior (not always selflessly: in 1439 the crucifix in the Carmine moved its head to avoid an artillery shot). Even figurines in Neapolitan *presepi*, the traditional—and very elaborate—nativity scenes that have been for centuries one of the city's most prominent forms of popular art, displayed such behavior: at least three times in the seventeenth century, statuettes of the Child Jesus moved or spoke, resulting in the conversion of witnesses to these miraculous acts.

The cult of saints and their relics focused on the miraculous powers of saints and saintly things and on the rituals through which individuals or groups (including a city as a whole) could direct that power to their own goals and protection. Images too not only were ways to commemorate the saint or express the faith of the pious, but also could, like relics, be themselves endowed with miraculous powers. In the early eighteenth century the Neapolitan essayist Paolo Mattia Doria complained that "Christians do to the saints' images what pagans did not dare do to those of their idols." The competition between religious orders and between aristocratic families, each of which pushed the images in its own churches, and its own saints or candidates for sainthood, as the most valuable intercessors, only intensified these devotions. There was a performance aspect to Neapolitan devotions and ceremonies, and the saint was seen primarily as a maker of miracles, not as a spiritual model. The supernatural was everywhere.

The lives of the saints always present them as triumphing over their enemies and offering powerful backing to their worshipers. This conception and the theatrical character of the rituals and devotions are evident not only in religious ceremonies and saints' lives but also in sermons. Churches served as stages for dramatic preaching, but preachers could also be encountered everywhere in the city and the kingdom, in markets and on street corners. Examples of demonic possession, traumatic death, and exorcism were often used in sermons as rhetorical devices for dramatic effect. Preachers extolled the power of the saints and of their relics and images both to reward and to punish. Many stories, for instance, surrounded the venerated image of the Madonna dell'Arco, in Naples's periphery, which always had a temper: its cult began when a gambler lost his game near the image, cursed it, and threw a ball at it. Blood spurted from the image and the gambler was paralyzed. A very popular story, dating to about 1590, was that of Aurelia Del Prete: this woman went on Easter Monday to visit the chapel of the Madonna dell'Arco, tripped, and in falling cursed the chapel. Her husband's dire warning upon hearing her curse proved only too true, as on the first anniversary of her blasphemy both of Aurelia's feet fell off, to be enshrined in the chapel in testimony to the image's power (in another version, Aurelia's sin was trampling on an ex-voto).

One final major element that characterized the religious life of southerners was (and is) the focus on the dead. The dead were endowed by popular belief with at least some of the power that saints exercised. They also engaged with the living in a contractual, exchange relationship similar to the one Neapolitans sought with their saints. The dead needed the support of the living, through masses or visits to cemeteries, and they reciprocated by interceding for the living with their more powerful heavenly neighbors. To this day, southerners offer ex-votos to churches in support of the dead, and many believe that their dead can communicate with them on matters from the mundane (such as what numbers to play in lotteries or whether rain is likely) to the spiritual. In the early modern period this cult of the dead was a dominant presence in southern life. Funereal imagery was common in the urban landscape, and guilds, confraternities, and other institutions devoted much attention to honoring their dead.

The souls of purgatory were at the center of these devotions. One of the most frequent images in Neapolitan popular art was the so-called Madonna of the Graces with the Purgatory. This Madonna was shown in the act of providing milk from her breasts to the souls of purgatory, who usually appear as small figures either imploring aid at the Virgin's feet or stuck in fiery holes in the ground, writhing in pain. The refreshing heavenly liquid gushing from Mary's breasts reaches them and provides solace in their sorrow. This image was widespread in the Naples area beginning in the late fifteenth century and flourished through most of the sixteenth century. The Counter-Reformation faced here one of its biggest challenges, as these images, mixing sacred themes with secular and sensuous tones, ran counter to its hope to enforce a more disciplined spirituality. The iconography of the bare-breasted, lactating Madonna appeared to many clerics to contain excessive elements, and they tried to prohibit its use.

Church leaders obtained the gradual disappearance of this type of image, but the cult of the souls of purgatory as a group, seen as powerful intercessors for the living, expanded. Churches, confraternities, and chapels were dedicated to the souls of purgatory in Naples, and large numbers of masses were addressed specifically to them. The dead appeared in many rituals: in May 1710, for instance, after San Gennaro's blood had ominously turned black, processions marched through the city "carrying skulls of the dead, dried bones, and even pieces of putrefied corpses, recently buried" to assuage the saint's apparent ire. Dying Neapolitans regularly requested masses for the salvation of their own soul and those of their relatives. In the seventeenth century there was a veritable inflation in the number of masses for the dead: it is not uncommon to find in testaments requests for thousands, or even tens of thousands. Bequests for perpetual masses for all souls also became common. The devotion to the souls of purgatory grew considerably into the eighteenth century. It satisfied a macabre taste that was central to the southern Baroque and that emphasized the role of churches as ossuaries. To this day, the souls of purgatory are popular figurines in Neapolitan presepi.

These elements of southern religious behavior reached their height in the seventeenth century, under the influence of Baroque tendencies to excess and drama combined with the decline of the more spiritual forces of the early generations of the Counter-Reformation. By the turn of the eighteenth century, new factors came to shape religious life. On the one hand, southern intellectual life began to react to the scientific and rationalistic movements that developed in northern Italy and Europe; after 1700, in part in response to these new trends, the royal government became more aggressive in its policy toward Church wealth and privileges. On the other hand, by the 1680s the Church itself, in Naples as elsewhere, again focused more intensely

Contemporary *presepe* figurines depicting the souls of purgatory

on spiritual renewal and on the suppression of ideas and practices it deemed threatening.

These shifts led to increased conflict between royal power and Church authorities and to stronger repressive actions on the part of prelates and the Inquisition. In Palermo in 1724 the Inquisition, in the presence of the viceroy, the archbishop, and a large crowd, held an auto-da-fé to burn a lay brother and a *bizzoca*, both jailed since 1699 and accused of heretical visions. In Naples the government resisted such Church activities. A synod in 1726 in which the archbishop affirmed an expansive view of episcopal jurisdiction caused such controversy that no archbishop managed to hold another synod until 1882. A dramatic example of tension occurred in Lecce. In 1709 a fight erupted over jurisdictional and fiscal exemptions the bishop claimed for some of his landed properties. The city's royal governor rejected the claim and the bishop excommunicated him. When the viceroy backed the governor, the bishop excommunicated the entire city government. The viceroy then ordered the bishop to leave Lecce and the prelate went to Rome, from where in 1711 he placed the entire diocese under interdict. This shut down all churches and forbade marriages and burials, allowing only the performance of baptisms and the hearing of confessions. A local chronicler wrote that "corpses were buried without tolling of bells, accompaniment . . . torches, priest, or candles." A compromise was not reached until 1719.

The period also saw, however, a renewal of spiritual energies and concerns. The life of Alfonso de' Liguori (1696–1787) reveals the more emotional, scrupulous, intense piety that spread across Europe then, as the growth of Methodism and Pietism in the Protestant world also show. Alfonso came from a provincial elite family, studied in Naples, and practiced law in the city's tribunals until becoming a cleric in 1723. As a young man he experienced profound moral scruples: he reportedly removed his glasses at the opera—which he enjoyed—so as not to see the singers, of whom he disapproved. He was sensitive to other worldly pleasures and wrote in a notebook that "speaking with women is not an occasion of sin *per se* even though it causes some sexual arousal." After renouncing his family's inheritance, in 1726 Alfonso was ordained a priest. His activities centered on two areas: moral theology, which was the main focus of his studies and writings, and pastoral care, with special attention to confession and missions, both to the urban poor and to rural areas.

In 1732, with other clerics he founded a society for missions to underserved rural areas, and by 1743 he was elected rector of the society, the Congregation of the Most Holy Redeemer. At the same time, Alfonso worked on his scholarship and in 1748 published his *Moral Theology*, which appeared in eight more editions during his lifetime.

Alfonso's approach emerged from his experience with missions. His focus was pastoral, not theoretical, and he displayed great sensitivity to the context of popular devotion: for instance, he argued that cursing on the part of ignorant, rural, poor people should often not be regarded—or punished—as blasphemy, but rather understood as the result of the harshness of rural life. In 1749 the papacy approved Alfonso's congregation as a new order, the Redemptorists, and the first house opened in Benevento in 1755. Unlike prior missionaries to rural areas, Redemptorists worked closely with the parish clergy, aiming to strengthen parish structures. By the end of the 1750s, however, Alfonso's health was weakening and he could no longer personally preach or engage in mission work. He continued to publish about his mission and confession methods, always emphasizing mildness, patience, and the use of simple language in sermons and confessions. Alfonso wished to bring a simpler, friendlier sense of the sacred to rural people and was dubious both of the emphasis on miracles on the part of many clerics and of the use of a threatening tone in sermons, wishing rather to instruct than to frighten listeners.

In 1762 he was appointed bishop of Sant'Agata dei Goti, a hilly village near Naples, where he pursued his pastoral and spiritual agenda until he retired in 1775 to Pagani, his order's headquarters at the foot of Vesuvius. By Alfonso's time, Catholic governments across Europe regarded the further expansion of Church numbers and wealth with suspicion and opposed any encroachment of papal authority into their territories. Thus, it was only in 1779 that the royal government of Naples recognized the Redemptorists, under strict regulations aimed at protecting royal jurisdiction. This caused a breach with Rome and the split of the order into two branches, which brought great sorrow to Alfonso's final years. In 1783 he resigned his leadership of the order. Alfonso's canonization trial began in 1795 and succeeded in 1839. Six other southern Redemptorists have also become saints. The Redemptorists spread to central Europe and by the 1830s to the United States. In 1871 the papacy proclaimed Alfonso a Doctor of the Church and in 1950 the patron saint of confessors and moral theologians.

The intense sentimentality of Alfonso's devotions, especially to the Virgin Mary, typifies devout spiritual currents that affected much eighteenth-century Christianity. Alfonso wrote short works on daily devotions and prayer. He was easily moved to tears by children and liked animals, for years keeping a pet cat called Mohamet. In spite of his theological accomplishments, the popular image of Alfonso remains that of an old, simple man of sentimental devotion. Like most southerners, he was especially fond of the emotions linked with Christmas: he composed "Tu scendi dalle stelle" (You Descend from the Stars), perhaps the most popular Italian Christmas carol. In the eighteenth century Christmas grew in prominence among Catholic feasts across the Catholic world, and in Naples the production of pre-sepi bloomed; foreign visitors noted the festive emotionalism of Christmas in Naples.

Alfonso's particular focus on the rural masses in missions, in confessions, and as a bishop also mirrored increased Enlightenment interest in the rural world. What Alfonso's missionaries found in the southern countryside troubled them greatly. The "Indies over here" had changed little since the first Jesuit missionaries visited rural areas of the South at the end of the sixteenth century. Given the prevailing settlement patterns, especially in areas of great feudal estates, many villages were remote, and their isolation posed great obstacles to the spread of new standards of piety and devotion. Missionaries and bishops found customs and emotions that struck them as violent and unchristian, especially by the morally more sensitive standards of the eighteenth century.

Respect for sacred spaces and rituals was a paramount concern: bishops forbade contacts between the sexes in church and inappropriate clerical appearance, and urged that "there be no frivolous talk, profane conversations, strolls, and great noise in churches." Educated outsiders repeatedly condemned the use of hired mourners and the wild screams of relatives of the deceased, which were typical of peasant attitudes to death; such behavior offended urban—and urbane—sensitivities and seemed to indicate disbelief in the afterlife. In 1664 a Puglia synod declared that "the wailing and clamor of relations shall cease [and] women shall not beat their breasts, tear out their hair." The archbishop of Reggio in 1672 urged women to avoid "extreme howling and immoderate sighs . . . [and] the laceration of cheeks and hair." Though over time these practices became rarer, as late as the mid-twentieth century visitors to the rural South reported similar behaviors.

A section of the famous Presepe Cuciniello,
from the Museum of San Martino, Naples

Wild rural customs were one expression of a trait that marked all of southern religion in the early modern period and beyond: its performative, dramatic aspect, apparent in peasant funeral customs as in urban processions and feasts. Visitors noted that popular devotion in Naples was "all exterior, demonstrative, and inconsequential." But even elite southerners partook eagerly in the beliefs and practices that many eighteenth-century visitors found distasteful, irrational, and superficial. The government's attitude toward the wealth and privileges of the Church became more aggressive in the eighteenth century, and Enlightenment intellectuals saw the Church as a major obstacle to progress. Yet the central role of religion and the Church in the life and beliefs of southerners declined little over the early modern period. The Counter-Reformation Church's stress on moral discipline and self-control met limited success in the South. But southern culture offered a fertile ground for many other elements of Baroque and Counter-Reformation Catholicism: its theatrical fervor, its ardent faith in the supernatural, its practical search for powerful protection. These traits flourished in urban and rural settings, contributed to an artistic boom that still gives many southern cities their dominant look, and shaped southern mentality and behavior in long-lasting ways.

It is easy, from a modern perspective, to find much of Baroque Catholicism in the Italian South somewhat entertaining in what to us may appear as its wackiness. But the seventeenth century witnessed a lot of religious strangeness across the Christian world. Members of many sects spoke in tongues—and Quakers quaked—in England; in Scandinavia, Germany, England, and Massachusetts— much more aggressively than anywhere in Spain or Italy—thousands of alleged witches were tortured and burnt at the stake by secular and clerical authorities; educated elites, and masses of the uneducated, had no problem believing that their neighbors flew at night to attend gatherings where they worshiped and copulated with the devil. The severe political instability, religious conflict, continuous warfare, famines, and economic crises of the age may help explain these behaviors and beliefs.

In that context, the religious practices of southern Italians may still appear excessive and somewhat primitive, but they also seem comparatively harmless, especially in terms of the numbers of victims of religious persecution. The practical help that so many southerners sought in their religious and ritual life appears the wiser course when confronted with what some contemporaries were doing. In the following century, during the Enlightenment, northern Europeans—in the name of rationalism—liked to scoff at southerners' approach to religion. Today, when church pews are often empty across Europe, but Pope John Paul II has declared more saints than his predecessors over the previous five centuries combined, six million pilgrims a year seek divine aid at Lourdes, and millions more visit other miraculous sanctuaries and shrines, the southern Baroque approach looks prescient.

Chapter VI

Paradise Inhabited by Devils
Culture and Society in
Baroque Naples

I go through the city and, apart from the innumerable artisans
who are about, and apart from all those who stay in their homes,
I see in each street, each alley, each corner such a multitude of
people who bump into me, who walk over me, that it is hard for
me to walk among them. I enter the churches during services, and
there are many, and I find them filled with people, and yet it does
not seem that anyone is missing anywhere in the city. I go into the
courts and it is a miracle to see there such gatherings, and the
streets, not one, not ten, but all filled with people walking, on
horseback, in coaches with a noise everywhere as if it were the
buzzing of bees.

G. C. Capaccio, *Il forastiero* (1634)

The city of Naples grew enormously under Spanish rule. Around
1500 its 100,000 inhabitants placed it about even with the populations of some northern Italian cities. By 1550 Naples had doubled in
size and was the largest city in Italy. By 1600 the number of residents
reached about 300,000, making the city, with Paris and London, one
of the largest in the Christian world. It remained such up to the devastating plague of 1656, which probably killed 60 percent of the
400,000 to 450,000 people who then inhabited it. Even after these
losses, Naples continued to be by far the largest city in Italy, and its
population grew to maybe 500,000 by the end of the eighteenth century. Throughout the early modern period it dwarfed all other cities
in its kingdom and was three to four times the size of any other Italian city.

A city of this magnitude posed enormous challenges, to which
were added the difficulties of Naples's particular geography. Its
coastal location, hemmed in by hills, allowed for far less growth of

urban space than the population warranted, even without the effects of misguided government controls over building. The roots of many of the most obvious problems besetting the modern city lie in its rapid growth: crowdedness, dirt, noise, crime, poverty, confusion, bad hygiene and health all became by 1600 inextricably linked with the experience and texture of Neapolitan life. When what order existed in Naples fell apart, the density of the population could also lead to astounding violence. The city's size, however, also meant that great wealth was concentrated there, and this fed education, art, music, and culture. The huge population developed rituals, associations, and customs that often struck observers as peculiarly tinted with drama, excess, or confusion. Nothing in Naples was small scale.

In 1527–29 the city faced both a serious plague epidemic and a siege by the French army. Yet in the first half of the sixteenth century Naples's population increase was especially fast. Urban growth across early modern Europe was mainly the result of immigration, since the poor health and hygiene of city life meant that the urban birth and death rates were, at best, even. The most obvious reason for Naples's growth was the abject misery of rural people, who were desperate for a better life, materially and morally. Campania, the region around Naples, was always the most densely populated in the kingdom, and almost 60 percent of those who moved to Naples came from this area; about 20 percent came from outside the kingdom. Poor people flocked to the capital to seek refuge from pirate raids and to avail themselves of the economic opportunities Naples offered and of the advantages granted to its residents. By 1500 Neapolitans paid lower taxes than all others in the kingdom, the royal government guaranteed the city's supply of cheap bread, and Neapolitans involved in judicial cases against other subjects of the Crown enjoyed procedural advantages. A Tuscan agent observed around 1590 that "people always come willingly to live in Naples, both for the great privileges they receive and for the opportunities open to the poor to earn a living, since there is at any time plenty of work to be found; and the rich can live quietly and escape the tyranny of the royal officials [employed] across the kingdom." The municipal secretary Giulio Cesare Capaccio pointed out in *Il forastiero* (The Foreigner), the guide to the city he wrote in 1634, that "[t]he city of Naples ennobles all those who come to live here. Speaking of the people from the kingdom, when some of them come here they seem to be reborn, and they change customs, and the roughness of the countryside becomes civilization and the liberty of Naples, [and] they become demanding, and want bread at good prices, and whiter and larger, and they forget the bread of barley or millet which they used to eat."

The elites also had many reasons to come to Naples. With the settlement of Spanish government it became essential for aristocratic families to spend at least part of each year in the city, near the strengthened royal tribunals that decided so many affairs crucial to elite patrimonies. Although the viceroyal court lacked the splendor of a royal presence, still in the capital there were patronage to be sought, offices or loans to be gained, and marriages to be arranged for one's offspring. By the later sixteenth century the flourishing of the Counter-Reformation also brought armies of clerics to Naples. Nobles and clerics were attended by servants and hangers-on. The Spanish government brought its own officials and soldiers. Naples was also the only large port in the kingdom and home to its only university, attracting traders and students from across the kingdom, and its eight public banks served the financial needs of all the kingdom's elites.

Finally, the foreign communities of Naples expanded. Genoese, Florentine, Venetian, Milanese, Catalan, Portuguese, Flemish, German, and French merchants, as well as Greek refugees from the Ottoman empire—all had their churches, representatives, neighborhoods. After England and Spain made peace in 1604, English sailors and merchants also arrived, despite the fears of Catholic prelates: in 1608 the bishop of Caserta vainly warned the viceroy against allowing the heretical English—a people "lively of mind, impatient of silence, impetuous and daring"—to settle in Naples "amidst a large, simple and ignorant people," in a city where one found "the greatest vices, great freedom of flesh and the senses, impatience with the yoke of virtue." To all these foreigners, Capaccio added "the Spaniards who by rule, marriages, offices, estates, fiefs, have become perpetual in this city and kingdom." Naples, he concluded, "is the whole world."

The size of the city caused problems, none as difficult and important as provisions. In 1634 Capaccio estimated that every year

Neapolitans consumed about 80 million liters of grain, 15 million liters of wine, 540,000 kilos of cheese, 1.35 million kilos of cured meat, and 1.8 million kilos of fish. A particular need was drinkable ice, what Neapolitans called "snow": especially in summer, Neapolitans consumed huge quantities of shaved ice, the trade of which the alert Spanish government soon taxed.

The growth of the city affected the consumption patterns of its population. Vegetables were the traditional staple of Neapolitan meals through the early sixteenth century. Orchards and vegetable gardens were common near the city and usually sufficed to feed it. Population growth and the expansion of the walls and of building areas made the provisioning of the city from nearby vegetable production increasingly difficult. In a 1509 edict we find the first mention of the production and consumption of "maccheroni" in Naples, though at that point they were most often eaten as sweets and on special occasions (the use of maccheroni as sweets survives in the English term "macaroons"). Initially, most pasta came to Naples from Sicily, the traditional source of wheat for the Italian South. But by 1546 a guild of maccheroni makers had separated from the bakers' guild in Naples. Twenty-two edicts issued between 1546 and 1600 addressed the production and trade of maccheroni. New presses developed in the early seventeenth century made production cheaper. The dry, windy climate of the Naples region facilitated the preservation of the product. By the 1630s Neapolitans were known across Italy as maccheroni eaters. Naples also began to export maccheroni. In the same decades the cultivation of tomatoes, first encountered by Europeans in America, spread to Italy. We still enjoy the results of the serendipitous encounter between these two developments.

Getting all needed supplies to the city was no easy task, but failure to provide for the city's masses risked their anger and could spark violence. As we have seen, the revolts of 1585 and 1647 began because of popular discontent with the quantity and pricing of the city's food. The danger of urban hunger riots was common across Europe, and some degree of urban discontent was endemic in early modern cities. The Spanish government was, however, especially sensitive to the risks posed by such a huge city where relatively few soldiers kept order. Losing control of Naples could place the entire realm in jeopardy, as happened in 1647. Guaranteeing supplies for the capital was thus inextricably linked with the control of public order and with the stability of Spanish rule.

Provisions and order were not the only challenges Naples's size posed to its rulers. From Toledo onward, Spanish viceroys attempted to regulate the life of the city, to minimize the danger of violence, to enforce a minimum of discipline in the chaotic conditions created by such crowds living in close quarters, and to make a worthy capital of what was the largest city ruled by the king of Spain. Toledo soon noted the street congestion: in order to expand their shops or homes, Neapolitans erected tents, balconies, and awnings everywhere, rendering the streets "narrow, dark, melancholy" so that "one could not see the sky." In 1533 the viceroy ordered all such things removed and "soon all the streets seemed a new world, spacious, open, clear." But, as often happens in Naples, it took more than one order to fix the problem, and the ban was repeated at regular intervals throughout the early modern period, until as late as 1768, when—perhaps more realistically, but no more successfully—it applied only to the city's main avenues. If Toledo visited the city today, he would not be happy on this score. His efforts, and those of later viceroys, to pave streets also often affected at best the main avenues. The old center still has many narrow, dark, badly paved roads (my own favorite is the ominously named Vico Scassacocchi, or Coachbreaker Alley).

Other edicts aimed at increasing the order and dignity of urban life met no greater success. In 1570 the viceroy ordered Neapolitans to sweep their streets once a week. In the 1610s Viceroy Lemos was especially eager to regulate urban life: he forbade Neapolitans from swimming naked at beaches near the city, which many were doing "without shame or modesty"; he ordered prostitutes not to go around in coaches or sedan chairs or in boats off the Posillipo coast (where leisured Neapolitans went in warm weather), "because one could not otherwise tell in Naples the good from the bad women"; and, in a much sadder example, he prohibited sailors from kidnapping children by luring them onto their boats "with fruits or sweet things" in order to sell the children as slaves outside the kingdom: forty-four children were lost to this scheme in 1610. The first two of these edicts had to be repeated by at least three of Lemos's successors.

Another target of the viceroys' reforming zeal was gambling. Dice, cards, games of chance, bets, all such potential sources of sudden wealth—and of the accompanying happiness—were extremely popular in Naples. The first ban on all games of chance came in 1568, to be repeated by almost all viceroys. In 1581 the viceroy was even forced to ban the unseemly bets Neapolitans were placing on the life of the pope. But this Neapolitan obsession, which continues unabated today, also provided the government with needed revenue. From 1621 the government taxed the sale of playing cards (about two hundred thousand decks of which were sold across the kingdom each year). In 1672 the government instituted a public lotto (private ones long preceded it). This built on precedents in other Italian and European states dating back well over a century ("lotto" had a meaning similar to the English "lot," or fate). Though it was suspended after the 1688 earthquake, as an act of repentance, the public lotto restarted in 1712, and clandestine lottos never declined. As is often the case with the so-called sin taxes of today, the struggle between morals and finances was brief. The colorful behavior of the crowds gathered for the lotto extractions (which grew in frequency until they became weekly in 1816) became one of the standard tourist attractions for foreign visitors to the area, just like the miracle of San Gennaro or the ruins of Pompeii. Today the Italian government offers multiple weekly lotto opportunities, and Neapolitans eagerly try their chances at all of them.

Gambling was linked to the broader problem of urban crime. Crime, both organized and petty, flourished as the city grew. In 1573 an edict tried to stop an illegal racket that forced prisoners in the Vicaria to buy oil for lamps at inflated prices, in one of the earliest signs of organized criminal operations. The term *camorra*, which today designates the Neapolitan organized crime network, first appeared at the turn of the eighteenth century to describe illegal gambling houses. Street theft was also widespread. The many church buildings of the city made it easy for all sorts of petty criminals to escape arrest by seeking sanctuary. Despite frequent thefts, however, city life was not particularly more dangerous to life and limb than elsewhere across early modern Europe. In 1701 a Venetian agent even marveled that in Naples one police guard sufficed to arrest two thieves.

Population growth sparked a building boom, which the government tried to regulate. Ecclesiastical institutions, elite families, the government itself, and speculating entrepreneurs grabbed spaces to satisfy their needs and those of all Neapolitans. Beginning in 1566 government edicts limited building within and especially outside the walls, to contain urban growth, to ensure the protection of the walled city, and to preserve agricultural production near the city. Though the oft-repeated prohibitions were frequently violated, they constrained Naples's growth and resulted in its peculiar urban landscape. Visitors marveled at so many buildings of five, six, or seven floors, which contributed to the dark streets deplored by Toledo. The imaginary foreigner of Capaccio's book avers that he is "stupefied when I regard the buildings of the city, which are so tall, as one finds nowhere else in the world."

Capaccio and many others credited local building materials, especially tufa: "Our method of building is so easy, that the houses rise to the sky. We have [tufa,] a light stone that comes from our mountains . . . the sand known as Pozzuolana is very strong when it is joined with the lime baked in the ovens at Stabia . . . it has such strength that it easily allows building up to the sixth or seventh floor . . . it makes buildings harder than marble." The softness and lightness of tufa allowed also the construction of numerous underground cisterns. These offered many Neapolitan buildings the convenience of internal wells and, aided by old aqueducts and underground sources, fulfilled the city's water needs; the cisterns, by then dried up, served as refuges during the bombardments of World War II, and some can be visited today. Hard, dark stone formed by Vesuvius lava was used instead for archways, foundations, and the solid and lasting *basoli*, slabs used to pave most streets that can still be seen in many old parts of town.

Government regulation was especially weak when it came to ecclesiastic building. Many monasteries and convents in Naples aimed to "form a block," as Neapolitans called the ecclesiastic practice of purchasing adjoining buildings, in order to expand the religious house, build a courtyard or garden, gain a belvedere, guarantee against excessive noise or garbage, as well as to acquire valuable real estate that could be rented out. This resulted in a veritable conquest of the city by religious buildings. Foreign visitors to Naples noted the predominance of church buildings. Ecclesiastic building ambitions led to clashes with noble families, the city and royal governments, and especially other religious bodies. In September 1696, for instance, the nuns of Donna Romita threw stones on the bricklayers who had began building a wall for the nuns of the adjacent convent of San Domenico; the rival sets of nuns were soon shouting insults at each other. In 1712 a convent argued in a dispute with a rival that "everyone on his own land can well erect buildings up to the stars." In 1728 the nuns of the Incurabili invaded the garden and neighboring monastery of Caponapoli, and there they stayed for twelve days, until the viceroy sent soldiers to remove the nuns, who pledged to resist until martyrdom. Similar episodes occurred across the kingdom, for instance in the Puglia town of Barletta, where in June 1728 the nuns of the Vittoria entered the neighboring Jesuit house carrying a crucifix, rosaries, "and under her habit each carried a stick." The Jesuits were routed.

Newer neighborhoods in and around the capital offered somewhat clearer spaces for all the new building, but the old center preserved the ancient scheme of narrow perpendicular streets, made all the more crowded by the height of the buildings: the density of the population was likely close to ten thousand people per square kilometer (in the kingdom as a whole it was about thirty-five people per square kilometer). In the old center all classes lived close together. The typical old Neapolitan residential building had (and often still has) very poor lodgings on the ground floor, the so-called *bassi*: windowless small lodgings accessible not from the inner courtyard but from the outside of the building. Bassi residents spend much of the day outdoors. The hot, inconvenient high floors housed poor tenants, while elegant, even princely, apartments occupied the middle levels. Neapolitans still call the first floor above the high portal the "noble" floor. The apartments located there afforded easy access, airiness, and the opportunity for grand entrances from staircases and courtyards.

The tall buildings increased the density of the population, and health and hygiene suffered as a result. Mercato, Porto, and Pendino, the poorest and most crowded neighborhoods of the old center, were home to 40 percent of the city's population in the seventeenth century, and living conditions there were abysmal. Estimates give a life expectancy of only twenty years in Mercato, and of twenty-four in Porto and Pendino. It was here that most of the many charitable institutions founded during the Counter-Reformation operated.

One of the most famous charitable institutions in Naples is emblematic of the social problems that accompanied the city's growth. The Annunziata, founded in 1587 in one of the city's poorest areas and soon the richest hospital in seventeenth-century Europe, housed up to two thousand people at any one time. The Annunziata cared for the ill, orphans, former prostitutes, and sundry other derelict Neapolitans. It was most famous for its acceptance of foundlings. As was customary in such institutions, a wheel passing through the entry wall allowed babies to be left anonymously and wheeled in when the bell rang. The Annunziata received about 500 foundlings a year in the seventeenth century, and 2,500 by the end of the eighteenth; in the famine year of 1764 it handled 4,675 foundlings. Modern Naples's most common surname, Esposito, derives from *esposto* (exposed), the term used for many foundlings. About six thousand other people lived in the city's other hospitals and orphanages. These cared for the urban poor while the government attempted to expel workless immigrants and vagrants. In 1550 an edict expelled from Naples those "who practice no trade, office, or work; who, though healthy, go begging; or who are not in the employ of anyone, or have no business to do." Seven similar edicts were issued by 1685.

The poverty and crowdedness of many lodgings and the overall warmth of the climate led many Neapolitans to spend most of their time outdoors throughout the year, producing huge crowds across the city. This was the feature of the urban landscape most frequently noted by visitors from northern countries. Life in Naples was spent in the open and this added to its dramatic, theatrical character. Everything—fights, gestures, shopping—was, or seemed, a performance and a competition, as eighteenth-century visitors noted with fascination. There were too many people and too much noise, and everyone sought to stand out. This image of the city as a huge and chaotic stage shaped comparisons with fabled eastern cities: in 1615, for instance, the agent of the duke of Urbino compared Naples to Cairo. Cervantes referred to Naples as "the richest, most vice-ridden city in the entire world."

Naples's growth and the residence there of nobles, foreign merchants, and countless clerics eventually stimulated the city's cultural life. Yet Naples was not a major center of Renaissance art or culture after the end of the Aragonese court in 1501. Artistic and literary projects continued in the city, but the important trends in sixteenth-century Italian art and culture developed elsewhere. The absence of a resident sovereign deprived Naples of sources of patronage, and Viceroy Toledo's policy of cultural and political control curtailed the intellectual liveliness developed under the Aragonese. Successful southern artists, writers, or musicians left the South as their careers advanced.

The two greatest Italian writers of the late sixteenth and early seventeenth century, Torquato Tasso (1544–95) and Giambattista Marino (1569–1625), were Neapolitan but achieved their greatest successes elsewhere. Tasso was the author of pastoral verse and drama and of *Jerusalem Delivered*, an epic and chivalric poem about the First Crusade that is considered the greatest work of Italian literature in the late Renaissance. Born in Sorrento near Naples, he spent much of his creative life at the Este court of Ferrara. Marino also sought courtly patronage outside the kingdom and worked in Rome and Turin before being called to Paris by Queen Marie de' Medici in 1615. While few read Marino today, his immense production was acclaimed in his time as the epitome of Baroque poetry. He was supremely skilled at verbal gamesmanship, and he was imitated in Italy and across Europe for a century or so. His *Adonis* (1623), a poem of over forty thousand lines about the lives and loves of the pagan gods, is the greatest work of Italian Baroque poetry.

Northern courts exerted a similar attraction upon Neapolitan musicians like Carlo Gesualdo (ca. 1560–1613) and Adriana Basile (ca. 1580–ca. 1642). Gesualdo was the son of the prince of Venosa (a large fief in Basilicata) and of a sister of Cardinal Carlo Borromeo, archbishop of Milan and one of the great Counter-Reformation saints. Gesualdo's paternal uncle Alfonso was also a cardinal and became archbishop of Naples in 1596. Gesualdo married a cousin, Maria d'Avalos, from one of the kingdom's noblest families. Contemporary accounts of the episode tell us that Maria fell in love with another nobleman, Fabrizio Carafa, duke of Andria, "perhaps the

most handsome and valorous knight in the city." In 1590 Gesualdo
learned of the affair and plotted revenge. He arranged to find the
lovers *in flagrante* and killed them both. A witness reported that on
entering the room, Gesualdo shouted to his men, "Kill this evil man
and this whore! Cuckoldry in Gesualdo's home!" The scandal was
great, but his rank and the notoriety of Maria's affair protected Gesualdo from judicial consequences.

After a brief retreat to his country seat, Gesualdo left the kingdom
for Ferrara, at the time one of the most splendid courts in Italy, where
music was especially pursued and celebrated and where Gesualdo
met Tasso, some of whose verses he set to music. Gesualdo married a
niece of the duke of Ferrara, a remarkable sign (given Gesualdo's mar-
ital past) of the esteem in which he was held. During his stay Gesualdo worked with other composers and virtuoso musicians at the
court and published his most important work: his first four books of
madrigals, poems set to music for instruments and multiple voices.
Gesualdo then retreated to his fiefs and spent the remainder of his
life there in a state of increasing melancholy, though he continued to
compose. In 1611 his last two books of madrigals were published by
a printer he had brought to his fief. Though his stay in Ferrara was
brief, it was there that Gesualdo matured as a composer and achieved
fame. His madrigals are the best examples of what was the dominant
musical genre of the late Renaissance in Italy.

Adriana Basile was part of a large family of writers and musicians,
and her fame advanced the careers of her brothers and sisters. She
profited from the rising popularity of singers in this early age of
opera. She probably began her career in the household of Neapolitan
aristocrats, but in 1610 she was hired by Vincenzo Gonzaga, duke of
Mantua, whose family had a long history as patrons of art and music.
On her way there, Adriana sang in Rome and Florence, where she met
many of the prominent Italian composers and poets of the time. Her
two sisters and her children sang with her at the Mantua court, and
her two brothers, Lelio and Giambattista, both poets and the former
also a composer, followed her there as well. Mantua was then the
greatest musical center in Italy, and it was there that Monteverdi's *L'Or-
feo*, the most famous early Italian opera, was first produced in 1607.
Adriana sang a varied repertory of songs and was also a composer and
a skilled instrumentalist on the harp and the guitar. Poets sent her

their verses to sing and she appeared in stage works. She traveled to Rome, Florence, and Venice for further performances. In 1623 several poets published a collective work in her praise (*Theater of the Glories of the Lady Adriana Basile*), and Marino extolled her singing in a stanza of his *Adonis*. In that same year she returned to Naples, where she gained the patronage of the viceroy. She spent most of the 1630s in Rome, still performing, often with her daughters, and she died in Naples around 1642.

Her brother Lelio (ca. 1575–ca. 1623) worked primarily in Mantua writing poems and composing madrigals. The elder brother, Giambattista (1566–1632), today the best-known member of this accomplished family, spent more of his life in the kingdom. In the early 1600s he briefly served the Republic of Venice as a soldier. In 1608 he returned to Naples, and though he was briefly at Mantua with his sister, much of his life was spent as a feudal governor in the service of Neapolitan aristocratic masters. This employment gave Basile the opportunity to encounter and appreciate the rural world, something contemporary Neapolitan authors often avoided or treated only as caricature. Basile wrote pastoral verse and works for the stage and around 1630 served as theater manager and librettist for the viceroyal court. His literary works in Italian follow standard Baroque topics and formats.

Basile's originality shone in his dialect works. In dialect he wrote nine eclogues, titled the *Neapolitan Muses*, and his masterpiece, *The Tale of Tales*, a collection of fifty popular tales, which was the first example in Europe of the literary adaptation of folktales. Both of these works were published by his sister after Basile's death. In the *Tale* one finds early versions of *Cinderella*, *Sleeping Beauty*, *Puss 'n Boots*, and other famous tales, adapted by Basile from popular originals from the South and other areas of the Mediterranean.

Giambattista Basile's career shows the new vitality of the Neapolitan artistic and intellectual scene in the early seventeenth century. With the danger of heresy now receding, some viceroys expressed greater interest in art and literature. Their court again became a source of patronage. In 1600 construction began on a new and grander royal palace. In 1605 a Neapolitan section of the Academy of the Lincei of Rome, one of Italy's most important scientific institutions, opened. Viceroy Lemos reorganized the university, and in 1615 he assigned to it a palace built recently for the royal cavalry, where the university remained for almost two centuries (it now houses the archeological museum). Lemos also supported the new Academy of the Idle (1611), which, contrary to its name, was actively interested in the latest intellectual trends. The very existence of several academies in the city (with the typically ironic names of the Furious, the Imprudent, and the Idle) reflects a more lively intellectual life, especially since Philip II had prohibited academies as recently as 1593. These informal groups of scholars, scientists, and members of the nobility and the professional elites met in elite homes to discuss issues and ideas of the day. By the late sixteenth century they constituted the main forum for Italian intellectual life.

By the early seventeenth century the arts also began to flourish in Naples. The rise of the Baroque across Europe emphasized dramatic effect, stark contrasts, and powerful emotions. In Catholic countries in particular, Baroque art stressed the awe and power of the faith in grand theatrical representations. These elements found fertile ground in Naples and in the character of its population, culture, and urban landscape. The cramped spaces of the city challenged Baroque artists to great daring and creativity. The city's building boom provided opportunities for artistic expression. Viceroys, nobles, and merchants collected art and befriended artists: the Flemish merchant Gaspar Roomer (d. 1674), the richest man in Naples, assembled in his splendid palace on the via Toledo the largest collection of paintings in the city and opened it to interested visitors. Even after the plague epidemic of 1656, when the city's growth stalled, noble and church building continued. Noble families competed for magnificence. Religious buildings expressed the plague survivors' thanks and sought to exorcize the return of contagion. Urban space in Naples and other southern cities was dominated by sacred and noble architecture, both of which sought an ostentatious, theatrical presence in urban life. All the figurative arts flourished, making Naples one of the greatest centers of Baroque art in Europe.

The best illustration of this artistic expansion is the Chapel of San Gennaro in the cathedral, the focus of great rivalries among artists. The chapel was begun in 1608 in fulfillment of a city vow to its main celestial patron, and the project was appropriately lavish. Together with the charterhouse of San Martino high above the old city, it was

Domenico Gargiulo, *Thanksgiving Prayers after the Plague Epidemic of 1656*
(ca. 1656), from the Museum of San Martino, Naples

the most splendid endeavor in a century of high artistic productivity
and profuse expenditure on the arts. Most Neapolitan artists were
involved, and the project attracted others from outside the kingdom.
Work on the chapel was an avenue to patronage from churches,
nobles, merchants, the viceroy, and even the royal court in Madrid.
The chapel caused great tension between the municipal authorities
and the archbishop, as the city government strove to maintain its
rights of patronage and control against the archbishop and the cathedral chapter. This slowed the overall project, which took a century
and was completed in 1706 with an altar in porphyry and silver. The
chapel is today an overwhelming sight: frescoes and altarpieces deco-
rate every corner of its large, imposing design; marble, bronze, and
silver statues fill every nook; and forty-plus silver busts of the patron
saints of Naples promise security to the pious.

The city's art scene was jolted by visits of artists from other regions.
Caravaggio (1573–1610), the greatest Italian painter of his time,
spent several months in Naples in 1606–7 and again in 1608–9 and
left there his *Flagellation of Christ* and *Seven Works of Mercy*, works that
posed a powerful challenge to the old local Mannerist tradition. In

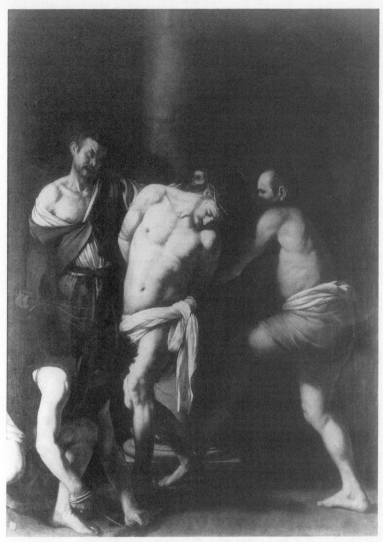

Caravaggio, *The Flagellation of Christ* (1607),
now in the Capodimonte Museum, Naples

Jusepe de Ribera, *San Gennaro Emerges Unharmed from the Furnace* (1646),
oil on copper, from the Chapel of San Gennaro in the Naples Cathedral

1616 Jusepe de Ribera (1591–1652) came to Naples, where he spent most of the rest of his life and furthered Caravaggio's legacy. By the 1630s a strong local tradition of painting emerged. Neapolitan painters such as Battistello Caracciolo (1578–1635), Massimo Stanzione (1585–1656), Mattia Preti (1613–99), Salvator Rosa (1615–73), Bernardo Cavallino (1616–56), and Luca Giordano (1634–1705) developed the dramatic and naturalistic style of Caravaggio, making Naples the only artistic center in Italy able to match Rome in the number and quality of its artists. By the end of the century, in fact, Naples was probably the leading school of Italian painting, and Giordano and later Francesco Solimena (1657–1747) were arguably the most successful Italian painters of their generations. Their works dominate the royal and elite collections of the Spaniards and then Austrians who ruled Naples until 1734.

Architecture remained the core of this artistic boom. In the mid-sixteenth century Viceroy Toledo broadened the urban walls and developed new neighborhoods. As war dangers faded, what had been separate suburban centers became fully integrated in the urban network and the walled gates ceased to be a true boundary between the city and its surrounding areas: Chiaia, Posillipo, Sanità, Materdei— all mainly rural areas in the previous century—were by the mid-seventeenth century full of splendid Baroque buildings and are today among the city's most interesting neighborhoods. There aristocratic families built palaces and villas, and religious orders settled. In fact, the new areas, with more open spaces, offered easier opportunities for architectural grandeur: decorated façades, high portals, large courtyards, gardens. The broad new via Toledo, in the newly walled area, the broadened via Costantinopoli, in the old town, and the via Foria, just outside the walls, afforded chances for displays of magnificence.

The career of Cosimo Fanzago (1591–1678) is emblematic of the opportunities and achievements of this urban expansion. This architect and sculptor, born and trained in northern Italy, came to Naples in 1612. After a decade working mostly as a sculptor and a church decorator, his first major architectural project was in San Martino, the old Gothic charterhouse. Renovation had started in the late sixteenth century. In his first years there (1623–31) Fanzago restructured a chapel within the church and completed the great cloister. These

Cosimo Fanzago, the great cloister of the
charterhouse of San Martino, 1623–31

projects display the fusion of architecture and sculpture and the the-
atricality and taste for visual effect that characterized Baroque Naples.
Over the next half-century Fanzago would leave his mark on just
about every major building project in the city. Even lower-class rebels
saw the need for suitable Baroque splendor: in 1647, when Masaniello
wanted a monument to commemorate the abolition of hated taxes,
he asked Fanzago to design it. After the revolt of Masaniello failed,
Fanzago prudently escaped to Rome, but he soon returned to Naples
and resumed work on multiple projects.

Fanzago always gave great attention to details in his buildings: in
San Martino he designed the marble floors, altar rails, marble screens,
vases, stairs, and so on. The marble intarsia in San Martino show his creative designs, as well as the skills of Neapolitan craftsmen. Throughout
his career, Fanzago also took time off from architectural projects to
design armoires, wooden statues, copper baldachins, and gates (such as
the one for the Chapel of San Gennaro). In addition, he took a close
interest in painting, worked with Ribera and others, and befriended
prominent art collectors, as well as working with generations of craftsmen specializing in marble, silver, gold, stucco, and cloth.

His success in San Martino brought Fanzago other large projects.

He designed the floor for the Chapel of San Gennaro. He directed the Baroque transformation of the Gesù Nuovo, the main Jesuit church whose fortress-like façade still reveals its original use as a noble palace. Fanzago worked there for about forty years, building chapels and windows, producing marble statues, and designing chandeliers and the sacristy decorations. The Gesù Nuovo shows his ability to create Baroque theatrical effects in a preexisting space: the grand chapels and lavish decoration mask the actual awkward plan of the church in ways that make a visit both awe-inspiring and intriguing. Here too he mixed sculptural and architectural elements to achieve an overall powerful effect. Fanzago's façades also blend architecture with urban design: stairways, terraces, and porticoes expand the façade beyond its function and make it a decorative element of the larger urban landscape. His work typifies the forceful effects sought by Baroque patrons, who wanted their buildings to express their power.

Religious orders surpassed noble families in their building patronage. Between 1561 and 1653 at least twenty-seven noble residences were transformed into churches and other pious institutions. But Naples also witnessed a boom in secular buildings, and Fanzago left his imprint on those too. In 1640–45 he directed his largest project, Palazzo Donn'Anna, a site that employed over four hundred workers. This majestic suburban palace, one of about fifteen strewn on the Posillipo coast and dramatically perched above the sea, ranks among the most theatrical of Naples's buildings: it was used mainly for parties and festive gatherings and was meant to be reached by water. The sea façade is thus the most scenic, and canals led visitors to the various sections of the building. Fanzago added a high loggia from which guests would enjoy games and view fireworks at sea. The loggia could also provide a natural backdrop for the performances held in the adjoining theater. The palace was left unfinished after Viceroy Medina de las Torres, who had commissioned it, left Naples (the palace was named after his Neapolitan wife, Anna Carafa). It was damaged in the 1647 revolt and again in an earthquake in 1688, so that by the eighteenth century, as a sort of modern ruin, it attracted visitors seeking picturesque sights. It still exerts a magical charm.

Fanzago's last grand secular project was Palazzo Maddaloni, finished in 1665 and meant to express the restored power of the feudal aristocracy after the 1647 revolt. The grand portal and façade, the stairway, and especially the terrace and loggia are again typical of his taste for the theatrical.

Fanzago also enjoyed the patronage of civic institutions. From 1637 to 1660 he worked on the *guglia*, or column, of San Gennaro, in a small square outside the new chapel, another votive offering of the city to its main patron, commissioned after the eruption of 1631. This was possibly Fanzago's most original work, as no similar monuments existed in Naples at the time, and it gave free rein to his imaginative mixture of sculpture and architecture. He proudly included his self-portrait in the column's decoration. His design proved so successful that when the plague of 1656 showed the need for further saintly intercession, another guglia was built in front of the church of San Domenico, and Fanzago worked on that one too. By the mid-eighteenth century there were four *guglie* in Naples, as the Theatines, Dominicans, and Jesuits all claimed their own. Others were built in provincial towns.

The guglie are among the few surviving examples of another element of the Baroque city: scenic decorations intended to mark important moments in the life of its rulers and people. The guglie were elaborations of traditional elements, such as obelisks, and also drew from more ephemeral structures, such as temporary triumphal arches or, in popular culture, carnival poles. They served as destinations for processions and gave order to the few open urban spaces crowded Naples offered. In the seventeenth century, statues and fountains also sprouted up all over the city, as each viceroy wished to leave his mark on the urban landscape. Fountains embellished the city and provided some relief from the fear of fires. On their streets Neapolitans would also frequently encounter temporary funeral or festive stages and sets designed and built for royal deaths, marriages, and births; victories and peace treaties; religious celebrations; processions; and secular games such as bullfights. In 1624, for instance, for the feast day of St. John's (June 24), a large "pediment with many choruses of angels" was built in a popular street: from this stage came the sounds of flutes and devotional hymns, a cloud opened, other angels descended singing, while the first angels rose through the cloud.

Such use of cities as stages for religious or political events was common across Baroque Europe. In Naples this practice occurred frequently, with theatrical flair. Since so much of life in Naples was in the open, rituals, processions, and performances were almost routine elements of the urban experience. These elaborate ceremonies offered opportunities for competition between church authorities, the viceroy, the city government, noble groups, and other urban elements. Fierce protocol battles often resulted in prolonged struggles for precedence and prestige. The events associated with the cult of San Gennaro and the procession of Corpus Domini in June (since the fifteenth century one of the major moments in the religious year) marked the urban ritual calendar. The great procession on September 8 to celebrate the miraculous image of the Madonna in the suburban church of Piedigrotta was also the occasion for a major feast and fireworks that attracted—noted a French visitor—"an immense multitude."

The public performance aspect was pronounced in many secular events as well. Executions followed well-established rituals, with elaborate processions (often along streets connected with the crimes being punished), episodes of theatrical repentance at the end, and, for the most heinous crimes, the exhibition of body parts of the condemned in places that referred to their evil acts.

Carnival—the celebration of excess that preceded the beginning of the Lenten season of fast and repentance—was perhaps the wildest secular ritual in Naples. It featured peculiar forms of the inversions that marked the feast across Europe: a chronicler reported, for instance, that on February 21, 1680, "all the mad people of the Incurabili [Hospital] came masked to the Palace . . . and there performed some dances such as they were, that is crazy." On the four Sundays before the start of Lent, frenzied crowds looted carnival poles and chariots laden with food placed near the tribunals in the old center. Later, toward the end of the seventeenth century, the chariots and poles were set up in the wide square in front of the royal palace. Violent fights often erupted over food. Elite members—and in the eighteenth century the king and his court—attended, though sedate Enlightenment visitors found the events shocking. The crowds served as both performers and spectators of this festive but unsettling ritual.

Fiscal privileges, guaranteed basic foodstuffs, repression, charity initiatives, and rituals helped maintain order and peace in this large, crowded city. Many new residents of the city lacked the family and community networks of support that often kept rural society stable. Associations such as religious confraternities and guilds provided an identity and social solidarity to old and recent residents. In an extremely hierarchical society, these associations offered poor and working Neapolitans a clear place in urban life.

Neapolitan writers heatedly debated the social hierarchies of their large city. Below the nobility was the vast Popolo, but clearly distinctions within it existed, especially—noted a historian—regarding those "who by birth do not fit in with the nobility, but by quality and wealth are very far from the plebs." There was, Capaccio wrote, "one People in name, but many peoples in fact." The elite of the Popolo owned estates and intermarried with the nobles. Some lawyers and judges rose to positions from which they could "order the nobility," and even merchants could achieve a "civil and generous life." Below these groups was the plebs—the "dregs of the commonwealth"—but even within this class were differences: printers, goldsmiths, architects, and many in the silk guild could be said to practice noble crafts. Further down, "some in their crafts live more civilly, some decline much from civility, and some in their basest labors are reduced to such lowness that they cannot aspire to any manner of true condition as Popolo."

Guilds—associations of all practitioners of a trade—gave some status and structure to the lives of even these lowliest workers. Guilds existed in most western European cities since the Middle Ages, and they typically regulated working conditions and dispensed group support. In Naples, guilds developed only at the end of the medieval period and never had the direct involvement in government that was frequently seen in northern Italian cities during the Renaissance. Nonetheless, their statutes offer vivid illustrations of the life of working Neapolitans.

For example, in the last weeks of 1611 at least 607 Neapolitan weavers gathered and agreed to revise the statutes of their guild's charitable endowment. They pledged to pay regular dues to this endowment and directed that it disburse its funds to sick members. They also agreed that the guild's chapel offer burial spots to deceased members and that dowry subsidies be made available to members' daughters. Finally, they planned for the establishment of a conservatory for the widows and unmarried daughters of members in which the women would be educated suitably. In October of 1679, 213 Neapolitan barbers agreed to revise their guild's statutes and settled issues pertaining to dues, dowry subsidies, and the procedures apprentices ought to follow to become masters in the guild. The large numbers of craftsmen who participated in guild meetings not only reflect the size of Naples but also illustrate how seriously weavers and barbers took these matters. These men—for they were all men—recognized their guild as a helpful forum to strengthen their mutual obligations, define and enact their joint decisions, prevent strife, temper competition, and give them an honorable identity within the larger society of early modern Naples.

By being members of guilds, craftsmen (and other groups we may today define as professionals) demonstrated that they belonged to the respectable Popolo of the city, albeit to its lower rungs. Through their guilds shopkeepers, craftsmen, and lower professionals such as notaries, pharmacists, and clerks enjoyed an acknowledged place in public ceremonies or festivals. This clearly separated guild members from the unemployed and unskilled, beggars, vagrants, and criminals, all of whom caused grave concern and fear to all authorities. Guilds also provided solidarity to the many Neapolitans working in crafts, retail, and services, and expressed their values and principles on matters pertaining to family and religion.

The Naples guilds depended administratively on both the royal government and the Eletto del Popolo. Guild leaders—the consuls—regulated all internal affairs and exercised the guilds' self-government and jurisdiction over their own members. Consuls collected dues and fees, inspected shops and workshops, and oversaw the exams by which apprentices became masters. The products created during these exams were sold to the guild's benefit. For instance, aspiring hat makers were required to make four hats of different materials for their examination, but they could only keep the costlier beaver hat, while the guild sold the other three. Over time, many guilds established separate endowments (Monti) devoted to internal welfare, and in some cases separate confraternities for religious activities. Eventually guilds became more important as pious institutions than as economic associations, reflecting the expansion of religious life in Counter-Reformation Naples.

As in the rest of Europe, the level of specialization of guilds, and thus their number, increased from the sixteenth to the eighteenth century. They varied enormously in size, including anywhere from a dozen to thousands of members: in 1650, at the height of the Baroque expansion and after the destruction of 1647, the builders' guild counted at least 2,816 bricklayers. The largeness of the city also afforded a chance at prosperity to groups of very specialized workers, such as the thirteen makers of playing cards active in 1619, and the forty-six men who made brass nails for coaches in 1651. As was customary across Europe, most guilds concentrated in specific neighborhoods, as is still reflected in many street names in Naples.

Royal regulation increased with the rise of the administrative state developed by the Spanish monarchy, which reflected a society increasingly specific and litigious in handling the duties and rights of its members. The state's role as mediator and arbiter of disputes helped increase royal authority throughout Europe. Regulation of the guilds, moreover, was essential to ensure the fiscal revenues of the state by minimizing smuggling and underground production and trade. The Annona guilds, which dealt mostly with food retail, were particular targets of government attention because they ensured the provisioning of the city with food and other necessities. The government issued hundreds of edicts that dictated who could engage in any commercial activity, where and how they could obtain the products they sold, what could be sold, at what prices, when and where, and in what quantities. The detail of regulation would warm the hearts of modern European Union bureaucrats. Nothing was too insignificant to be regulated: women could not weigh goods in fruit vendors' shops; traders in used clothes could not buy anything after the evening Ave Maria; and broccoli could not be sold unless the leaves were first removed.

The guilds' own rules aimed to limit competition and to support the livelihood of existing members, by enforcing standards of quality and membership and by emphasizing the need for harmony. Selling goods outside of shops or workshops was generally prohibited except for very few licensed traders such as greengrocers. Numerous rules dictated minimum distances between workshops or retailers' shops: "[t]he proximity of shops"—a 1710 statute observed, as any Neapolitan could still today—"has often caused differences among greengrocers." Consuls in many Annona guilds bought goods wholesale and distributed them to each retailer to prevent anyone from gaining what was seen as unfair advantages. Some larger guilds were also divided by neighborhood, and rules prohibited seeking customers in other members' areas. For instance, bearers of sedan chairs (portable chairs that offered the rich faster rides than going by coach across Naples's crowded streets) were divided in four areas, and they were forbidden from poaching customers in areas other than their own unless they carried a fare outside their area, in which case they were allowed to pick up a fare for the trip back.

Guilds recognized the competitive pressures that set members against each other, and guild against guild as well, and accommodated the circumstances of specific trades. Sausage makers, for instance, were allowed to close their shops after Carnival (when no meat could be eaten) and even briefly to exercise another job, without having to pay a fee when they reopened. Conversely, in 1586, fishermen and fish sellers were allowed to set their prices freely during Lent, when demand for their product would be highest, though they were required to donate to city hospitals any fish they failed to sell within twenty-four hours. The usual rule that prohibited work on religious holidays was waived for mattress makers for the period around May 4, when new rental contracts traditionally started (and often still start) in Naples and people moved, many needing new mattresses. But generally guilds sought to protect the interests of members against the dangers of the free market. In 1720, for instance, button makers lamented "the disunion among masters, which has meant that each one, in order to sell more buttons, has been content to sell at very low, cheap prices" and pledged now to sell at "just" prices. The guiding principle was that every worker was entitled to a fair chance to succeed and maintain a livable balance between work and rest. Such healthy attitudes persist: my Naples barber told me that rules "fortunately" prohibit barbers from working on Mondays; otherwise, he said, soon someone would work every day of the week, and then all barbers would have to follow suit.

Guilds also attempted to ensure the success and renewal of their membership, which they saw as best guaranteed by hereditary transmission and the careful integration of new members. Masters' sons were exempted from entry exams and paid lower fees, as crafts were best learned at a father's feet. These privileges extended to apprentices who married masters' daughters, in another sign of the familial atmosphere that pervaded guilds. Guilds also charged higher fees on noncitizens of Naples and higher still on foreigners to the kingdom. This was one of the few instances in which the government's approach, which favored the immigration of skilled workers, was at odds with the guilds' interests. Often the authorities urged the guilds to reduce the fees for all entrants.

With the spread of Counter-Reformation concerns, guild charity increased and became more discriminating. Guild welfare policies aimed not just to help but also to reform, encourage, and ultimately mold the recipient. Charity aimed to alleviate the poverty of members weakened by age, incapacitation, work crises, or illness, as a form of solidarity among companions, and to avoid embarrassment for the association. Of equal importance was the members' honor. In line with Catholic and Mediterranean conceptions of honor, guilds aimed to shore up the morality of their members' behavior and the morality of their families. All benefits for guildsmen's children were limited to those of legitimate birth.

The first concern was for the impoverished worker himself, because of his immediate claim to the solidarity of his brethren, and because the guild's image would suffer from the abjection of any member. The oldest forms of support (death rituals and aid to the infirm or imprisoned) went to the men themselves and to the healing and protection of their own bodies, whether these bodies be sick, dead, or confined by force. Ransoming those captured by the "infidel" was also a top priority. Aid to the disabled and those incapable of work was one of the most important ways in which guilds played a role useful to the government.

Guild aid usually came with conditions attached and reflected concerns for spiritual as well as physical well-being. The ill were to be visited by their colleagues and received short-term financial support. The undeserving infirm comprised a clearly defined category, just as the undeserving poor, and guilds gave no aid to those incapacitated by wounds (likely the result of brawls) or suffering from venereal infection, the "Gallic disease." Aid to the imprisoned was also not unconditional. Prisoners, with no income from work, needed money to support themselves in jail, as each prisoner had to pay for his food, bedding, and clothes. Guilds assisted only those jailed for "honest" causes, which excluded grave crimes and especially debts due to gambling or drunkenness. Only debts due to economic fluctuations, business troubles, or family needs were worthy of communal solidarity. The model put forward of the proper guild member was therefore the responsible, if perhaps unlucky, family man who may suffer because of the physical and financial burdens of his work life but who did not engage in illicit sex, gambling, or excessive drinking.

Only one guild (the cane-chair makers) explicitly admitted women as masters in their own right and billed them reduced dues. But most guilds gave welfare benefits to wives or daughters of members, which focused on controlling women's honor and respectability, traditionally linked to their sexual reputation by both Neapolitan culture and the Counter-Reformation Church. The marriage or cloistering of daughters and the guarantee of their chastity were paramount. As was common across Europe, guildsmen hoped that widows would remain unmarried, though the marriage of a master's widow to her late husband's apprentice was not discouraged. Often the largest benefit offered by the guild in terms of cost was the contribution toward members' daughters' dowries. Concern for the proper marriage of young women was widespread in early modern Italy. In the Kingdom of Naples, aristocratic clans, guilds, charitable associations, local governments, and many other groups established dowry funds to which both parents and donors could contribute. In Naples in the early seventeenth century, 665 dowry subsidies were distributed every year to women of low or middling status, for a total of about thirty thousand ducats, or an average of forty-five ducats per subsidy, a fairly substantial amount: around 1650 one ducat bought about thirty-five liters of grain or forty-five liters of wine, and a master craftsman's annual income might have been around fifty ducats. Providing dowries for young women, especially those endangered by poverty and thus on the brink of perdition ("teetering," as it was often described in Naples), gained merit in the eyes of the Church and relieved some of the worst anxieties of Mediterranean fathers. Many guilds also offered subsidies to daughters who chose a religious life.

Another form of help was the establishment of a conservatory specifically reserved for members' daughters, to prepare them for marriage or the cloister. These conservatories also hosted orphaned daughters and in some cases widows. Usually conservatories were established by the most ambitious or wealthiest guilds, like notaries or goldsmiths, but in 1700 the shoemakers had forty-five girls in their guild's conservatory. Conservatories provide one of the best examples of the guild as a suprafamilial institution that guarded the respectability of women whose behavior might affect the association's image.

Solidarity between members was expressed even more forcefully in the obligations guildsmen had toward each other at the moment of death. Assistance to the dying and dead was financial but included spiritual and symbolic support as well. The guild offered masses for the dead, both regularly throughout the year for all its dead and at the time of death for individuals; it covered the cost of funerals; and it offered a common burial space. All members were required to participate in the rituals that accompanied death. Just as it would shame the guild if any of its members were seen begging in the streets, the public display of piety and solidarity in funeral rituals upheld the worth of the association and offered each departed member the proper support of the living that Catholic piety deemed highly beneficial in the achievement of eternal salvation.

The rituals of death were (and are) prominent in Neapolitan culture and formed a significant business. Masses after death had specific price tags, depending on their level of solemnity. Burials were also sources of income, and various institutions fought over ownership of corpses. When someone died in a hospital, for instance, the hospital would be entitled to receive the fees from the burial. Parish priests also jealously guarded the revenue they were entitled to when parishioners died. Guilds, therefore, set policies for how to negotiate with various claimants and give the deceased a communal funeral and burial. The biggest problem came with sudden deaths. Dying suddenly was a major fear of all Catholics at least since the Middle Ages, because the inability to confess one's sins on one's deathbed gravely endangered one's soul. To this spiritual fear in Naples was added a financial cost. After 1403 the cathedral chapter of Naples enjoyed the right to perform the funeral, and to receive the related fees, for all those who died without having chosen a burial place. Many guilds urged their members to declare officially each year where they wished to be buried, to prevent this problem. The process of dying itself was another central concern. Several guilds offered masses for the spiritual well-being of those in agony, to facilitate the so-called good passage. This benefit too had a specific cost, and each guild member was entitled to it only once: if he survived and later went into agony again, he was on his own.

Guilds also encouraged accepted forms of devotion and demanded participation and conformity from their members. Most of them held common devotions, such as annual masses on the day of the guild's patron saint, or annual processions with candles or torches, for which members were required to contribute set amounts of wax or other provisions. Many guilds urged members to practice the works of mercy and warned about leading a good Christian life, teaching Christian doctrine to one's neighbors, and not playing cards or dice. Moral demands increased in frequency over the seventeenth and eighteenth centuries. Until new ideas about free trade and free labor brought their abolition in 1821–25, Neapolitan guilds operated as fraternal communities of respectable, if often poor, men who assisted each other both in the practical challenges of work and family life and in fulfilling their, and their relatives', spiritual and moral duties.

Economic historians often deplore that Spanish Naples was not a productive center: it certainly lacked the prominent textile crafts that made many western European cities rich in the Renaissance and early modern periods. But, like modern London or Washington, it flourished as a government center, as a center of trade and finance, of education and culture. It also housed large, wealthy elites, and met their demand for buildings, goods, services, and entertainments.

All the problems that faced early modern cities—hunger, disease, chaos, violence, social instability—were magnified in Naples by the size and density of its population. The same intensity marked more beneficial elements of urban growth: the artistic and intellectual fervor; the dynamism of urban associations; the liveliness of cultural and religious life; the ferment of spiritual and charitable renewal; the diversity of trades and people. The Baroque mentality, both learned and popular, put a premium on outward signs. Churches, aristocrats, artisans—all sought a visible, spatial affirmation of their status or power: in the grandeur of their buildings, in the luxury of their palaces, in the size, sign, or stock of their shops. Urban space was so scarce that its control and manipulation, through means as exalted as a church façade or as humble as a shop awning, were crucial to everyone's life.

Excess and drama became Spanish Naples's most prominent traits. The artistic flowering in a place of such natural beauty, the emotional religious practices and rituals, and the unruliness and occasional violence of the crowds easily explain the European popularity of the remark, coined in the fourteenth century and later a cliché, that the city was a paradise inhabited by devils.

∽ *Chapter VII* ∾

Reason Truly Is Always Beautiful
The Southern Enlightenment

[Through my studies] I saw with amazement how, on the foundations of a humble and true religion, which despised earthly
things, such a vast and high construction had been raised; no
other religion in the world, however much it may have aimed at
earthly success, ever could aspire to this, let alone reach or equal
it. . . . Instead of a heavenly kingdom, [priests] built for themselves on earth a new earthly kingdom, entirely unknown to the
ancients.

Pietro Giannone, *Vita scritta da lui medesimo* (1736)

*E*arly on January 9, 1693, a violent earthquake shook southeastern Sicily. Two days later, an even stronger one hit and lasted
about four minutes, during which people found it impossible to
stand. Over twenty aftershocks followed over the next four weeks and
almost two thousand tremors within eighteen months. The devastation was great. About fifty thousand people died (or 5 percent of the
island's people), including four thousand in Syracuse (one-third of
its population) and eight thousand in Catania (two-thirds of its
inhabitants). Sixty percent of buildings across the affected area were
destroyed, including virtually all of Catania, its cathedral, and its university—Sicily's only one. The towns of Noto and Avola were also
destroyed. The tremors left enormous challenges, both immediate
and long-term: from burying thousands of corpses to housing and
feeding thousands of homeless, from preventing disease and infection to reconstructing homes and infrastructures.

Earthquakes and volcanic phenomena have occurred with deadly
frequency in the southern regions of Italy over the centuries. Few
southerners have not experienced at least one major earthquake. The
late seventeenth century was a particularly unhappy time from this

point of view, with significant earthquakes hitting the Naples area in 1688 and again in 1694. Yet the tragedy that took place in Sicily was the worst in those years. The catastrophe came at the end of Spanish rule in the South. Finances and administration on the island were weakened by the pressures of decades of distant wars and by the revolt of Messina in the 1670s. Spanish leadership was preoccupied with the succession problem facing the monarchy. The immediate response to the crisis showed awareness of its immensity, but over time the government's actions proved hesitant and haphazard. Most taxes were suspended (they probably would not have been paid anyway), and property confiscated from the Messina rebels was used to make up the lost state revenue. The viceroy directed resources to the rebuilding of fortifications in various towns. But the efficacy of the government's response was limited. In most areas reconstruction was extremely slow and depended more on local initiative and funds than on any coordinated intervention. In some areas, it was almost ten years before large-scale rebuilding started. No significant reform or policy shift resulted from the disaster.

The intellectual response was also mixed. Some Sicilian scholars examined the events from a scientific standpoint and rejected supernatural explanations. But many Sicilians saw the earthquake as a divine punishment and a harbinger of the apocalypse. An old prophecy circulated that Aetna would cause the descent of the entire island into a sea abyss. In Catania, the city's most precious relic—St. Agatha's breast—was displayed. When that failed to stop the tremors, all the cathedral's relics were marched through the city. Even the combined powers of the heads of Sts. Cataldo, Margaret, and George, two thorns from Christ's crown, a splinter of the Cross, a hair of the Virgin, the throats of Sts. Paul and Blaise, and sundry fragments of eleven other saints failed to achieve the desired goal. This kind of reaction matched what happened in Naples: there the 1688 earthquake was the subject of poems and narratives and contributed to the proclamation of new patron saints for the city, but inspired no scientific analysis. Noto was eventually rebuilt in a uniform late Baroque style that makes this little Sicilian town an architectural gem, but the overall response to the catastrophe was evidence of the limits—intellectual and practical—of southern culture and government at the end of the Spanish period.

Less than a hundred years later, on February 5, 1783, a devastating earthquake hit Calabria Ultra (the southernmost province of the Kingdom of Naples), destroyed its capital Reggio, and gravely damaged Messina, just across the strait. In Calabria Ultra thirty thousand people, or 10 percent of the population, died. About five thousand more died in the following weeks because of aftershocks and disease, and about one thousand others in Sicily. While nature's power to harm was the same as in 1693, southern society had changed. By 1783 the South was intensely interesting to travelers and foreigners fascinated not only by antiquities but also by natural phenomena, and the earthquake received much scholarly attention. Scientific reports and analyses were published in various languages across Italy and Europe, while few of the apocalyptic reactions that characterized the 1693 disaster made their way into print.

The 1783 earthquake also came when ideas for structural and institutional reforms were spreading among the Neapolitan ruling and intellectual elites. Participants in the Neapolitan Enlightenment saw the catastrophe as an opportunity to change southern agriculture and society and rid them of primitive elements. Writers urged the royal government to take over Church and feudal land in the region, to improve land management, and to help peasant and nonnoble landowners. The government expropriated about fifty-six thousand hectares of Church land and formed the Sacred Fund (Cassa Sacra) to manage it. The plan was to distribute land to new owners in the hope that they would use it more efficiently. This would also enlarge the province's tax base, both because land previously exempted would now be taxed and because new owners would increase the output of local agriculture. In Sicily resistance to change was more entrenched and the intellectual movement less developed. But even there the destruction led to the lifting of some trade regulations and of traditional dues on exports and imports that had long been a target of economic reformers.

One should exaggerate neither the inadequacy of the official response to the 1693 earthquake nor the effects of the reforms that followed the earthquake of 1783. But the two catastrophes provide clear evidence of the changes that had come to the South in both intellectual and practical terms.

Across Europe the intellectual movement known as the Enlightenment, characterized by belief in progress and science and the application of reason to concrete problems, led to reform projects. Enlightenment thinkers began to examine traditional institutions and practices from a rational and historical perspective. They found that the privileges of Church and aristocracy, the prejudices that discriminated against individuals or groups, and the policies that did not lead to a demonstrable public good were hard to justify under the cold scrutiny of reason. Above all, Enlightenment thinkers advocated a secular and optimistic perspective. Improving human life ought to be the goal of the state and of public policies. Greater human happiness on earth was to be the guiding principle of all reform. Reward or punishment in the afterlife and beliefs about divine intervention in human affairs could not legitimate prejudices or privileges that lacked a rational basis.

The foundation of this approach was a new method of inquiry and analysis developed by scientists across Europe between the mid-sixteenth and the late seventeenth century, during the Scientific Revolution. The new method was based on experiment, observation, and the rejection of supernatural explanation. Hypotheses developed from experimental data were subjected to further empirical proof, in a gradual process that fostered more cooperation between scientists. The scientific method was applied to the study of the natural world, from astronomy to physics to the functioning of the human body. Scientists rarely suggested, at least explicitly, the broader intellectual implications of their method for other fields of human study. But a long struggle ensued nonetheless with religious—and often also political—authorities worried about the threat the new method might pose to traditional understandings of religion, as well as to established systems of power. By the early eighteenth century, after this struggle led to the spread of scientific knowledge beyond scholarly circles, European thinkers began to explore the implications of the new method of analysis for social, economic, and political realities.

Naples offers a dramatic example of this struggle and transition. The ideas and reforms that flourished in the eighteenth century were rooted in earlier intellectual and spiritual struggles that focused on the relationship between scholarship and faith. After Viceroy Toledo closed academies and strengthened censorship around 1550, intellectual life in Naples was dominated by Scholastic views and methods. The Counter-Reformation made Scholasticism the official culture of the Church, and the University of Naples fully embraced this tradition. Scholasticism relied on a Christian reworking of Aristotle's ideas, and its main method of analysis was abstract logic, applied to authoritative and sanctioned texts of the past (religious texts and secular ones long approved by the Church). In Naples, as elsewhere in western Europe, the first challenge to this intellectual orthodoxy came in studies of nature that placed more emphasis on evidence gathered through the senses than on logical deduction. Bernardino Telesio (1509–88) in his *On the Nature of Things according to Their Own Principles* (1565–67) argued that all knowledge is based on sensation.

His materialistic approach was pursued by his pupils Giordano Bruno (1548–1600) and Tommaso Campanella (1568–1639). Both, like Telesio, came from provincial southern towns; both entered the Dominican order; and both went on to European careers as scholars and troublemakers. Bruno, a playwright and philosopher, traveled across Europe and managed to be condemned by both Calvinists and Lutherans before being burned at the stake as a heretic in Rome. Campanella wrote philosophical essays in support of Telesio's views and political tracts, most famously *The City of the Sun* (1602), a brief utopian essay. He also wrote a defense of the scientific work of Galileo and in a letter expressed his eclectic rejection of traditional authorities: "in my youth I had no teachers except for grammarians, and two years of the logics and physics of Aristotle, which I soon rejected as sophistry; I studied all the sciences by myself . . . and I walked through all ancient and modern schools of philosophers, doctors, mathematicians, jurists and other scholars in the rhetorical, practical, and theoretical arts, and the sacred and profane arts of all kinds." In 1599 Campanella was involved in an anti-Spanish conspiracy in his native Calabria, tortured, and jailed for decades by the Spanish government. Eventually released, he ended his days in France.

Another challenge to established ideas came from the study of magic and its links to nature, pursued in Naples especially by Giambattista della Porta (1535–1615), whose interests in the natural world made him in 1574 the subject of an Inquisition inquiry. Della Porta also wrote plays and late in his life enjoyed the patronage of rulers from across Europe. At the turn of the seventeenth century, however, Scholastic philosophy, supported also by the Jesuits and other religious orders, remained dominant in Naples's intellectual life. Books prohibited by the Church were once more burned in 1610. In spite of these obstacles, interest in nature and its secrets spread, and by the 1610s there were in Naples a few scientific collections where the curious could examine instruments, plant and animal specimens, geological materials, and so on; the most famous belonged to Ferrante Imperato "who"—wrote a contemporary poet—"alone holds in a study / all the good things done / by great human reason." Viceroy Lemos (served 1610–16) supported scholarly interests, and private academies for scientific and philosophical discussions again opened in the city.

Over the next generation, as a result mainly of Galileo's work, Italian interest in nature focused more sharply on experimentation. Galileo's

The Museum of Ferrante Imperato,
print from his book *Historia Naturale* (1599)

decision to write in Italian rather than Latin broadened the impact of his ideas. The empirical method entered Naples in midcentury. In 1649 Viceroy Oñate appointed Tommaso Cornelio (1614–84) to the mathematics chair in the university. Cornelio had studied medicine and mathematics with a pupil of Campanella and brought to Naples the ideas of Descartes and Gassendi, French thinkers whose theoretical analyses of scientific inquiry complemented Galileo's empirical studies. Cornelio became the center of a group of intellectuals that included lawyers, historians, medical doctors, natural scientists, aristocrats, and ecclesiastics. In 1652 he presented a paper to a private academy in which he provided a mathematical analysis of eclipses, introducing Neapolitan scholars to a new approach.

Intellectual life advanced in fits and starts. Censorship was still a strong obstacle. Viceroys varied in their support for free inquiry. Private and monastic libraries offered limited opportunities for research. In the seventeenth century, about forty book-printers and -sellers operated in Naples, though jurisprudential works were much more numerous than scientific ones. On the other hand, even legal scholars began to employ new methods of inquiry, based on empirical comparison of laws and institutions more than on Scholastic logic.

In 1663 the men of Cornelio's circle founded the Academy of the Investigators, which in its name reflected both the experimental method advocated by its members and their view that truth was not yet known and had to be researched. In 1664 the Academy entered a debate about the causes of an epidemic of fever then raging in Naples. Traditional doctors were blaming linen manufacturers who soaked their products in the waters of nearby Lake Agnano, allegedly polluting the air. Members of the new Academy disproved this notion by conducting chemical experiments, emphasizing their commitment to empirical explanations. As one member later put it, "[T]he principle of things must be sought nowhere but in the things themselves." Debates about science continued. Foreign journals and books arrived in Naples and foreign scholars came to visit in greater numbers. In 1691, somewhat late for a city of its size, the first library open to the general public began operations. Neapolitan intellectuals became increasingly aware of the provincialism of their culture and sought inspiration no longer in Spain but in France, England, and the Netherlands, in spite of the Protestantism of the latter two.

Galileo's experimental method, natural philosophy, and Descartes' theories were all sources of ideas for Italian intellectuals. The Church fought an increasingly desperate struggle to vanquish them. By the 1680s some Italian scientists were pursuing atomistic conceptions of the universe and a belief in the accidental character of natural processes. This challenged an understanding of the world as ordered by Providence and could provide the basis for skepticism, agnosticism, and even atheism.

Such was the context for the "trial of the atheists." This prolonged legal fight proved the climax of the long struggle between Church authorities and the new culture, and the last significant setback for new ideas. It came about after, on March 21, 1688, Francesco Paolo Manuzzi, a young provincial lawyer studying in Naples, denounced himself and his friends Basilio Giannelli, Giacinto de Cristofaro, and Filippo Belli to the Inquisition. The friends were all young (the four were born between 1660 and 1667) minor figures in the legal world of Naples. De Cristofaro was the oldest and most established, as his father was a prominent lawyer in the city, while the others came from provincial families. Manuzzi declared that his friends, because of their atomistic views, denied the divinity of Christ and claimed that men had existed before Adam and that the world was eternal. The Inquisitor gave Manuzzi mild spiritual penalties (mostly prayers) and little else followed for a while, partly because of a period of turnover in the leadership of the Church in Naples. Everything changed when a new Inquisitor had de Cristofaro arrested on August 12, 1691 (as was customary then across Europe, detention served to guard the defendant awaiting trial and was rarely used as a penalty after conviction). The city government and elites had long resisted not only the introduction of the Spanish Inquisition but also the use of the secretive Roman procedure, and insisted that only the archbishop, using ordinary procedure, could prosecute Inquisition cases. The jailing of de Cristofaro was thus an act of ecclesiastic defiance of state and society.

The trial became a matter of dispute between three parties: the city authorities, pushing for the abolition of the Inquisition; the papacy, insisting on its jurisdictional power; and Madrid and the viceroy, struggling to prevent unrest, especially at a time of war between Spain and France. Manuzzi and Giannelli, traveling in Spain for work, were briefly detained and interrogated by the Inquisition there and received minor penalties for their ideas. But the situation in Naples degenerated, and in February 1692 a petition supporting the city's position quickly gathered over six thousand signatures (a remarkable number in a city with perhaps a hundred thousand adult male residents, most of them illiterate). Both the viceroy and the archbishop regarded the initiative with concern. In November 1692 Belli was also arrested. He and de Cristofaro denied all accusations. De Cristofaro expressed special outrage at being accused of denying the miracle of San Gennaro, apparently considering this a worse stain on his character than denying the immortality of the soul.

Madrid's calls for moderation and the insistence of Pope Innocent XII (who had been archbishop of Naples and took special interest in the city) prevailed on the city's combativeness. No definitive proof was found to convict the accused, and the witnesses against de Cristofaro offered only contradictory, circumstantial evidence. Belli was released in 1695 after abjuring the opinions under trial; he received minor penalties. Eventually even de Cristofaro's remarkable resolve faltered, and in April 1697, after almost six years of imprisonment, he too recanted the ideas he stood accused of having advocated. He was released with spiritual penalties. He went on to a modest legal career and to the pursuit of mathematics, a field in which he published two significant works before his death in 1725. The other three protagonists returned to their native towns and left no further mark in history, except Giannelli, who published some poetry and was murdered by a servant.

The Neapolitan "atheists" were probably no such thing, but their trial shows how dangerous the Church considered scientific interests. All scientific study, and the very principle of the freedom to investigate nature (what intellectuals called the freedom to philosophize), was suspicious, and the trial was clearly intended to send a message to all Italian intellectuals. "All Rome is up in arms against mathematicians and physicists," wrote a Roman Jesuit to a Neapolitan friend during the Naples trial. Prominent defenders of the accused argued strenuously that there was no necessary contradiction between modern science and Christianity. But the conclusion of the trial showed the strength of Church authorities. It also established, temporarily at least, a more rigid intellectual climate across Italy. In the long term, however, the Naples trial proved the last defeat of modern thinking under the old regime. A few years after its conclusion, the end of Spanish rule in Italy led to a freer flourishing of new ideas. Southern writers began to articulate new criticisms of Spanish policies that began to have an impact on actual reforms.

In November 1700 King Charles II of Spain died, the last male of the Spanish Habsburgs. The event was not unexpected. He had been sickly his entire life, and it is likely that neither of his marriages was ever consummated. The king was the unfortunate product of generations of royal inbreeding: he had only ten great-great-grandparents while most of us have sixteen. For at least a decade, European powers had been negotiating over the succession. Spain was no longer the power it had been a century before, but the inheritance—Spain itself, the Italian dominions, the southern Low Countries, plus a colonial empire stretching from the Philippines to South and Central America—was still well worth having. Both the French Bourbons and the Austrian Habsburgs had dynastic claims, and English King William III proposed a partition plan. But Charles II left a will designating Philip of Anjou, grandson of French King Louis XIV, as his sole heir, and France accepted the will. Philip V thus became king of Spain, as well as of Naples, Sicily, and Sardinia. An aristocratic conspiracy in Naples against the new king failed in 1701, and the young ruler visited his Italian domains in 1702, the first time since 1536 southerners saw their sovereign. That year, however, also brought the start of a general European war against France and Spain: the War of the Spanish Succession.

It now became clear that the Italian states, once the center of European politics, played a marginal part in European affairs. None of the Italian states had the military, diplomatic, or economic ability to affect the progress of events. In a series of European wars through the 1760s, the various principalities of the peninsula found themselves not only the pawns of the balance-of-power schemes of the great powers but also the battlefields. When Austrian forces invaded Italy, the Spanish dominions fell with little resistance: Milan in 1706, Naples in 1707, and Sardinia in 1708. The peace treaty in 1713 gave the Kingdom of Sicily to the duke of Savoy, who ruled the northwestern parts of Italy, elevating him to the highest rank among Italian princes (in 1720 another treaty swapped the two island kingdoms, giving Sardinia to Savoy and Sicily to Austria). Philip V kept his Spanish crown, but Spain lost all its Italian possessions.

Austria's rule in the South represented in some ways a strong continuity with the past. A Habsburg king once more ruled in Naples (and soon Palermo) through viceroys, and the kingdoms served an imperial agenda formulated in a distant capital. Spaniards still played a prominent role, since the Austrian court was full of Spanish exiles who had backed the Habsburg side in the war and were rewarded with offices in the former Spanish dominions. Spanish remained the language of government. But the political change had profound effects on the intellectual climate. Especially in Naples, the intellectual ferment that had increased at the end of the previous regime now produced numerous projects for reform. Writers, in and out of government, debated the grounds for papal and Church authority in the kingdom. They began to apply a dispassionate analysis to practical situations and to reject traditional authorities and supernatural explanations for the problems that beset the kingdom. They became ever more critical of the conditions surrounding them: the poverty of the masses, the backwardness of the economy, the wealth and privileges of the Church, the confusion and corruption of the administration. Even the new rulers saw the need for reform, to reflect new ideas circulating in Austria and to increase the financial contribution the southern kingdoms could offer to their masters.

Reforms were hesitant and not always coherent. But this marked the first time that the ideas developed over the previous decades actually effected change in policies and institutions, and a sense of optimism and progress began to spread in Neapolitan culture. The togati (the lawyers and judges who staffed the central state institutions) became the leading group in the government, and the Collaterale Council in particular gained the most authority, surpassing even the viceroy's. The main areas of reform were commerce, finance, and the position of the Church.

Austrian leaders embraced mercantilist ideas, which considered a positive balance of trade essential to state strength. Mercantilism tended to neglect agriculture and to see real wealth in manufacturing, trade, and in particular bullion. The Austrian government in Naples thus gave fiscal assistance to fairs and markets, supported the expansion of mining, and entered trade agreements with neighboring powers. Trade treaties with the Ottoman empire and the Barbary states lowered the threat of piracy to the southern coasts. In 1728 Messina was made a free port, abolishing all customary dues (it later lost this status and then regained it after the 1783 earthquake). Both the commercial and military fleets were expanded, though they remained small. Smuggling continued to be common, and foreign ships still handled most of the kingdom's foreign and much of its internal trade. Very little investment came forth for the kingdom's woeful roads and bridges. Overall, the South's exports continued to consist mostly of agricultural and raw goods, such as silk.

The government also attempted reform of the administration by establishing new committees to supervise areas of special concern, such as commerce, transportation, and guilds. This new type of administrative structure, circumventing the entrenched bureaucracy of Spanish government, became the norm later in the century. A new census was begun in 1732, although never finished. The southern population increased in the early eighteenth century, a sign of improved economic and especially agricultural health. The government launched a program, and founded a public bank, to buy back fiscal revenues assigned in previous years to the monarchy's creditors, though this remained a limited effort given the continuing pressure to finance Austria's wars. Nothing was done to restrict Church wealth or immunities, but the government did extend the Spanish policy of resisting clerical encroachment on royal jurisdiction. There were no serious attempts to rein in the power or privileges of the feudal nobility, and the government continued to tax trade heavily, though in 1718 the old restraints on building in and around Naples were lifted.

Military expenses limited the government's action: over the Austrian period military costs always absorbed more than half the royal revenues (low compared to France and England, but still quite substantial). The reform program collapsed altogether as war again consumed the energies of the monarchy in the 1730s. The dynasties that for two centuries had ruled the duchy of Parma and the grand-duchy of Tuscany were about to become extinct, and this opened up new opportunities for shuffling power in the peninsula.

Charles of Bourbon, the eighteen-year-old son of Philip V of Spain and his second wife, Elisabetta Farnese, and already the designated heir to those principalities, led a Spanish army into Italy and entered Naples on May 10, 1734, bringing Austrian rule to an end. The next year Charles added Sicily to his conquest. Though in the peace settlement Charles had to abandon his claims to Parma and Tuscany, Naples now had a resident king for the first time in 230 years. He was crowned in Palermo in June 1735 and thereafter ruled Sicily through a viceroy.

Overall, the Austrian reforms in Naples were less significant for their results than for the shift they signaled: the government recognized the serious problems in the kingdom and was willing to listen to proposals for solutions. It was also willing to appoint several of the critics of existing conditions to positions of influence. Censorship diminished and more opportunities opened up for scholars and thinkers. In 1732, for instance, a private academy of sciences was founded by prominent Neapolitan scholars and officials, devoted to the circulation of new and foreign ideas. This was the novel environment in which the likes of Giambattista Vico flourished.

Vico (1668–1744) is today the best-known Italian philosopher of his time. In his main work, the *New Science* (1725), he presented a controversial conception of history as fundamentally cyclical. He also rejected Descartes' conception of man and the universe as machines operating by mechanical laws. Vico's emphasis on cycles and recurrences, on the power of life forces in history, on poetry and emotion, and on an organic rather than mechanical approach to history and nature put him at odds with the prevailing eighteenth-century trust in reason, experiment, and linear progress. His ideas greatly appealed to the Romantics, and he has been variously interpreted as a precursor to Hegel, Marx, and other modern thinkers. Today in the United States an institute and a journal are devoted to the study of Vico; the text of *New Science* is also available online. But what made Vico so intriguing to later centuries left him a marginal figure in his time, when his ideas seemed conservative and confusing. His contemporary Pietro Giannone (1676–1748) offers a better example of the daring that informed the work of Neapolitan intellectuals in the early eighteenth century—and of its sometimes tragic consequences.

Giannone's early life was typical of the main avenue for social mobility open to young men of the provincial and middle classes: a legal career. Born and raised in a provincial town, he came to Naples at the age of sixteen to study law. After graduating in 1701 he quickly established a fruitful law practice and entered the learned circles of the capital. He studied the classics, history, and natural science and engaged in lively controversies on scholarly and legal issues. With Austrian rule, many of Giannone's friends ascended to influential posts, and Giannone himself prospered. He bought a suburban villa, brought his widowed father to Naples, and fathered two children. In March 1723, encouraged by his learned friends and with a license from the Collaterale, Giannone published *Civil History of the Kingdom of Naples*. Because the work attacked Church jurisdiction, Giannone did not seek the archbishop's permission to publish; in his autobiography he claimed that such permission was not needed.

Civil History was the most coherent Italian expression of the position called jurisdictionalism. In the sixteenth century, many Catholic rulers obtained substantial powers to appoint bishops and tax Church revenues within their kingdoms. Over the course of the seventeenth century, French, Dutch, and German political thinkers articulated a view of a secular state that rejected papal claims to universal jurisdiction and asserted each sovereign's right to supervise the administration of the Church within his state. But major areas of struggle remained, such as Church sanctuary rights, fiscal and judicial immunities, episcopal control over intellectual life, and papal influence in international affairs.

By the early eighteenth century, Church power was ebbing across Catholic Europe, compared to its earlier might. Yet it remained especially strong in the Italian states. The Kingdom of Naples, formally a papal fief, was in a particularly difficult position in its relationship with Rome. Giannone based his attack on Church jurisdiction on a thorough historical reconstruction, demonstrating the political and intellectual impact of new scholarly methods of research and analysis. He offered an innovative approach to political history, centered on the history of institutions. His focus on the secular autonomy of the state helped start a national consciousness in Naples.

Response to the work was swift. Such was the scandal aroused by some of Giannone's conclusions that the viceroy intervened to suspend sales. Within weeks Inquisition proceedings began. Clerical authorities excommunicated the printer and Giannone, and placed the book on the Index of Forbidden Books. A vast campaign against the author began, as Giannone reported: "as far as Neapolitans were concerned, the calumny best apt to the perverse ends of [my enemies] was invented, namely to have people believe that I denied the miracle of San Gennaro's blood." Giannone's friends worried that should the miracle not happen at its appointed time in early May, Giannone would be in jeopardy, and urged him to quit the city. He fled to Puglia, and though he heard reassuring news of the miracle, he sailed thence to Austria, where he hoped to receive protection. In Vienna, by June, Giannone was granted a pension from the emperor and joined the large local Italian community. Under straitened circumstances, and unable to work regularly, he remained there for eleven years, during which he composed numerous essays pursuing the themes of his work and drafted much of the *Tri-kingdom*, which would appear posthumously. In 1729 an English edition of *Civil History* came out in London to positive reviews.

When Austria lost its Italian realms in 1734, things got much worse for Giannone. His pension was revoked and he was asked to leave. He sold most of what he owned, including his books, made his way to Venice, and petitioned the new government of Naples for permission to return. At this point Giannone became a pawn in a much bigger game between the papacy and various Italian states. Charles of Bourbon was eager to receive papal acknowledgment of his rule in Naples and denied Giannone's request. Giannone stayed on in Venice, where his son joined him from Naples. His plan to publish a new edition of *Civil History*, which might have improved his increasingly difficult financial circumstances, raised further opposition from Church authorities. On the evening of September 13, 1735, as he returned home, he was arrested and escorted to the borders of the Venetian Republic. He managed to avoid being caught in papal territory and escaped to Modena and soon Milan. Doubtful of his safety and in need of sustenance, he moved on to Turin and crossed the Alps to Geneva. This was not an easy trip, in midwinter, for a bookish lawyer of sixty.

Giannone hoped to publish in Geneva both a new Italian edition and a French translation of *Civil History*. He claimed that he had no intention to convert to Protestantism, and in fact he did not during the three months he and his son spent in the Calvinist city. Unbeknownst to Giannone, the government of Charles Emanuel III of Savoy was under papal pressure to arrest him. He was lured into Savoy territory by false friends, who told him he could attend Easter Catholic services there. In the night of March 24, 1736, he and his son were arrested and taken to the first of several prisons. Again, he found himself a tool of princely negotiation, as Charles Emanuel struggled with Rome over a new concordat between the papacy and his kingdom. The conditions of Giannone's imprisonment progressively worsened. For the first few years he still produced essays on ancient and medieval history. His autobiography, begun in jail in 1736, ends with the poignant realization that he would never be set free. He may not have known that *Civil History* was finally published in French in 1742. Giannone died in jail in Turin in March of 1748, never having been tried for any crime.

Giannone's life presents a classic tale of success followed by tragedy, itself followed by posthumous redemption. The *Tri-kingdom*, a brilliant and virulent text that reviews both ancient and early Christian history to demonstrate the illicit bases of papal authority over both the Church and the secular powers, was not published until 1890, though parts of the manuscript were known before then. But *Civil History* enjoyed great success in the second half of the eighteenth century, when Church power considerably diminished across Catholic Europe. A German edition came in 1758–70. Seven additional Italian editions appeared before 1800. In 1769 Giannone's son was granted a pension by the king of Naples as the son "of the greatest, most useful to the state, and most unjustly persecuted man that the Kingdom has produced in this century." That Giannone conceived his work and felt confident to publish it shows the intellectual ferment and optimism that spread in Naples under Austrian rule. The reaction to the work and the Church's ability to pursue its author across Europe show how far intellectual freedom and political reform still had to go.

The government of Charles of Bourbon (1734–59) greatly expanded the reform agenda of the Austrian viceroys, aiming at economic revival, administrative rationalization, judicial reform, and limitation of ecclesiastic powers and privileges. Much more than in the previous generation, the reforms resulted from the overlap between royal aspirations and intellectual trends. Charles and his ministers were inspired by a desire for absolutist rule, modeled on the French example of Louis XIV, which called for expanding the authority of royal courts, officials, and laws, and for asserting royal power over Church and aristocracy. Enlightenment principles also played a major role in government reforms. Naples became one of the major Italian centers of Enlightenment studies, and for two generations an active reform program and flourishing new ideas reinforced each other.

In its first years, the new government even dared challenge feudal powers: in 1738 Neapolitan barons lost their jurisdiction over capital crimes in their fiefs and it became easier for royal tribunals to claim cases from feudal courts. These measures proved short-lived, however, as they were repealed in 1744, when the king needed his barons' support during yet another war that threatened to bring the Austrians back into power. But they showed the ambitious scope of the reform agenda and the search for new solutions to the kingdom's problems.

To rein in the power of the bureaucratic elite, in 1735 the government replaced the Collaterale with a new organ, the Chamber of Santa Chiara, which the king could more easily mold. The monarchy also increased the use of committees dedicated to specific problems and especially to economic development. In 1739 a new Supreme Magistracy of Commerce was established to stimulate trade. This was the first organ of the central government to include nonlawyers, namely, a few merchants, and to employ the Italian language (instead of Latin or Spanish). In 1742 a royal factory of porcelain was opened to produce luxury goods that would increase the kingdom's exports (Charles's queen, Maria Amalia of Saxony, aimed to emulate the works of her native land in this field). Other luxury industries to enjoy royal sponsorship were ceramics, silk, and tapestries. The government also expanded the Austrian policy to buy back alienated fiscal revenues.

The government curtailed the old Spanish policy of selling fiefs and offices and began to buy some back. In particular, when a fief reverted to the Crown because of a baronial family's extinction, the government kept it in the royal domain. By 1788 there were 388 communities under royal jurisdiction, compared to about 50 in the 1720s. Other initiatives show a commitment to public utility, a central element of the Enlightenment mentality. Swamps were drained near Naples, and a new aqueduct ensured better water for the capital. In 1751 Charles began the building in Naples of an enormous poorhouse, the Albergo dei Poveri, to gather and sustain the capital's destitute multitudes. The kingdom's dreary road system also became an object of concern. The new Royal Road of Calabria and improved roads to Puglia and Abruzzo expanded the capital's links to the provinces. However, progress was limited, and at the end of the eighteenth century the kingdom had less than a thousand kilometers of paved roads, compared to forty thousand kilometers in France.

One of the major projects came in the 1740s and 1750s when the Catasto Onciario was undertaken. This massive enterprise (it produced over nine thousand volumes of documents) was a complete fiscal and demographic survey of the kingdom: all citizens were listed by household, and all real estate, livestock, investments, and other assets were to be reported, with the goal of establishing a more accurate and fairer tax system. Feudal and clerical assets were also listed, though they remained subject to separate fiscal regimes.

The southern economy improved, and both trade and manufacturing grew. New crops, such as citrus fruits, were exported. The kingdom's population grew from about three million early in the century to about five million at its end. The period also saw social differentiation, as new rural and urban elites began to rival the traditional feudal aristocracy and the administrative elite.

The royal court affected relations at the top of the kingdom's social hierarchy. The Bourbons increased noble participation in government to balance the power accumulated by the togati under Austrian rule, though the Neapolitan nobility did not shine as administrators: in 1746 the archbishop wrote that "the noblemen who are in [the Council of State] know nothing and understand less." The rituals and protocol of court life attracted aristocrats to royal service, which granted prestige and access to the king. The development of a lavish court followed the French absolutist model: the king used court favors and etiquette to keep the nobility under a careful watch and to separate noble factions. At the same time, the splendor that came from proximity to the king gave the aristocracy higher status and reinforced its sense of social superiority to the administrative elite. In 1738 the new chivalric Order of San Gennaro created further hierarchies in the court and noble sphere. The king asserted his position as the arbiter of noble status. A 1756 edict defined the requirements and ranks of nobility. Between 1730 and 1800 the Crown controlled the expansion of the Naples Seggi, which more than doubled their member families to about 250. Thus, the presence of a royal court in Naples allowed for more balance between various elements of the elite and enhanced royal ability to shape and control them.

Charles also engaged in a more assertive policy toward the Church. In 1736 the university, traditionally a bastion of Church influence, was reformed and new chairs in the sciences were created. In 1740 the government limited Church building. In the same year, Charles again allowed Jews to settle in the kingdom, although this was revoked under Church pressure in 1747. In 1741 a concordat was concluded with the papacy, for the first time taxing clerical wealth with some regularity and restricting its further growth. The number of clerics was also limited, though it remained quite high, and sanctuary rights were curtailed. Church benefices in the kingdom were restricted to Neapolitan subjects, thus curbing the amount of Church income that left the kingdom. These decisions limited Church property, which in 1734 amounted to about 15 percent of the kingdom's land. In 1746 the archbishop's attempt to import the secretive procedures of the Roman Inquisition united secular forces and led to the abolition of the Inquisition in Naples.

Over time, anti-Church policies grew. In 1767 the Jesuits—seen everywhere in the eighteenth century as the most devious and powerful agents of the papacy—were expelled from the kingdom, as happened also in France, Spain, and Portugal around that time. Their property was distributed among secular owners. Until the pope agreed to disband the Jesuits altogether in 1773, the Naples government occupied the papal enclaves of Benevento and Pontecorvo. In 1777 the university moved into the Jesuit monastery of the Salvatore, where sections of it remain to this day. Freemasonry, though formally condemned by the king in 1751, flourished in the following decades in spite of Church opposition. The royal government strictly enforced its right to approve all papal decisions affecting the Church in the kingdom, and in 1786 expanded it to include the religious orders. In 1787 the right of ecclesiastic sanctuary was abolished. In 1788 the king stopped sending to Rome the yearly tribute of the chinea, the white mare that symbolized the kingdom's status as a papal fief. Finally, in the changed climate of the 1790s, when the papacy and the monarchy needed each other's support against revolution, the pope granted the king the right to make all episcopal appointments in the kingdom.

In the policy toward the Church we can see another effect of the presence in Naples of a resident monarchy, namely, more emphasis on the independence of the kingdom, on its identity as a state and a nation, and on the prestige of its monarchy. Charles pursued a stronger foreign policy. The Neapolitan diplomatic presence in the Adriatic and the Levant was expanded. The government concluded trade treaties with Sweden, Denmark, and Holland. Ponza and Ventotene, uninhabited islands off the Roman coast, were settled and claimed by Naples. The military also received new attention. In 1735 the Naval Academy was created. In 1769 the artillery and engineering academies (founded in 1744 and 1754, respectively) were joined in the Royal Military Academy. In 1773 the Nunziatella school opened to train noble officers. Ferdinand IV, Charles's successor, continued to spend considerable sums on the Neapolitan navy, and in 1784 he established a new arsenal in Castellammare, on the Bay of Naples. The government aimed to develop weapons production and improve the kingdom's ports. By the 1780s the hope was to have about sixty thousand men under arms, and by 1790 military costs amounted to two-thirds of royal revenues. But neither the navy nor the army could compete with those of larger European powers, as would become evident in the wars of the 1790s.

Finally, Charles and Ferdinand launched an ambitious program of royal building and patronage, designed to celebrate the monarchy and surround it with suitable splendor. The city of Naples was the main stage for royal magnificence, and it benefited also from increased elite numbers and wealth. The new opera theater of San Carlo opened in 1737. Streets were broadened, new ones were opened and paved, and new elegant neighborhoods expanded outside the old walled city. In 1788–90 the first public garden opened, the Villa Reale, along the seashore west of the old city. The area of Chiaia, around the Villa, emerged as the most popular among nobles and new bourgeois elites. The urban upper classes competed with the court to employ painters, architects, and decorative artists.

The kingdom acquired new royal palaces. The one in Portici, just east of Naples, had a large hunting park; numerous aristocratic villas sprouted nearby. Capodimonte, on the hills behind Naples, housed much of the splendid art collection Charles had inherited through his mother's family. A new royal library opened at the university. The magnificent new palace and gardens in Caserta, about thirty kilometers north of Naples, lived up to Charles's hope to establish a Versailles of Italy. These projects drew artists from outside the South and stimulated a new flourishing of architecture and the decorative arts, which added to Naples's attractions for tourists. With the same aim to glorify the monarchy, Charles sponsored the archeological excavations that began during his reign at Pompeii, Herculaneum, and Paestum. Following the model of French absolutism, Charles and Ferdinand founded royal academies devoted to the sciences and arts: in 1752 the Academy of Fine Arts, in 1755 the Herculaneum Academy (to spread information from that site), in 1762 the Academy of Architecture, in 1778 the Royal Academy of Sciences and Letters, in 1779 a new medical school at the Incurabili hospital. These institutions, regulated by the government, spread knowledge and celebrated the monarchy.

Just as in France, freedom for intellectual exploration bloomed in the 1750s, as Church censorship lost its grip. The University of Naples, noted a French visitor, "is the only one in Italy to enjoy a real freedom." Intellectuals began to articulate a cohesive critique of traditional privileges and practices that inspired and underpinned royal reforms affecting commerce, taxation, and religion. The 1750s marked the start of a mature phase of intellectual development in Naples and of more intense exchange with thinkers across Europe. Until then the leading intellectual figures came from legal studies and were close to the administrative elite. By midcentury a new generation of intellectuals applied a more practical, economic, and statistical analysis to the kingdom's problems. Younger thinkers produced concrete studies of the capital, the provinces, and economic trends. For the first time, a clear group of intellectuals, sharing a new culture, emerged as participants in the political life of Naples.

The symbol of this evolution was the appointment in 1754 of Antonio Genovesi (1712–69) to the first professorship in political economy in Europe. To the scandal of traditionalists, he was the first professor in Naples to lecture in Italian rather than Latin. Genovesi prodded Neapolitans on the path to reason: "[Reason] truly is always beautiful, but where she is not active she is yet unripe and can, if you wish, adorn men, but not be of use to them. . . . Reason is not useful until she has become practice and reality, nor can she be such until she has so spread in customs and crafts that we employ her as our sovereign rule, almost without realizing it. . . . [We Neapolitans] still love disputing more than doing. . . . A certain vanity of mind still attaches us to things more specious than useful, we still believe ourselves greater when we are admired as incomprehensible than when we are held as useful."

He and other thinkers argued for freer trade, state support for manufacturing, legal and judicial reforms, and reform of the feudal system. They critiqued the position of Naples within the kingdom: they saw the size of the city—it was the huge head of a frail body, many wrote—and its privileges as factors in southern economic backwardness. Too many tax revenues and goods came to the capital from the provinces through exploitative, coercive means. Population distribution was also inefficiently skewed: over two-fifths of the kingdom's people lived within sixty kilometers of Naples, while many provinces were underpopulated. Genovesi also argued for a system of public education, to improve the kingdom both economically and morally. Projects for public education increased after the expulsion of the Jesuits, who had run many schools.

When Charles inherited the Spanish Crown, he maintained the autonomy of the southern kingdoms, and taking his second son to Spain as heir to that Crown, he left Naples and Sicily to his third son, Ferdinand IV. In what may be a unique occurrence in the annals of European royalty, Charles excluded his oldest son, Philip (1747–77), from the succession because of the boy's mental retardation and left him to live out his days in Naples. Since the new king was only eight, Charles set up a regency council in Naples, led by Bernardo Tanucci (1698–1783), a Tuscan lawyer who had served Charles virtually since the start of his rule in Naples. Tanucci pursued Charles's policies and maintained close contact with the old king. Even after the formal end of the regency, Tanucci remained the dominant figure in the Naples government until he was removed from office in 1776 under pressure from Ferdinand's queen, Maria Carolina of Austria, who found Tanucci

Anton Raphael Mengs, *Ferdinand IV as a Child* (1760),
from the Capodimonte Museum, Naples

too beholden to pro-Spanish positions. Tanucci's fall marked a shift in the international alignment of the kingdom: after 1776 Austria and Britain gained influence in Naples, while France and especially Spain lost it.

The biggest crisis of Tanucci's years came with the famine of 1763–64. Bad harvests across the Mediterranean world, the inadequacies of southern agriculture, and the delays, privileges, and corruption of the Neapolitan administration resulted in a tragedy of devastating proportions. By early in 1764, about forty thousand starving rural immigrants huddled in Naples, where they added to the lack of bread and the worsening health conditions. Tension and violence spread across the kingdom as the year advanced, although no general revolt occurred—which surprised many observers. Processions and devotions to San Gennaro intensified. By March, starvation and miserable hygiene brought diseases. A Neapolitan doctor reported that "everywhere one sees wandering in the streets not men, but living corpses, pale, emaciated, dressed in rags, and exhaling a rancid, most disagreeable vapor. Some fall and faint out of sheer starvation, abandoned to certain death if they are not promptly restored and aided by the pity of some generous soul; others die in the streets . . . ; others fall face down on the road and die vomiting their scarce and ruined blood, or a bloodied foam dirty with the grass they have devoured." About two hundred thousand people died in the kingdom as a result of famine and contagion; thirty to fifty thousand of them died in Naples. The number of dead led to the establishment of Naples's (and Italy's) first cemeteries, as the government prohibited the traditional burials inside churches, which it feared would spread disease.

The disaster marked a crucial point in intellectual analysis and government action. Tanucci was convinced that traditional structures were corrupt and inefficient: the city's oligarchic government, the kingdom's cumbersome system of regulated and heavily taxed trade, the deficiencies of credit institutions—all aggravated natural shortages that came from the backwardness of southern agriculture. New enormous grain depots were built east of Naples. Intellectuals, led by Genovesi, drew from the crisis a systematic critique of feudal power, of the capital's abnormal size and of the privileges that opposed it to the provinces, and of the Church's misuse of its landed wealth. Genovesi and others began to argue for free trade, which was increasingly practiced in Britain, France, and Spain. Tanucci saw an increase in royal power as the only way to eliminate the entrenched inefficiencies of bureaucracy and privileged groups, and he limited the powers of the Naples Eletti.

Actual changes, however, were resisted by nobles and officials and fell short of the proposals of intellectuals. In midcentury Naples, about twenty-five thousand people worked in the legal and judicial field: they represented over 6 percent of the city's population, an even higher percentage than in Washington today. A formidable pressure group, they often sided with the nobility, whose ranks many of them joined. Their reaction to the famine showed that elite lawyers, judges, and officials, once active participants in the intellectual explorations leading to reform projects, were now more likely to curtail them. Reflection on the famine's causes and effects, on the other hand, accelerated the pace of intellectual analysis and pushed a new generation to pursue more daring ideas. After the famine, what had been a common culture of reform embraced by all educated elites became an increasingly contentious issue setting bureaucratic and other powerful groups against economists, historians, and other intellectuals.

In the 1770s and 1780s the intellectuals continued to enjoy the support of the monarchy. Neither the king nor his wife was particularly learned. Ferdinand was indeed notorious for his boorish behavior and his limited skill with the Italian language, to which he preferred the Naples dialect. The Irish singer Michael Kelly was amazed to see the king gulp down maccheroni with his fingers. But the royals saw the Enlightenment as a fashionable culture: Queen Maria Carolina even joined the Freemasons, hoping to share the radical chic of her brothers, Emperor Joseph II of Austria and Tuscan Grand-Duke Leopold, who were the very models of enlightened rulers. In the eighteenth century in Naples as elsewhere, Freemasons organized in secret lodges dedicated to philanthropy and science. They were among the strongest advocates of new ideas and especially supported anticlerical measures. Meanwhile, Ferdinand devoted much time and money to San Leucio, a utopian colony he founded in the 1770s near the royal palace in Caserta. The inhabitants worked in silk production and formed a model community in which Enlightenment ideas of equality and philanthropy prevailed: its statutes mandated gender equality, free public education, and concern for public health and hygiene.

Cooperation between innovative ideas and monarchical absolutist goals reached a high point. Economic, commercial, and military reforms were expanded, and censorship further diminished. Contacts across Europe brought a broader scope to Neapolitan discussions. A coherent approach to legal and judicial reform widened the range of government initiatives. Neapolitan writers, in line with the most advanced European thought of the time, advocated the end of feudal jurisdiction, torture, and the death penalty. In 1774 the government required judges to justify their sentences with explicit references to existing laws, a major demand of judicial reformers concerned about the arbitrariness of the justice system. Clearer law codes were proposed in the 1780s, also aimed at making justice more reliable, and torture was abolished in 1789.

The response to the 1783 earthquake, with its expropriation of Church land intended to stimulate modern management and accelerate social dynamics, was part of this advanced phase of reform. In 1781 an enlightened aristocrat, Domenico Caracciolo (1715–89), was sent as viceroy to Palermo, where he implemented many of the reforms that had been enacted in Naples over the previous decades. In 1782 he abolished the Sicilian Inquisition (its jail yielded only three women detained for sorcery). John Acton (1736–1811), an Englishman who succeeded Tanucci as the royal favorite, continued efforts at modernization and rationalization of commerce and the military. A new Supreme Council of Finance, created in 1782, rationalized the fiscal system, and trade in olive oil and raw silk was liberalized. In 1788 the government lifted regulations on provincial provisioning and trade, in 1792 it abolished privately held street tolls throughout the kingdom, and in 1795 it eliminated the Naples Annona. In 1794 a national bank was opened by fusing the seven existing Naples banks.

This high point of political activity coincided with the greatest achievements of Neapolitan intellectuals and with their rising European fame. Gaetano Filangieri's life and work typify this phase of the Neapolitan Enlightenment. Born in 1752, the younger son of a noble family, he served in the royal army and received a good education, thanks to his enlightened uncle, Serafino, archbishop of Palermo and later of Naples. By the time he was twenty, having witnessed the poverty of Sicily and a Palermo riot, Filangieri had developed critical views of the conditions of the South. In 1780 he published the first volumes of his great work, *The Science of Legislation*, a critical analysis of legal and judicial issues. The success was instantaneous and only grew when the next volumes, in which Filangieri more pointedly attacked the feudal system ("which gives the people many tyrants instead of a single king"), appeared in 1783. Filangieri's reputation soared among enlightened minds from Philadelphia to St. Petersburg. In 1782 he sent Benjamin Franklin the first sections of his work, and Franklin asked to receive multiple copies of all ensuing volumes. Franklin sent Filangieri French translations of the American state constitutions as well as a draft of the federal constitution.

Filangieri's reverence for Franklin was part of his admiration for America, in which he saw a promised land of justice and freedom, where a better society would be built. For example, after criticizing the American imposition of the death penalty on military deserters, whom Filangieri regarded as poor, troubled young men, he noted, "Free citizens of independent America, you are too virtuous and too enlightened not to know that by winning the right to govern yourselves you have contracted in the eyes of the universe the sacred duty to be wiser, more moderate and happier than all other peoples."

Personal reasons also attracted the young Neapolitan to America. Filangieri loved a Hungarian woman who was a governess at the Naples court, but his modest income as a second son and her relatively low social status made marriage difficult. In a letter of December 2, 1782, Filangieri asked Franklin whether he knew of any employment available in Philadelphia, "the only place where I might be happy" with a "lady, whose virtues would bring her distinction even in Philadelphia." Once in "the refuge of virtue, the land of heroes, the city of brothers" Filangieri was sure he would never wish to return "to a country corrupted by vice and degraded by serfdom." He echoed here the general popularity of Philadelphia in the 1780s: after the 1783 earthquake, a destroyed Calabrian village was rebuilt and renamed Filadelfia, still its name today. Franklin suggested that Filangieri seek a diplomatic post when the Kingdom of Naples established relations with the United States, and the correspondence continued until Filangieri's death in 1788, after which his widow—the virtuous lady whom he had eventually managed to marry—sent Franklin her husband's last writings.

Filangieri's work was criticized in Naples by conservative writers, and in 1784 Rome placed it on the Index of Forbidden Books. But the success of the work only increased with the later volumes. Filangieri, who by this time had left both the court and the army, published more volumes in 1785. A visit to the young reformer became as much a must for educated tourists as a tour of Pompeii or Vesuvius. In 1787 Goethe praised Filangieri's "delicate moral sense which pervades his whole personality" and his commitment to the "happiness and freedom of mankind." Goethe added that he "had never heard Filangieri say anything commonplace."

Comparing Filangieri's ideas and success with Giannone's illustrates the progress that had occurred in the intervening decades. Filangieri's criticism of his society and its problems is much broader than Giannone's, and although he too attacked Church privileges and wealth, his anticlerical views are part of a larger analysis of the entire edifice of southern society and culture. Filangieri's ideas cannot be reduced to anticlerical or antifeudal polemics, although those were the grounds on which his critics attacked him. Rather, his work presents a thorough project of renewal that advocated specific reforms but also aimed at an overall improvement in both the material condition and the moral welfare of mankind:

> Man becomes used to anything. An unjust government familiarizes the spirit of its subjects with injustice, and gradually leads them to regard it without horror. Without a long habit of being oppressed, we would shudder at the sight of the evils that surround us, of the violence that overcomes us from all sides, of the dangers to which our innocence is exposed. We would try to put an end to our woes. . . . But, senseless under the weight of our chains, most of us would not even dare think that our woes could be cured, and that our condition could be better. . . . Nature has not created us as the plaything of a few powerful men, but has endowed us with all necessary means to be free and happy.

The work brims not only with moral indignation but also with optimism and confidence in progress. It is imbued with the highest moral and intellectual aspirations of the Enlightenment. Filangieri engaged all the most advanced ideas of his time, reflecting the scope and breadth of the European Enlightenment at its zenith while often focus-

Etching portrait of Gaetano Filangieri by Raffaello Morghen, 1780s

ing on his own troubled land. In introducing his critique of the feudal system, Filangieri wrote, "May I be forgiven if, almost forgetful of the universality of my subject, my fatherland will occupy a large part of this horrible depiction. My heart rules my hand, and I cannot resist it." The text also reveals the profound humanity of Filangieri's thought. The appealing personality of its author, which Goethe celebrated, shines through its pages and is part of what makes *The Science of Legislation* a humane, engaging book. After describing a cruel judicial procedure, Filangieri concludes, "Here is how the life and freedom of man are judged among us. Who is not indignant against this perfidious system has either no mind or no heart."

Filangieri's work was attacked, as was Giannone's, and his hopes for far-reaching reforms were frustrated. But the success of his book among cosmopolitan readers (it soon appeared in French, Spanish, German, and English) and the fact that Filangieri was never seriously harassed for his ideas also show the changed climate compared to Giannone's times.

Filangieri died young "with no fortune"—his widow wrote to Franklin—"except the memory of his virtues and reputation." The reform period was at its end. Though much had changed in the South over these decades, its fundamental problems proved resilient to reform. In spite of new crops and more commercialization, the rural economy lagged behind its northern Italian counterpart. The productive sector remained limited in spite of government encouragement to manufacturing. Olive oil remained the kingdom's main export. The subservience of southern commerce to foreign capital and interests continued. Although in the 1780s feudal jurisdiction was the object of minor reforms, the monarchy did not challenge the social dominance of the old aristocracy or its fiscal and other privileges. The wealthiest ninety barons still lorded over about two million vassals, and total feudal income in the kingdom was about the same as the entire royal revenue.

Persistent feudal power, weak manufacturing and trade, and the dreadful poverty of many southern peasants helped to shape northern Italian views of the South. During the eighteenth century, areas of northern Italy, especially Lombardy and Tuscany, experienced significant change. In Milan and Florence governments led by the brothers of the queen of Naples implemented bold policies of free trade and political and fiscal reform that favored savings and investment. Lombard agriculture in particular advanced because of effective irrigation; the spread of new crops such as rice, corn, and fodder; and freer commercialization. Textile plants such as hemp and flax—and at the end of the century cotton—helped develop rural manufacturing. New

roads and canals lowered transportation costs and made trade easier
and more profitable. Though the southern economy had lagged
behind the North's for centuries, the gap may have widened in the
eighteenth century, and it led many educated Italians to regard the
southern regions with increasing dismay.

The period of cooperation between progressive ideas and government reforms ended dramatically, in Naples as elsewhere. The start of
the French Revolution in 1789 marked a crucial transition. As in 1707
and 1734, sudden political change led to a shift in the intellectual climate, and this time it broke the link between government and intellectuals that had grown tighter over the century. Almost overnight the
Naples court became hostile to Enlightenment ideas and the reform
agenda ground to a halt. Increasing fiscal demands—also due to the
return of war—spawned tension across the social spectrum. Censorship, political controls, and fear of change dominated the 1790s. The
1793 executions of Louis XVI and Marie Antoinette (sister of the
queen of Naples) and the entry of French armies into northern Italy
in 1796 further roused the Naples government to resist reform. At the
end of 1798 Ferdinand IV deployed the Neapolitan army in defense
of the papal government, and the failure of that initiative added to
the tensions and suspicions between the Crown and many of its subjects. A French army entered Rome in December of 1798 and soon
threatened the kingdom.

Government anxiety and repressive measures coincided and
clashed with the enthusiasm with which many Neapolitan intellectuals welcomed French developments, especially after the end of the
most radical Terror in the summer of 1794. The younger generation
of Neapolitan thinkers and students embraced ideals coming from
Paris and argued for legal equality, economic and social opportunity,
and constitutional government. In 1794 the government unveiled a
conspiracy among radical intellectuals: dozens were tried and exiled,
and in October three young men who had participated in the plans
were executed. Neapolitan radicals began to go into exile to northern
Italy and France. The monarchy, so recently the main supporter of
progressive and intellectual forces in the kingdom, was now their
enemy.

⌥ Chapter VIII ⌥

The Grand Tour Heads South
Nature, Ruins, Music, and Folklore

The beauty and sweetness of [the South]'s climate, so celebrated at all times, and so prized by the ancients; the antique monuments that it contains and which, without being as numerous or as magnificent as those in Rome, are of a particular type and character; finally a multitude of phenomena of interest to physicists and naturalists; all of this makes the Kingdom of Naples worthy of the attention and research of observers and of men of taste, as much or more than the rest of Italy; it even has the advantage of stimulating curiosity all the more, because it is much less well known.

J. C. R. de Saint-Non, *Voyage pittoresque* (1781), introduction

These observations, by a French traveler who authored a beautifully illustrated, four-volume description of Naples and Sicily, are typical of eighteenth-century visitors to the South. The age of Enlightenment was an age of tourism, when travelers sought pleasure, knowledge, and new experiences. Over the course of the century, Naples and the South acquired a prominent and special place in the European imagination. The new vogue for antiquities and the archeological discoveries sponsored by the Bourbon kings made the region an obligatory stop on the Grand Tour (Greece, under Ottoman rule until 1829, was much harder to reach). Interest in natural science made the southern volcanoes tourist attractions. A visit to Pompeii (about which Goethe wrote that "there have been many disasters in this world, but few which have given so much delight to posterity") combined archeology and natural science. In addition, Naples became one of Europe's greatest musical centers. The return in 1734 of a resident monarchy helped maintain a high level of artistic activity, which included the building of royal palaces, gardens, theaters,

and collections of art and antiquities. The monarchy also drew foreign ambassadors to the city, producing both a more cosmopolitan
social atmosphere and a better safety net for foreigners should they
run into trouble.

Moreover, Europeans were fascinated by southern Italian people,
who to many visitors appeared to embody a different human type.
Enlightenment travelers shared a material, scientific approach to the
world. This included a conviction that climate and geography shaped
culture and temperament. Southern Italians—who supposedly lived
in such an easy, pleasant natural world—were thus further differenti-
ated, morally and materially, from northern Europeans, whose less
generous surroundings required harder toil and stimulated industri-
ousness and thrift.

Perceptions—or, perhaps better, clichés—ranged widely: some
travelers were repelled by the violence, primitiveness, and loose
morals of southern life, especially in the countryside, while others
were charmed by the southerners', and especially the Neapolitans',
insouciance, liveliness, and happy acceptance of life's natural
rhythms—what Goethe called the city's "universal gaiety." Across this
spectrum of views, visitors saw the South as different: this was not
like visiting other parts of Europe, but rather a voyage into a peculiar
way of life, one that was best understood through a folkloric lens. The
people of the South were at once the true heirs of the ancient Greeks
and the most savage of all Europeans. One may wish to civilize the
southerners, or one may wish to share in their blessed and happy
simplicity, but one could not be indifferent to them or regard them
as fully part of the modern world that was developing in northern
Europe. (According to Goethe, Neapolitans returned the compliment
and summarized northern European life as "always snow, houses
made of wood, great ignorance, but a lot of money.")

Certain features of the South, primarily its wonderful climate and
natural beauty and abundance, including the particular appeal of the
Bay of Naples, were well established in the European imagination
even before the Renaissance. Goethe—who visited in 1786–88, when
he was already famous as the author of the best-selling novel *Werther*
(1774)—observed that "one can't blame the Neapolitan for never

The Bay of Naples, print from the *Voyage pittoresque* of Saint-Non (1781–86)

wanting to leave his city, nor its poets for singing the praises of its situation in lofty hyperboles." The French visitor J. J. de Lalande wrote that "one cannot imagine anything more beautiful, grander, more varied or singular in all ways than the view of Naples from all sides." The Romans had styled the Naples region "Happy Campania," and Sicily had been Rome's granary. No evidence of the poverty of southern agriculture managed to counter this picture until well into the nineteenth century. Compared especially to the climate of northern Europe, the South appeared the land of sun and plenty. In 1494 Charles VIII of France, after conquering Naples, wrote that the gardens near the city "lacked only Adam and Eve to be an earthly paradise." The Neapolitan Renaissance poets Pontano and Sannazaro were widely read across Europe until the eighteenth century, and their works spread the image of the South as an enchanted garden. Sannazaro's picturesque tomb was itself a regularly visited site. This idyllic view of the South appears again and again in visitors' reports. Few travelers visited the inland and mountainous regions of the South or Sicily, or even the dry plateaux of Puglia, and so this opinion persisted.

Travelers to the South—particularly French, English, and other merchants, sailors, and diplomats—began to be more numerous in the second half of the seventeenth century. Before about 1650 Church authorities could make a trip to the South quite dangerous for Protestants, but afterward, as religious tension abated, the danger ebbed. Foreigners traveled mostly by sea and few covered much distance by land. Usually they limited their visits to Naples and the surrounding area and were awestruck by the size and riches of the city. Although Protestant visitors were harshly critical of clerical wealth and ignorance, they—no less than Catholics—admired the sumptuousness of the city's religious buildings. Details that differed from their own lands impressed northerners: the flat roofs of Neapolitan houses, where the residents enjoyed the evening cool air; the large numbers of idle people about the city; the urban habit of evening promenades (to this day a common activity); the high consumption of shaved ice; and the rarity of drunks, which particularly surprised English and Irish travelers, who expected the urban poor to be heavy drinkers. Learned Englishmen, like Gilbert Burnet in 1685, expecting little modern knowledge in such a Catholic land, were surprised to meet men "of learning and good sense" and to attend sophisticated intellectual discussions.

Catholic travelers also admired the intense devotions they witnessed in Naples, and even Protestants were captivated by them. The number of relics in the city amazed foreigners, and the miraculous liquefaction of San Gennaro's blood was always high on their list of Neapolitan events. In 1494 the successful performance of the miracle in the presence of Charles VIII helped make the French king acceptable to the Neapolitan populace. André de La Vigne, the king's chronicler, reported that this was "one of the greatest miracles man has ever seen, and all the French people, nobles and others, greatly marveled at its sight." Later Protestant visitors approached the ceremony with anxiety, because should the miracle not happen in their presence, they might find themselves the target of popular fury. But most visitors did not want to miss the event and were generally astonished by it. It was not until the eighteenth century that skepticism or irony entered foreigners' descriptions.

The curiosity of seventeenth-century visitors led them on a set itinerary in and out of the city. At these common destinations they found the first tourist infrastructures, such as inns and guides. Vesuvius was one attraction, especially after the devastating eruption of 1631. But the most significant attraction was the Phlegrean region just west of Naples, which already Charles VIII had visited during his short reign in Naples. This area was full of ancient echoes: many protagonists of Roman history lived and died there; ancient poets sang of the area's beauty; Roman ruins were everywhere, even underwater. Because of a large presence of sulfur, a substance and a smell associated with demons in many cultures, the ancients had placed the mythical hell there. Nearby was the cave of the Cuman Sibyl, one of antiquity's most renowned diviners. Already in the 1340s, at the dawn of the Renaissance, Petrarch had made a point to visit "the places Virgil described." Vapors, flames, and tremors added to the visitors' fascination with this area. The Solfatara, a crater that still bubbles with stinking fumes and is full of red-hot rocks, also intrigued visitors. Finally, in September of 1538 an earthquake resulted in the sudden appearance of a new mountain, the aptly named Monte Nuovo, and this recent natural marvel added to the area's appeal and mystery.

A particular site in the Phlegrean region transfixed seventeenth-century visitors: the so-called Grotto of the Dog, where low-lying deadly fumes allowed for the kind of amateur scientific experiment beloved by the curious minds of the age. The cave, located next to Lake Agnano, was safe for humans but poisonous to smaller creatures. When Charles VIII had visited it, an ass and a cat had been killed to show this phenomenon to the king: the animals' noses were kept low by force, and quick gasping death followed. Even more cruelly, Viceroy Toledo supposedly watched as two slaves were the victims of this demonstration. By the seventeenth century the phenomenon had given rise to a veritable business: a local inn catered to the curious and helped them find dogs for the purpose, as reflected in the cave's name. Over time visitors became somewhat more humane. Several report holding the dog down until the animal gasped for air, and then quickly throwing it into the nearby lake, where the cool water would restore it to life. In 1664 a traveler called John Ray tried this, but when he threw the dog in the lake, the poor animal was so weak that it drowned. Rather mercilessly, Ray continued the experiment and killed a hen, a frog, and a snake. In 1610 the English traveler George Sandys reported that "it is a sport to see how

The Grotto of the Dog and Lake Agnano, from Joan Blaeu,
Nouveau Theatre d'Italie (1704)

the dogs thereabout will steale away, and scud to the tops of the mountaines, at the approch of a stranger." In the eighteenth century a keeper rented out dogs for these experiments.

By and large, seventeenth-century travelers had limited anthropological interests. They did not regard the southerners as especially intriguing or different. A few comments about drinking or idleness, and about the dangers of overland travel for the few who ventured away from the metropolitan region, sufficed. English visitors remarked on the high number of prostitutes in Naples (thirty thousand according to Sandys, twice as many according to Fynes Moryson in 1617). The remark did not, however, lead to much comment about Neapolitan mores, and Moryson's concern was only how much income the tax on prostitution brought to government coffers. Sandys, one of the travelers who saw the most of the South, was intrigued by the effects of tarantula bites on Calabrians—those bit danced frantically until collapsing from exhaustion—and by the remedies available to the afflicted. The 1647 revolt also greatly interested foreigners. In England, for instance, Scipione Mazzella's 1601 description of the kingdom was translated and published in 1654, with an addition on the revolt. Masaniello and the great power the fisherman had briefly enjoyed were especially fascinating: Mazzella's editor noted that "the [Sultan] was never obeyed and feard in Constantinople as [Masaniello] was in Naples." Still, this interest led to no particular analysis of the Neapolitan character, as it would in the next century.

Only the few travelers headed for, or returning from, the Levant saw much of Sicily. These were all merchants, and so they focused on harbors, sea routes, and goods available for trade. The constant activity and occasional dramatic eruptions of Mount Aetna, the mythical Cyclops's abode, attracted some sightseers, and a few travelers made a point of sailing by the volcanic islands of Vulcano and Stromboli, in the Aeolian archipelago north of Sicily. The Sicilians themselves—and their island's abundant ancient ruins—were of limited interest, beyond John Ray's observation that "the Sicilians . . . have not undeservedly the reputation of being uncivil and rude to strangers."

Visitors to the Phlegrean region were familiar with its classical heritage, but its natural marvels attracted more attention. This and the lack of interest in the ancient sites of Sicily point to a relative indifference to antiquity on the part of seventeenth-century travelers, most of whom in any case came to the South of Italy for business or other practical reasons. Only in the eighteenth century did the search for antiquity become a prominent motivation for travel. Over the century new archeological sites were discovered in the South. Collectors, and soon the monarchy, arranged for the exhibition of new finds, opened the first public collections of antique objects, and disseminated knowledge through publishing. All of this went hand in hand with the emergence of Neoclassicism as the dominant artistic and intellectual style across western Europe. When British, French, Germans, and others embarked on the Grand Tour of the continent, which in the eighteenth century became an obligatory element of the education of young gentlemen, the South of Italy and its ruins and ancient collections were high on the list of attractive—indeed, necessary—destinations.

In 1738 the royal government of Naples began funding archeological excavations at Herculaneum, and ten years later at Pompeii. The first digs were purely looting expeditions, but by the 1750s parts of both sites were opened to visitors, and foreigners flocked to them. The royal collection of antiquities opened in Naples, and the Herculaneum Academy, established in 1755, published information about and reproductions of the ancient cities. After she married Ferdinand IV in 1768, Maria Carolina of Austria attracted German and other northern artists to Naples, and they further spread Neoclassical taste and ideas. In 1780 the government brought the large Farnese collection of antiquities (which was part of the royal family's inheritance) to Naples and displayed it in the old university building, adding to the city's classical must-sees.

The new sites offered a much fuller impression of ancient life than the Phlegrean area, which now took second place among tourist interests. Goethe still went there first and felt "tossed about between the acts of nature and the acts of men," but he found the new sites more deserving of repeated visits. In the 1770s Paestum also became very popular. This site, with its remarkably preserved Greek temples, was not as developed by the government and so visitors found there the true picturesque ideal: beautiful ruins immersed in a lush overgrown

The Temples at Paestum, print from the *Voyage pittoresque* of Saint-Non (1781–86)

countryside, surrounded by peasants, herds, and open fields. Prints of the temples, with cattle and shepherds resting amidst the columns, became popular.

By this point prints were an essential element of tourism. They were what postcards and photos are now. Visitors also brought or hired draftsmen to record what they saw so they could share it with friends back home. Tourists as well as scholars were fascinated by Herculaneum and Pompeii, which offered varied objects, buildings, and paintings to enjoy and study. Paestum's attraction was different and reflected an advanced phase of Neoclassicism, when Greek art came to be prized even more than Roman works. Greek art, especially of the archaic period to which Paestum's temples dated, was seen as stark, severe, and pure. Paestum, mostly abandoned and unregulated, farther from Naples and devoid of most tourist comforts, offered visitors a direct contact with both antiquity and the natural world. It especially appealed to the early Romantic taste for nature of the 1780s. Goethe, who brought with him a painter friend to sketch the site, was typical in his reaction: "At first sight [the temples] excited nothing but stupefaction. I found myself in a world which was completely strange to me. . . . Our eyes and, through them, our whole sensibility have become so conditioned to a more slender type of architecture that these crowded masses of stumpy conical columns appear offensive and even terrifying. But I pulled myself together, remembered the history of art, thought of the age with which this architecture was in harmony, called up images in my mind of the austere style of sculpture—and in less than an hour I found myself reconciled to them." Even Sicily's Greek ruins, which Goethe but not many others saw, could not match the impact of the temples at Paestum.

Grand Tour travelers had an eclectic mind and their curiosity included the natural sciences. They did not simply seek natural oddities, as many had in the previous century, but brought a scholarly approach to the world around them. Many visitors collected mineral and plant specimens. Vesuvius in particular, which Goethe called "this peak of hell which towers up in the middle of paradise," became an obligatory stop on any trip to the South. The volcano obligingly rewarded this interest by intensifying its activity to a level never matched before or since. Saint-Non, visiting in 1780, listed six major eruptions before the year 1000, another six by 1600, four in the seventeenth century, six between 1700 and 1750, five between 1751 and 1767, and eight in the 1770s, or nearly annual ones. Volcanic activity affected tourist plans. In November of 1786 Goethe, then in Rome, reported that "most of the foreigners are wildly excited over the present eruption. . . . [They] have interrupted their sightseeing tour and are hurrying off to Naples." Though he stayed put then, when he went to Naples he climbed Vesuvius three times in a month.

Guides and coachmen took tourists to the crater of Vesuvius. Many visitors also lauded the good wine produced on the volcano's slopes, though a few were scandalized by its blasphemous name, Lachryma Christi, or Christ's tear. Aetna, while also of interest, remained harder (and more dangerous) for most to reach and climb. The first foreign description of an ascent to Aetna appeared in German in 1771, and the first decent hotel in Catania, the nearest town, opened in 1774. More tragically, the Calabrian earthquake of 1783 was also the object of passionate foreign interest. Numerous travelers went to the area to report on the situation and study the phenomenon.

Eighteenth-century travelers approached antiquity and natural phenomena differently from their predecessors. Both matters of interest were also exploited by the developing tourism industry. Porcelains with designs inspired by antiquity became popular souvenirs. Images of Vesuvius, from prints to watercolors, from porcelain to fans, became keepsakes for tourists.

The abundance of music in Naples, and its quality and style, also contributed to a new interpretation of the Neapolitan character and shaped foreigners' perceptions of southern identity. In 1739 Charles de Brosses, a French magistrate, wrote in his travel memoirs, "Naples is the capital of the musical world." Such a sentiment, expressed by many visitors, was based principally on the flourishing of opera in the city. Opera was, to eighteenth-century eyes and ears, the musical genre par excellence, the highest form of musical expression, and an artform equal to theater and poetry. Many European cities were famous for their opera productions, but Naples stood unrivaled through most of the century. In particular, Naples played a crucial role in shaping the new genre of comic opera, which was at the core of Enlightenment ideas about theater.

Opera as a separate genre had started at the Medici court in Florence in 1600, the result of attempts on the part of Florentine intellectuals to revive an ancient Greek theatrical style. Opera was a staged sung-through performance, with continuous musical accompaniment and often dance. Its plot, always based on classical myth, was serious but invariably ended happily. It usually included explicit or allegorical praise of the ruler whose deep pockets financed the lavish staging. Mythological topics guaranteed the noble tone expected of court performances and minimized the problem of implausibility: gods and heroes may be allowed to sing their way through their adventures, a mode of expression rather ridiculous in ordinary mortals. The aim of opera was not only the combination of all artistic expressions (song, dance, music, acting, scenery), but also the enhancement of poetry and acting. Opera embodied the new Baroque aesthetic of monody, the idea that a single sung line, by strengthening the power of the words, would move the emotions of the listeners more effectively than the traditional polyphony of Renaissance music.

Early opera was a courtly product meant to celebrate, and to convey to a captive audience of courtiers the wealth, culture, and power of their rulers. In 1637, however, the first commercial production of opera took place in Venice, a mercantile republic without an extravagant court but with a large elite public accustomed to theater. Since this audience had to be lured into the theater and enticed to buy tickets or rent boxes, the *impresario*, or theater manager, had to cater to its taste. That taste, to the dismay of poets, inclined not to beautiful verse affectingly expressed, but rather to astoundingly skilled singing and exceptional stage effects. Daring stage machinery and vocalizing—especially the celebrated vocal legerdemain and high-pitched powerful sound of the *castrati*—filled the theaters. This horrified many moralists, who saw women on the stage as dangerous temptresses and associated the castrati with traditional condemnations of eunuchs. All over Italy poor parents with sons who were promising boy sopranos began to regard the boys' castration as their ticket to fame and wealth. Singers, especially castrati and female sopranos, became the stars of the opera world, while librettists, instrumentalists, and composers were interchangeable. Even the Church, which refused to allow women to sing during masses and other services, often employed male sopranos: castrati sang in the Sistine Chapel choir from 1599 to 1903.

Opera in the commercial theater expanded its repertory and range. Comic elements entered the plots, as did historical or literary settings (mostly ancient, but also chivalric) and human characters. The public cared little about verisimilitude, provided the singing was good. Costumes, stage effects, and virtuoso singers made the texts virtually irrelevant, and the focus of attention became the arias. These were highly artificial set pieces in which a character expressed his or her emotion or reaction to a plot development in song that included word repetition and vocal flourishes. Popular arias were often encored, transferred from one opera to another, and applied to different texts or sung by different characters. Duets and other ensembles were rare, as were choruses, while two or three star singers could make almost any work a success. The public, which went to the opera theater to be entertained, to see and be seen, and to socialize in open and well-lit boxes, paid irregular attention to the stage except when the stars sang their arias.

In this general form, Italian opera triumphed across the peninsula. By the early eighteenth century it conquered audiences from Vienna to Handel's London, where an English public delighted in absurd plots sung in Italian to music composed by a German. The fact that the great heroes of history, myth, and epic romance—Alexander, Caesar, Roland—were sung by castrated men did not trouble anyone. Even in Paris, where there was a rich tradition of lyrical tragedies in French, by the early eighteenth century Italian opera was fashionable, though the French public never accepted the castrati.

Tastes began, however, to change. Literary and artistic trends developed toward greater simplicity and away from what were now seen as Baroque excess and artifice. Similarly, writers and composers began an attempt to "reform" opera, to make it more dignified, more balanced in its various elements, and more reflective of real human actions and emotions. The Enlightenment stressed that simplicity and naturalness formed the path to truth, beauty, and ultimately virtue, which ought to be the goals of all artistic expressions. In opera this meant simpler and better texts, fewer arias, nobler themes, fewer characters, more decorum, and more honest, simple sentiment. These were the traits of the numerous libretti penned by Pietro Metastasio (1698–1782), a Roman butcher's son who for over fifty years served as imperial poet in Vienna. His elegant, charming verse plays were intended to bring opera closer to spoken tragedy and were set to music—often repeatedly—by virtually all eighteenth-century opera composers.

These reforms aimed at improving and ennobling opera but did not rethink it as a theatrical or musical genre. At the same time, a completely new form of opera emerged in Italy and quickly spread across Europe: comic opera, or *opera buffa*. Comic elements had been present in early operas, especially in those for the commercial theater, but by the end of the seventeenth century, comic elements had been discarded to avoid mixing genres. Comic opera was linked to other, humbler, theatrical traditions, especially the *commedia dell'arte*, an improvisational comedy filled with stock characters and plots and marked by physical and farcical elements, which had been popular on Italian (often makeshift) stages since the Renaissance.

At the turn of the eighteenth century, in the Naples theaters that catered—by their use of dialect—to a less sophisticated audience, simple stories of ordinary characters with their blemishes and foibles, caught in ordinary events, were set to music and performed mostly by second-rate singers and musicians. In part because of their lesser skills, and in part because of the different aesthetic that came with comic opera, the singing and acting were as different from those deployed in serious opera as the characters and stories represented. Small orchestras sufficed. Duets, ensembles, and choruses were much more frequent and gave new dynamism to the productions. Solo parts required much less ornamented vocalization. Dialogue and language were more varied and moved away from the noble tone and themes that dominated traditional opera. Singers engaged in farcical actions and interacted much more with each other on the stage.

The singers themselves changed in comic opera. Castrati were too expensive for comic opera, and anyway they were the target of growing criticism as the embodiment of the artificiality of traditional opera. Instead, prominent roles became available for what developed into the signature voice of comic opera: the so-called *buffo* bass, whose low tones served marvelously for comic sound effects. In comic opera simple melodies, initially based on folk tunes and songs, predominated. Such easy melodies reflected, critics argued, the natural tendencies of the human voice, and thus were better able to stir the naturally tender feelings of the audience. Even in ensembles, melodic lines were passed from one singer to the next in ways that maintained the lyrical momentum of the music. Solo virtuoso singing was rare in comic opera.

Several reasons help explain why this new form of opera found fertile ground in Naples. Eighteenth-century observers thought that the Neapolitan character, shaped by the warm climate and the good food, was naturally given to song, dance, and general happiness, and hence predisposed to comic opera. Lalande observed that "music is above all the Neapolitans' triumph . . . the entire nation sings; the gesture, the inflection of the voice, the prosody of syllables, even the conversation, everything there marks and breaths harmony and music." But there were more mundane reasons. Naples was the largest city in Italy and the residence of a rich aristocracy, many soldiers, clerics, merchants, and foreigners. A large, diverse public was available to be entertained. The viceroyal court, many aristocratic households, and the city's countless churches, convents, and monasteries employed musicians of all sorts. Opera had started in Naples around 1650 at the viceroyal court, and many commercial theaters operated by the late seventeenth century; by the turn of the eighteenth century several stages offered theater in the local dialect. The first great southern composer, Alessandro Scarlatti (1660–1725), directed music and wrote scores of operas for the viceroyal court from the 1680s onward.

There were four conservatories in Naples, founded in the sixteenth century and devoted originally to the care of orphans. Conservatories were supported by the city's elites and by the royal and municipal governments and were part of the proliferation of charitable institutions in Counter-Reformation Naples. Music education was one of the opportunities conservatories offered their wards to develop skills that might earn them an honest living. By the mid-seventeenth century this had become the main focus of the four schools, which began to attract boarders and regular students, in addition to taking in orphans. Boy singers were in especially high demand to fulfill the needs of sacred and secular musical events in the city. The Naples conservatories flourished. Operas were performed in them beginning at the end of the seventeenth century, and in the course of the eighteenth century over forty future opera composers studied at these institutions.

Interior of the San Carlo theater, first built in 1737

In 1709 the first comic opera in Neapolitan dialect was produced in a theater (the first one in a private home was given in 1706). Soon three theaters specializing in comic opera operated in the city. The advent in 1734 of Charles of Bourbon opened up new opportunities for the cultural and musical life of the city. In 1737 the splendid theater of San Carlo—named after the king's patron saint—was built adjacent to the royal palace. This large horseshoe-shaped theater seated twenty-five hundred people, had six rows of boxes, and soon attracted courtiers, aristocrats, and travelers. The San Carlo was devoted to the performance of serious opera, but added enormously to the overall musical life of the city. Its musical productions became an obligatory stop on the Grand Tour. All the star singers of the century sang at the San Carlo, and foreigners flocked to admire them, even though most northern Europeans were shocked by the castrati who still dominated serious opera.

Initially, the audience for comic opera was different from that for serious opera. King Charles never attended the comic opera, and foreigners—because of the dialect and the lower technical level of the performers—also stayed away from it. But by the 1750s comic opera was recognized as a major form of musical expression, and both courtiers and foreigners attended its performances. Ferdinand IV attended comic opera productions and had many staged in the small theater in the royal palace.

The earliest examples of comic opera, in Naples and elsewhere, were short pieces, sometimes performed as intermission features during serious works. Such *intermezzi* continued to be produced throughout the century. Pergolesi's *La serva padrona* (Maid Mistress) of 1733, probably the best-known comic work to come out of Naples, was originally an intermezzo. Pergolesi (1710–36), though born in central Italy, came to Naples in 1726 to study in one of the conservatories and spent most of his short career in the city. His lovely two-character piece, in which a curmudgeonly bachelor realizes he loves his pert, bossy maid and ends up marrying her, sparked the Enlightenment debate about theater that raged in Paris in 1752–54 and is known as the *Querelle des Bouffons*. This was a heated pamphlet war in which Rousseau and others attacked serious French opera as artificial and unnatural in comparison to the grace, lightness, and simplicity of Pergolesi's work and to what they saw as the artless melody of the Italian language. The Paris Opéra orchestra burned Rousseau in effigy in the Opéra courtyard, but the dispute was crucial in advancing new ideas about both theater and opera—all thanks to a little comic intermezzo from Naples.

As the genre developed, comic operas in Naples came to consist of full sung-through theatrical works, most often in two acts. Apart from simple plots and situations, the stories often involved, for comic effect, regional types, as well as disguises, children, silly servants, or odd costumes. As the audience became more aristocratic, the genre lost some of its more popular aspects. By the 1730s only servants and other purely comical characters sang in dialect. The main characters began to resemble the sentimental bourgeois families of Enlightenment drama. A few eccentricities and foibles remained as the source of what dramatic and comic tension the plots required, but the fundamental goodness and nobility of sentiment of everyone were rarely to be doubted. Farcical elements gradually disappeared. With time, solo arias regained some of their primacy, especially to express the more tender feelings or nobler emotions of more serious characters (such as young but pure lovers or respectable parents), but comic opera remained much more varied and dynamic than the rigid serious genre. Orchestral music also acquired a more prominent role, especially in overtures and ensembles.

A good example of a comic opera on the Neapolitan model and by a southern composer is *La Cecchina, o sia la buona figliola* (Cecchina, or The Good Girl), by Niccolò Piccinni (1728–1800), which premiered in Rome in February of 1760 and enjoyed enormous success: it was the most performed opera of the 1760s across Europe. The libretto was by Carlo Goldoni (1707–93), a great Venetian playwright who reformed Italian comedy to make it simpler and worthier of the esteem of moralists and serious writers. The story of *Cecchina* is loosely based on Samuel Richardson's novel *Pamela, or Virtue Rewarded* (1740), whose protagonist, a virtuous maid who resists the advances of her master and is rewarded by his final agreement to respect her purity and marry her, was one of the first sentimental heroines of the century. *Cecchina* includes standard elements of the genre: tearful, noble melodies for the main characters, envious and mischievous servants, proud noblemen, lively ensemble scenes. The opera also revised the story to make its happy ending more acceptable to socially conscious Italian audiences. Unlike Pamela's in the novel, Cecchina's master is virtuous from the start, and the "good girl" is discovered at the end to be in fact the lost daughter of a noble German colonel. This allows both for a comic German soldier (who sings with a funny German accent) and for an indisputably suitable marriage at the end.

Comic opera appealed to the Enlightenment ideals of nature, reasonableness, and sensibility. Yet, somewhat paradoxically, over the course of the century comic opera actually moved even farther than its serious counterpart from the focus on the text. Purely musical effects—stuttering, panting, fast repeated sounds, nonsense words, exaggerated vocal leaps—developed as comic features. In ensembles the words became wholly unintelligible. Comic opera developed a strictly musical language, autonomous from the text, and thus a truly independent musical theater—discarding, after almost two centuries, opera's initial goal and pretense of being a form of theater in which music played just a secondary and supporting role.

Thus, comic opera, born and shaped in Naples more than anywhere else, played a central role in the changes in theater and music that reflected Enlightenment values. In fact, the reform of serious opera that took place in the last third of the century borrowed many of its components from comic opera: the decline of virtuoso solo singing (and the gradual disappearance of the castrati), the increase in ensemble and choral parts, and the larger role of the orchestra. Comic opera shaped the transition from Baroque opera to the nineteenth-century model with which most people are familiar today. At the end of the eighteenth century, Italian comic opera on the Neapolitan model was the most successful form of opera in Europe. When Mozart and his Italian librettist wrote *Così fan tutte* (So Do They All, 1790), one of the century's few operas not based on a preexisting text, they set the action in Naples, the natural home of comic opera. Many of Mozart's operatic rivals were, in fact, southern composers: besides Piccinni, other southerners at the pinnacle of the cosmopolitan opera world included Niccolò Jommelli (1714–74), Tommaso Traetta (1727–79), Giovanni Paisiello (1740–1816), and Domenico Cimarosa (1749–1801). In Vienna in February of 1792 the latter's *Matrimonio segreto* (Secret Marriage) had what is likely to remain the greatest opening night of any opera, as it was encored in its entirety immediately after its first performance.

Thus, throughout the century Naples was closely identified with opera and song. In the entry on "genius" in his 1768 *Dictionary of Music*, Rousseau urged young musicians to "run, fly to Naples." The visit to Naples by Charles Burney, one of the greatest musicologists of the time, is typical of what the city offered to tourists and music lovers. Burney spent a remarkably busy three weeks there in the fall of 1770. Like any proper tourist, he visited the Phlegrean region, Pompeii (which gave him "more pleasure than any antiquities [he] ever saw"), Herculaneum, and the collection of antiquities in Portici; he ascended Vesuvius; he dined with English and French residents of Naples; he admired the views from everywhere and the "bustle and business" of the city; he visited churches and saw the royal palace and art collections at Capodimonte. He also did his musical homework. Burney visited the conservatories and inquired into their curriculum and methods. He attended operas in three different theaters, including the San Carlo, a "noble and elegant structure." He listened to music in churches and private homes and was especially intrigued by Neapolitan street musicians. Finally, he met composers, singers, instrumentalists, and music scholars.

By the 1790s financial and political crisis had weakened the Naples conservatories. The cultural climate of the city became stricter as a result of revolutionary events. Fewer composers came out of the local schools and theaters, and fewer visitors came to the city. Still, however, there were three opera houses. The San Carlo remained one of the greatest theaters in Europe, and it was rebuilt after a fire destroyed it in 1816 (astonishingly, reconstruction took less than a year). Rossini was based at San Carlo in 1815–22. Famous works such as Donizetti's *Lucia di Lammermoor* (1835) and Verdi's *Luisa Miller* (1849) continued to premiere there. Bellini, Donizetti (sixteen of whose operas premiered in Naples), and Verdi, all from other parts of Italy, were eager to have their works produced in Naples. Censorship grew with the 1830s. After the political troubles of 1848, the resources for culture decreased and the Bourbon government regarded all artistic expressions with suspicion. After Naples ceased to be a capital city, the San Carlo slid further into the ranks of ordinary opera theaters. But for over one hundred years, music lovers had found in Naples one of Europe's greatest musical cities.

Antiquity, music, and natural phenomena were thus the most prominent attractions Naples offered to foreigners. Sir William and Lady Emma Hamilton embodied this world of cultural contacts and in their remarkable lives came to personify the attractions of the South. William (1730–1803) came to Naples as the British ambassador in 1764, was knighted in 1772, and stayed in Naples nearly to the end of his life. He was a discerning art collector and dealer: when he left the city in 1798, his palace held over 340 paintings, one-fifth of which represented southern locations or scenes. Moreover, Hamilton was a skilled violinist and gathered musicians and music lovers in his home, where the first Lady Hamilton presided over weekly concerts.

Hamilton was also a talented amateur scientist and joined the Royal Society in 1767. He set up an observatory in his villa in Portici to study Vesuvius and in 1769 he climbed Aetna. In 1776 he published *Campi Phlaegrei*, an illustrated guide to the volcanic phenomena of southern Italy. He saw volcanoes neither as a symbol of hell, as they had been seen in the previous century, nor through a Romantic sensitivity as images of the sublime powers of nature. Rather, he studied and presented them purely as scientific phenomena. He also published a thorough report on the 1783 earthquake. An amateur botanist, Hamilton urged and aided the Naples royals to develop an English garden in the new palace at Caserta.

Hamilton's even greater accomplishment was as a scholar of antiquity. He owned the largest collection of Greek vases in Europe and between 1767 and 1776 published an illustrated survey of his collection that greatly spread knowledge of these works across Europe. In 1781 Hamilton publicized his discovery of the long-standing practice, in the church of Sts. Cosmas and Damian in the small mountain town of Isernia, of presenting wax phalluses as votive offerings to local shrines. Here, confirming all English preconceptions of Catholicism, was proof of its pagan basis and evidence of the link of southern culture to ancient traditions. Hamilton bought the phalluses and donated them to the British Museum. This donation and his publications—all of them quite expensive to produce—show Hamilton's vision of his role as a cultural mediator.

Hamilton's fame as a cuckold sadly trumps all these achievements. Amy Lyon, the daughter of an English blacksmith who soon renamed herself Emma Hart (ca. 1765–1815), became in her teens the mistress of Charles Greville, an impoverished English gentleman. When in 1786 Greville's debts mounted beyond repair, he appealed for relief to his uncle, the widowed Sir William, who paid off his nephew's debts and received fair Emma as compensation for his pains. Greville assured his uncle that he had never had a "sweeter and cleaner" bed partner than Emma. She took Naples by storm. Goethe wrote that Sir William "has now after many years of devotion to the arts and the study of nature, found the acme of these delights in the person of an English girl of twenty with a beautiful face and a perfect figure. He has had a Greek costume made for her which becomes her extremely. . . . In her, he has found all the antiquities, all the profiles of Sicilian coins, even the Apollo Belvedere."

The illusion wore off quickly for Goethe, who later referred to Emma as a "soulless beauty" and "frankly, a dull creature." However, Sir William—"this friend of art and girlhood"—made of Emma his muse and the embodiment of what northern Europeans admired in the South. Attired as an ancient goddess, she danced and sang for his guests. He had her painted over fifty times, often in ancient garb, by the major artists of the time: Emma was the most portrayed woman of her era, more than any queen. In 1791 Hamilton married her.

Emma thus entered the court world as the Naples monarchy increasingly relied on British support in the revolutionary 1790s. When in 1798 Admiral Horatio Nelson (1758–1805) came to Naples after the Egyptian campaign against France, Emma threw him a birthday party with eighteen hundred guests and danced one of her ancient dances for him. The ancient dance led to timeless pursuits, which Sir William seems to have accepted with remarkable outward equanimity. When the scandal of the liaison between Emma and the admiral became excessive for the staid Naples court, the trio returned to England, where they carried on with their arrangement, in spite of Nelson's wife's remonstrances. Emma's daughter Horatia bore in her name her adulterous parentage. After both men died, Emma squandered what she had inherited from both, was briefly jailed for debts, and died in penury in Calais. For over a decade, Emma had turned her ability to go native—to be more ancient and musical than any Neapolitan—into success and fame. While, in Goethe's judgment, her musicianship was dubious, she fully understood the local color.

Local color was the final attraction the South offered in spades. The city of Naples, the first and main location of most visits, was a shocking sight, even for those inured to Paris or London. It was not just large and crowded; it was noisy, chaotic, dirty, and full of people running hither and thither, shouting, begging, fighting, and—most remarkable to northern Europeans—wildly gesticulating. This "infernal movement," as Brosses called it, made the first and most lasting impression. Saint-Non developed this image:

> [H]owever large the streets may be, they are so cluttered, so noisy, the multiplied gestures and the turbulent pantomime of passions throw so much movement and activity in them, that one has to collect oneself for a moment in order to discern anything. . . . [Gestures] are so diverse, so characteristic, so dedicated to each movement of the passions, that, if one had a perfect knowledge of their expressions, one could from sight alone and without the aid of hearing

City Plan of Naples, print from the *Voyage pittoresque* of Saint-Non (1781–86)

follow the animated conversation of two Neapolitans. . . . [In via Toledo] coaches, surreys, pedestrians, people on horseback, a populace excessively screaming and gesticulating, make a *brouhaha* that Paris cannot surpass, or perhaps even equal.

Goethe also found that "lively gestures" gave "such extraordinary fascination" to southern speech. Some years later, the French novelist Stendhal called via Toledo "the busiest, most joyful thoroughfare in the entire universe."

It was not the city's buildings that foreigners admired. Taste had changed since the previous century. The architecture of Naples now displeased visitors used to simpler, more refined beauty, and to more open, regular urban spaces. The Baroque excess and ornamentation earlier visitors had praised was now criticized. In 1728 Montesquieu noted that in Naples "it is easier to spoil one's taste than to form it" and that one could see the city "in two minutes." Winckelmann, the greatest European advocate of Neoclassicism, lamented that "Neapolitans generally are mortal enemies of any straight line. They are disgusted when it is not divided into curves of various sorts that form varied angles." This negative judgment was embraced by enlightened Neapolitans themselves, one of whom wrote in 1765 that the "bad taste" of the city's buildings was caused by "the natural awkwardness of Neapolitans, who incline to ostentation, but without elegance."

But this distaste was closely linked with the attraction of the city. Naples was exciting: from Brosses in 1739 to Stendhal in 1817, visitors noted that it was the only Italian city that looked and felt like a capital; no other city in the peninsula approached it in size, variety, or cultural life—certainly not Rome, where the papal court imposed a provincial and moralistic atmosphere. Naples was vulgar and fascinating in its difference from the elegant cities of northern Europe. Increasingly one finds mentions of Naples's Asian or African character. The city, and even more so its inhabitants, were simply not European; at least they were not like anything or anybody in northwestern Europe. One traveled there to visit the ancient sites that were the cradle of European civilization and of European taste, to experience being in the places ancient authors had celebrated; one also found superb musical performances and cosmopolitan intellectuals. All these features that foreigners prized made the contrast with the physical experience of the city and its people all the more intriguing and, depending on the visitor's temperament, appalling or appealing.

What gave Naples its special character was its people, their behavior, their temperament. Travelers noted the theatrical, competitive, performance aspects of Neapolitan popular life, and marveled at its loud, external character. "Naples"—Goethe found—"proclaims herself from the first as gay, free, and alive." Most foreigners explained the southern temperament through the climate they admired so much: Neapolitans were sunny, happy, and naturally given to song because they lived amidst such natural warmth and plenty. They were lazy and lively because they needed little work to survive, because they lived outdoors most of the year, and because the sun and the sea always smiled on them in what Saint-Non called the "garden of Europe."

This was, of course, a cliché, but a powerful one. It was especially applied to the Neapolitan lower classes, known as *lazzari*. The term was originally worrisome: the lazzari formed the urban mobs whose violent excesses in 1585 and 1647 echoed across Europe. In 1739 Brosses referred to them as "the most abominable canaille, the most disgusting vermin that ever crawled on the face of the earth." But over the course of the eighteenth century, the term, and the men it identified, became tamer, at least in the eyes of visitors. Foreigners were fond of imagining that the lazzari formed a sort of parallel society, with its own institutions and leaders, and this too shaped a less frightening image. The resigned submissiveness of the crowds during the 1764 famine contributed to this more benign view. The gentle sentiments of comic opera also helped change the perception of Neapolitans from troublesome rebels to wistful folk who gracefully and even wisely enjoyed life. Visitors observed the wild behavior of lower-class Neapolitans—the street fights, the insults, the shouting, the sexual ardor, the forceful dialect, the passionate gestures—but with more fascination than fear. Lalande noted that murders were rare and that "Neapolitans scream a lot and threaten each other constantly, in a tone that makes one fear for their life, but this rarely has effects; they make much noise and little evil." Even petty crime, though a nuisance, was hardly a great danger. Burney almost admired the pickpocket who stole his handkerchief: "the pickpockets of Italy as the politicians . . . are superior in subtilty to those of other countries."

Eighteenth-century visitors to Naples developed an image that in later times—from the Romantics to novelists like E. M. Forster—northern Europeans would apply to all Italians: lazy but violent, joyful, sexually passionate and omnivorous, primitive, extroverted. Most visitors sentimentalized these traits as those of simple, happy savages. Saint-Non wrote, "[V]ery little-dressed, [lazzari] feed on fish and dry legumes, have no property and want none, sleep outdoors . . . and pass thus their life sweetly without cares or thoughts." Neapolitans were easy to quarrel but also gregarious and quick to reconcile. Everything that happened in the street immediately became everyone's concern. The popular masked theater character Pulcinella—a foolish but witty layabout, always hungry for maccheroni—embodied the foreign image of lower-class Naples. More thoughtful observers like Goethe realized that the lazzari worked hard, but he too admired how they "work not merely to *live*, but to *enjoy* themselves." Neapolitans were able to "get the most out of the least" and showed "the most ingenious resource, not in getting rich, but in living free from care"; the city was a "school for easy, happy living." Goethe's admiration is mixed with typical condescension: "[The common people] are like

PULCINELLA

The Neapolitan popular mask Pulcinella, from Francesco de Bourcard,
Usi e costumi di Napoli (1858)

children who, when one gives them a job to do, treat it as a job but at the same time as an opportunity for having some fun. They are lively, open and sharply observant. I am told their speech is full of imagery and their wit trenchant."

Foreigners were aware and critical of bad government in the South, though they tended to blame the old Spanish rule and be optimistic about Bourbon reforms. They also saw the poverty of the crowds and lamented their ignorance, their superstitious faith in miracles and relics, and their wild rituals from funerals to Carnival. But they still found the experience of the city overwhelming and invigorating. The English writer Henry Swinburne in 1780 reversed the common saying "see Naples and then die" and argued rather that "after living in Naples it is impossible not to wish to live that one may return to it." Naples made visitors think differently about their own life and values, led them to reconsider their priorities and appreciate life more fully. Goethe noted that "the longer one stays here, the idler one gets"; he had gladly studied in Rome, but in Naples he wanted "only to live": "Naples is a Paradise: everyone lives in a state of intoxicated self-forgetfulness, myself included. I seem to be a completely different person whom I hardly recognize. Yesterday I thought to myself: either you were mad before, or you are mad now."

Naples dominated the impressions of foreigners; until midcentury, very few dared visit the provinces, where bandits, bad roads, and few decent accommodations awaited. Lalande said he "did not penetrate the interior of the kingdom; rarely do travelers have this curiosity, because the roads are most difficult." To foreigners not used to the countryside of southern Europe, the lack of infrastructure was stunning: as late as 1863, two-thirds of southern villages lacked a paved access road. Sicily was worse. Even King Charles, when he traveled to Sicily for his coronation in 1735, went from Messina to Palermo by sea, because—wrote the later historian Pietro Colletta—"the asperity of the places, void of inhabitants and savage" argued against a land route. The medieval and Baroque architecture that prevailed in provincial towns, even ones more accessible from the coasts like Salerno, Amalfi, and Lecce, also held little interest for Enlightenment travelers with classical tastes. The backwardness of the provinces repelled visitors. The Venetian adventurer Casanova, after an unhappy stay in Calabria in 1743, noted that he met no man "who could boast of writing decently, and still less of any taste . . . there was not a single bookseller"; moreover, "how ugly were the women!" Health was another concern: Messina was the last city in western Europe to experience an epidemic of the plague, in 1747.

For much of the century, rural southerners were regarded simply as barbaric. Neapolitan Enlightenment intellectuals, who themselves rarely visited the distant provinces, deplored the barbarism and backwardness of their rural neighbors. The economist Genovesi noted that on exiting the capital, one encountered Patagonians or Hottentots. Such shocking parallels to faraway savages were meant to call southerners to action and reform. The idea that the farther South one went the more one abandoned Europe was widespread. If in earlier centuries Jesuits had compared the rural masses to the "savages" of the New World, now it became common to regard them as African. A French traveler in 1801 stated that "Europe ends in Naples, and it ends there rather badly. Calabria, Sicily, all the rest, that's Africa." Calabrians and Sicilians had a particular reputation for savagery.

By the 1770s, however, slight improvements in crime control and transportation and a shift in taste brought more foreigners to Paestum and even to Sicily. In these later decades of the century, northern Europeans began to treasure the very primitiveness of the rural South and of its population. Here was a wild world of ancient passions, dramatic landscape, and brooding peasants that appealed to the first stirrings of Romanticism among northern Europeans. The first English Gothic novel, Horace Walpole's *Castle of Otranto* (1764), was set in a highly fictionalized South, as were some of Ann Radcliffe's equally stormy novels from the 1790s.

By the end of the century visitors who ventured into the provinces reported that the rumors of danger were exaggerated. The first extensive descriptions of Sicilian travel appeared in the 1770s. Saint-Non noted the poverty of rural inland areas but described the Calabrians as "happy and peaceful" and praised Sicilian hospitality. Even bandits were sentimentalized, and by the early nineteenth century some foreigners saw them as dashing rebels. The notorious bandit Michele Pezza (1771–1806), who fought against French forces in 1799, even became the subject of a popular French Romantic opera titled after his nickname, Auber's *Fra Diavolo* (1830). Neapolitans themselves continued to regard the rural population with fear and distaste and to describe it as hostile and fierce, but many foreigners found rural people charming and intriguing, though the ferocious acts of rural crowds during the political troubles of 1799 led to some change in that opinion.

A few visitors came to see Sicily as the apex of southernness. Its climate, food, and vegetation were even more beguiling than those of the continental provinces. Its people appeared to be the physical embodiment of the ancients and certainly closer to the Hellenic type than any other people in Europe. Palermo, like Naples, offered tasteless architecture and noisy crowds, but also—wrote Saint-Non—"a warm climate, lively passions, beautiful women, and sybaritic customs: . . . a stay [there] must be agreeable to foreigners." The few who visited rural areas (where the arrival of foreigners "was an event") were stunned by their poverty and had trouble finding decent inns. Unlike in Palermo, the women were homely "because misery is always ugly." But the island's volcanoes and ancient sites (especially Segesta, Taormina, Agrigento) astounded visitors. Lemon and fig trees, and the lush gardens near Palermo, delighted them. Goethe had originally been dubious: "to me Sicily implies Asia and Africa." But, once in "the land where the lemon trees blossom," he concluded that "to have seen Italy without having seen Sicily is not to have seen Italy at all, for Sicily is the clue to everything."

The people and places of the South thus attracted foreigners more and more as the century progressed. Still, travelers retained a negative image of the southerners' character, convinced that the inhabitants of Naples were shockingly immoral, especially in sexual matters. Already in the 1650s James Howell noted that "[t]he Neapolitan being born in a luxurious country is observd to be the greatest embracer of pleasure, the greatest courtier of ladies, and the most indulgent of himself of any other nation." This view was commonplace in the eighteenth century. Even the marquis de Sade—hardly a shrinking violet—claimed in 1776 that the city's corruption and debauchery were "physically impossible to imagine." Public displays of affection and lust troubled foreigners, as did the common sight of kissing or hugging between men. It was probably thrilling to some to find in this yet another element of ancient Greek heritage in southerners, but the overall reaction was negative. While foreigners rarely examined the misery of the urban masses, they deplored the availability of sex for sale.

Sexual immorality was linked to religious deficiencies. Southern religious practices were regarded with disapproval and at times horror. Protestants had always enjoyed finding among Italians the superstitious behavior they associated with Catholicism. As the eighteenth century progressed, even Catholic visitors marked their skepticism and distaste for the emotional, irrational rituals of southerners. Everyone wanted to see the miracle of San Gennaro and to report about it with heavy irony. Brosses noted that "miracles are not a rare merchandise in Naples." Goethe disliked the "tinsel trappings of Catholic worship." When he witnessed Easter rituals in Palermo, he noted that "to ears unaccustomed to such a rowdy worship of God, the noise was quite deafening."

Much of the southerners' behavior was offensive to the moral and aesthetic sensibilities of northern Europeans. Eighteenth-century travelers, much more than their predecessors, analyzed the ways in which southern Italians differed from themselves. As products of the Enlightenment, educated Europeans believed progress to be linear and rational and to follow universal standards. They saw differences between societies as indicators of developmental stages. To travel outward from France or England—the obvious centers of advancing civilization—was also to travel backward in time, to regions and peoples that were not on a different path to progress, but rather were behind on the one, rational path from the state of nature to material and cultural success.

And yet, as the century ended, the primitive southerners became not only a symbol of how far other Europeans had progressed, but also of what they may have lost in the process. Certainly the South was behind in material, economic, and technical advances, and in moral and religious awareness. But southerners were close to the natural world and able to enjoy it. Europeans, at the start of the Romantic movement, were beginning to regret their loss of that closeness to nature. The backwardness of the South was closely linked to its picturesqueness, and it thus afforded an aesthetic pleasure. Southerners were savages, but good—almost noble—ones, and moreover good savages with a special link to the ancient world. Hamilton, when he studied ancient vases and votive phalluses, relished continuities between ancient rituals and the southern culture of his own time. In a later (1832) study, the Neapolitan cleric, archeologist, and museum curator Andrea de Jorio (1769–1851) compared Neapolitan gestures to those he saw on ancient vases and paintings. Neapolitan culture, he concluded, perpetuated ancient life in living, bodily form.

Chapter IX

Feast, Flour, and Gallows
Revolution, Restoration, and the End of a Kingdom

In the Kingdom of the Two Sicilies, in the country known as the Garden of Europe, people are dying of hunger and live worse than animals, the law itself is caprice, progress is retrogression and barbarization, and in the name of Christ a Christian people is oppressed.

Luigi Settembrini, southern patriot, 1847

In November 1798 the royal army of Naples marched into Rome to fight the Republic just established there by French arms and to restore papal government. The invasion proved disastrous. A satirist said of the king of Naples that "he came, he saw, he fled." French forces followed the defeated Neapolitans back south. On December 23, Ferdinand IV and his court, having stripped the city's banks of their cash and the museums of many precious items, left Naples for Sicily, escorted by British ships. It was the first time the king visited his island realm. Ferdinand left behind as vicar general the old aristocrat Francesco Pignatelli, but as French forces approached, the political situation in Naples quickly collapsed into chaos. On January 16, 1799, Pignatelli also fled to Palermo.

On January 22 local republican groups gained control of Castel Sant'Elmo and proclaimed the Neapolitan Republic. Thus, on the next day, the French entered Naples as protectors and not as conquerors, as they had done in Rome and elsewhere in Italy. The Republic produced a flurry of reforms and debates, but its life was short. By June 1799 a mostly peasant army brought back the monarchy. The divisions that exploded in those few months shaped the rest of the existence of the South as an independent political entity.

The leaders of the 1799 Republic embodied both the achievements and the limits of the southern Enlightenment. Most were young lawyers, scholars, journalists, noblemen, or clerics, all imbued with reform ideas. Since 1789 they had watched with dismay as the monarchy, nervous about the progress of the revolution in France, suppressed the discussions that had flourished in previous decades, halted all reforms, and executed young radicals. The soon-to-be republicans embraced French Jacobin principles of rule of law, free press, equality of opportunity, and a secular state. They believed that they could alleviate the disgraceful poverty of the rural masses; bring modern constitutional government, rational administration, and fair justice to the South; and earn the trust and love of their fellow citizens.

Yet the Republic dramatically failed to accomplish its goals. Debates over the constitution dragged on, reform of the feudal system remained incomplete, political divisions proliferated. More dangerously, the Republic never developed loyal military forces independent of French support and never established control of most provinces. Counterrevolutionary insurrections and conspiracies flared up across the South. Already on February 7 Cardinal Fabrizio Ruffo (1744–1827), from a prominent aristocratic family, landed in Calabria and gathered a monarchist army. The Holy Faith Army, as it became known, attracted peasants and provincials and steadily advanced on the capital. The British fleet blockaded the Bay of Naples and helped strangle the Republic. In late April most French forces were recalled by the Paris government. On June 21 republican leaders surrendered, accepting Ruffo's promise that they would be allowed to leave for France.

Vincenzo Cuoco (1770–1823) participated in the Republic and from exile tried to make sense of its failure. His *Historical Essay on the Revolution of Naples* (1800) offers a severe and poignant analysis of the republicans' aspirations, merits, and flaws. Cuoco's main argument is that the revolution never managed to expand its ideas and values past the narrow intellectual, urban elite of the Jacobins. He rejected the rationalist approach of his revolutionary friends, who argued that French ideas and institutions reflected universally applicable principles of reason and justice and should thus be followed in

Naples. Instead, Cuoco believed that each nation through its history acquires a specific character, and that only institutions and government practices suited to each people's particular nature will gain the loyalty of citizens. Moreover, no revolution imported from abroad could succeed: "vainly one founds a republic in a nation which constantly needs the help and protection of another." This focus on history and nature and on the specific character of each nation was typical of the budding Romantic movement, and it made Cuoco's essay—soon translated into several languages—influential in the following decades.

Cuoco saw the southern masses as passive in regard to the revolution occurring in Naples with French support: "a revolution cannot be made without the people, and the people are moved not by rationality, but by need. The needs of the Neapolitan nation were different from those of the French." The monarchy's senseless repression in the 1790s made French ideas attractive to southern intellectuals. Cuoco despised the royal government, which suppressed the best elements among the population and kept the masses "without jobs and without education." Even after the court fled, however, the people "still loved their religion, loved their country, and hated the French." Cuoco's main point was the unbridgeable separation between masses and intellectuals, the product of centuries of southern history:

> The views of the patriots and those of the people were not the same; they had different ideas, different habits and even two different languages. . . . The Neapolitan nation can be seen as divided into two peoples, different by two centuries of time and two degrees of climate. Since the learned part had been raised on foreign models, its culture differed from what the entire nation needed, which could only be hoped for in the development of our own talents. . . . Thus the culture of few had not profited the entire nation; and the latter, in turn, almost despised a culture for which it had no use, and which it did not understand.

Mutual misunderstanding and lack of respect was the root of the Republic's failure: "we cannot profit our country if we do not love it, and we can never love our country if we do not esteem its people."

Thus Cuoco explained the failure of the ambitious reform program of the republicans. Their focus on abstract principles—freedom of opinion, freedom of religion—meant little to the poor. The very language of republican laws and proclamations, with its references to reason and ancient history, was alien to uneducated masses that needed to improve their material lives. The abolition of the feudal system, which might have earned the Republic the loyalty of the peasantry, was delayed by debates about how much feudal land to leave to the barons, and never implemented. Efforts to diminish clerical wealth, which answered long-standing needs, became unpopular when the republican government tied them to reforms of Catholic practices. Changing the names of streets to reflect revolutionary values, redrawing provincial boundaries according to abstract geometry, and adopting the French revolutionary calendar were other policies that sacrificed southern history to French models. Naples neighborhoods gained names such as Masaniello, Giannone, and Humanity, but this hardly endeared the Republic to the masses. The diarist Carlo de Nicola noted that "the government and the French do not know how to make people love the revolution." As the months passed and the threat from counterrevolutionary forces increased, the government engaged in harsh, but ultimately futile, repression that further tainted it in the eyes of the Naples masses.

Especially harmful, as in the 1647 revolt, was the failure to link republican interests in the capital with provincial concerns. Early on, several provincial towns joined the revolution: they erected liberty trees, proclaimed the Republic, and adopted its flag and calendar. But these rituals and symbols could not command the loyalty of most provincial and rural people. Often, local contrasts exacerbated the conflict between republicans and monarchists. The crisis of feudal authority opened the way to the expression of violent rural animosities. Though some clerics supported the Republic, the irreligion ascribed to republicans was particularly unpopular. Myths emerged to express celestial opposition to the Republic: crucifixes and statues of the Virgin or saints discharged sweat or blood to mark their displeasure; when the liberty tree was erected in Lecce, a nearby statue of St. Oronzo, the city's main patron, "turned its face the other way and raised a leg . . . as if to leave." Even San Gennaro got into trouble for his alleged support of the Republic (his blood performed the usual miracle under the Republic): after the return of the monarchy, the residents of one of Naples's poorest streets displayed an image of

Gennaro being beaten by St. Anthony, the patron saint of the Holy Faith Army.

Cuoco criticized the patriots' intellectual and political failings. Yet he admired their love of country, their selfless, if misguided, concern for those they governed, and their courage. Their views may not always have been practical, but under the Republic fervent discussions and progressive ideas enlivened Naples and other cities. Projects for public education, the opening of clubs and associations for political debates, and the printing of texts in dialect to explain government initiatives attest to the patriots' sincere effort to reach the masses they aimed to serve. Individual leaders exhibited the grand noble behavior they had learned in their classical educations. Aristocratic officers such as Admiral Francesco Caracciolo eagerly served the Republic. Mario Pagano, the last of the great southern Enlightenment jurists, drafted a new constitution and aimed to make the justice system free of cost to all. The young lawyer and political philosopher Vincenzio Russo—about whom Cuoco wrote that "it was impossible to push love of country and virtue farther than he did"—was the greatest orator of the Republic. They and many others faced execution stoically.

Ruffo's Holy Faith Army, on the other hand, embodied what Cuoco saw as the worst elements of southern society as it had developed during centuries of poverty and oppression: "impunity, theft, looting, easy promises, superstitious fanaticism, all contributed to increase [Ruffo's] followers." The advance of Ruffo's forces through the kingdom was marked by great violence. The bishop of Potenza, who supported the Republic, was murdered in his see at the end of February and his severed head paraded through his town; many other clerics and administrators met similar fates. By April the republican government lost control of most provinces. British ships led by Admiral Nelson patrolled the coasts. British, Russian, and even a few Turkish troops assisted Ruffo's advance (thus, none of the Holy Faith's foreign allies were Catholic). Ruffo's army entered Naples on June 13 (the day of St. Anthony). One of his officers, Domenico Pietromasi, wrote that Neapolitans, in seeing the "respectful manner" of the Russians and "the serious but handsome English," were "universally pleased." But what de Nicola called "the horrors of popular anarchy" quickly began. The Republic's leaders and the remaining French forces took refuge in the city's castles, while Ruffo tolerated an explosion of popular fury against republicans: Cuoco commented that "the Neapolitan people . . . committed acts of barbarism that make one shudder."

Ruffo and foreign representatives guaranteed the conditions under which the republicans surrendered on June 21, but the court refused to abide by those terms. The queen urged Lady Hamilton to "recommend Lord Nelson to treat Naples as if it were a rebellious city in Ireland." Nelson, Cuoco wrote, "prostituted his honor, the honor of his arms, the honor of his nation"; Cuoco also quoted one of Nelson's aides as writing, "[W]e commit the most horrible infamies to put the stupidest of kings back on his throne." With British support, the court unleashed a severe repression. Thousands of people were jailed, including 132 ecclesiastics. Thousands fled or were exiled, many were summarily killed. One hundred and twenty people were executed in Naples and 50 more in the provinces. The 120 included 13 nobles, 26 lawyers and jurists, 10 priests, 1 bishop, 6 other clerics, 16 university professors, 17 military officers, but only 7 artisans and 1 farmer.

Two of the executed were women. Eleonora Pimentel Fonseca was a committed revolutionary and editor of the most prominent republican newspaper, the *Neapolitan Monitor*, "from which"—Cuoco wrote—"breezes the purest and most ardent love of country." The second woman was Luisa Sanfelice, a somewhat more reluctant heroine. Through one of her admirers, Luisa learned of a monarchist conspiracy against the Republic. She passed the information on to another suitor, who reported it to the authorities. Luisa's role was heralded in the *Monitor*, but it cost her a death sentence at the monarchy's return. By feigning pregnancy, Luisa managed to delay her execution until September of 1800 and became the last victim of the repression.

A generation of the intellectual elites was decimated. Two-thirds of those exiled were under thirty-five years old. Cuoco celebrated the heroism of the victims: "We have suffered the gravest woes; but we have also given the greatest examples of virtue. A just posterity will forget the errors committed, as men, by those to whom the Republic was entrusted: but among them it will vainly seek a coward, a traitor. Here is what we must expect from men, and here is what forms their glory." In addition to the human and material costs of the failed revolution, Cuoco lamented "the loss of all principles, the corruption of all customs," and "a court which from now on regards the nation as alien, and which believes that it can find its own safety in the misery and ignorance of its people." The rupture between the monarchy and the progressive elements of the population was complete and poisoned subsequent political and intellectual developments in the South. In 1999, the bicentennial of the Republic produced a flood of scholarly and popular writings celebrating the "martyrs of 1799" as the South's last, failed chance for a better history.

Ferdinand IV stayed only briefly in Naples after the end of the Republic, purged the administration of republican sympathizers, and showered his supporters with gifts. In September, at a lavish party in the Palermo royal palace called "Nelson's Triumph," the king gave the English admiral the laurel crown of victory and a diamond-studded sword that had belonged to Charles III. Chaos continued in both the capital and the provinces for well over a year, however, as royalist troops, bandits, and lawless police looted and raided with impunity. Prisons overflowed and violence was common across society. In December of 1799, de Nicola noted that "the populace is ever more insolent and unchecked, thieving and murderous." The government wavered between repression, concessions, and suspicions of everyone, especially military officers. In 1803 the government set up the police, which until then depended on different tribunals, as an autonomous agency. A holding pattern prevailed: the few remaining progressive elements of the Naples elites were hostile to the monarchy, and the reform projects of the previous century were either irrelevant now or tainted in the monarchy's eyes by the recent events. The court did not even return to Naples from Sicily until the summer of 1802.

The monarchy saw the events of 1799 as a betrayal by the nobility and intellectuals. The reaction was to expand absolutist policies, punish the nobility, and suppress intellectual freedom. In 1800 the monarchy abolished the old Seggi, the municipal government of Naples dominated by the city's nobles. Abolition of the feudal system was halted, but fiscal pressure on feudal estates grew considerably. The government strengthened censorship and granted the Church broad control over education and culture, arrested another eleven university professors, and raided and shut down bookshops. Artists and writers sympathetic to the Republic were punished. Earlier laws limiting ecclesiastic privileges and wealth were repealed or weakened. In 1804 the Jesuits returned to the kingdom, recalled by the same monarch who had expelled them in 1767.

In the meantime, the international context shifted dramatically. By the end of 1799 Napoleon ruled France and soon French power grew again in northern Italy. In 1801 the southern kingdom had to give up the Presidii, the bases on the Tuscan coast that Naples had controlled since the sixteenth century. Napoleon also demanded that Ferdinand grant an amnesty and allow the return of many exiles. At the end of 1805 Napoleon resoundingly defeated Austria and the latter withdrew its forces from northern Italy. Napoleon was king of Italy and master of all territory north of Rome. In November of 1805 the Naples court allowed British and Russian forces to return to the kingdom, violating its pledges of neutrality. Napoleon declared that "the existence [of the Naples Bourbons] is incompatible with the peace of Europe and the honor of my crown." French forces moved toward the kingdom. On January 24, 1806, the court again sailed for Sicily, and on February 14 the French were back in Naples.

This time things were different. France was more powerful, more moderate and stable, and more interested in dominion over all of Italy to pursue Napoleon's fight against Britain. The Kingdom of Naples maintained its autonomy but received a new king, Napoleon's brother Joseph. When France conquered Spain in 1808 and Joseph moved to the Spanish throne, Joachim Murat, one of Napoleon's finest generals and husband of his sister Caroline, came to reign in Naples. Britain's navy defended Sicily, and British and Sicilian forces held a few towns in Calabria and the island of Capri in the Bay of Naples until 1808, but the French controlled the continental South. Though unrest and banditry persisted, most peasants, clerics, and provincials acquiesced to French rule. Murat ruled Naples until 1815.

The French Decennio (decade) transformed administration, justice, and social and economic structures in the South. In 1806, still over 70 percent of the southern population outside of Naples was subject to feudal jurisdiction and frequent abuse. Confusing institutions, overlapping jurisdictions, and widespread venality characterized royal justice and government. The old ideas of the Neapolitan Enlightenment were insufficient to confront these problems. The

Antonio Calliano, *Portrait of Joachim Murat, King of Naples, with a View of Vesuvius* (1813)

French brought coherent approaches and ambitious reforms to most aspects of southern life. Their reforms would modernize the southern state and largely survive the return of the Bourbons.

One of the first and most significant reforms was the abolition of the feudal system, decreed on August 2, 1806. After seven centuries, feudal dues, monopolies, rights, and jurisdictions ended. Full private property of land became the norm and a free market for land developed. The reform did not, however, primarily benefit the poorer peasantry. Old feudal domains, which in many villages were open to partial use by villagers as pastures, woods, or meadows, were now divided up and distributed among village residents. These divisions, controversial and managed by local leaders, often increased the holdings of local elites and deprived landless peasants of an important communal resource. The most common result was the strengthening of the rural bourgeoisie, which controlled local offices and became the dominant social group in the southern countryside. The misery of the rural masses persisted.

The old aristocracy lost its feudal powers but kept its old estates and gained as full property a share of the old feudal domains. The separate noble orders that used to dominate municipal government in Naples and other cities no longer existed. Yet the hereditary nobility remained a prominent social group and continued during the Decennio to occupy most leadership positions in the armed forces and in provincial administration. Murat granted offices to members of the traditional nobility and bestowed new titles of nobility on loyal members of the Naples elites. Overall, the Decennio accelerated the integration of the old nobility with rising elements of the administrative, business, and landowning elites.

The main features of the administrative model implemented during the Decennio were centralization and uniformity. The kingdom was divided into fifteen provinces of roughly equal size, modeled on French departments. The city of Naples lost its administrative uniqueness and became part of one of the provinces. The government appointed provincial intendants who implemented uniform administrative practices, central methods of tax collection and record keeping, and, in 1811, the decimal system. Old organs of government were abolished and replaced with a central, professional bureaucracy. The central government's activities were organized around new ministries (such as Justice or Interior) on the French model. Record keeping and information gathering improved. In 1811–12 the Interior Ministry conducted a general inquiry on the population and economy of the kingdom.

Property replaced rank as the central element in determining participation in public life. All Napoleonic governments regarded propertied social groups as the necessary backbone of the state. From the smallest village to Naples itself, communes were managed by councils and mayors selected from men with incomes above set minimums. Similar criteria were used for members of provincial councils. This system was quite innovative but remained problematic in small communes, where most residents were poor and illiterate. Propertied men and craftsmen formed new urban and provincial militias, based again on French models and charged with domestic order and defense. Property also became the basis of the fiscal system. The old head tax was abolished. A uniform tax on real estate was established, for the first time applying equally to property held by nobles and clerics, though insufficient records created opportunities for fraud. Some indirect taxes (and royal monopolies on salt and tobacco) remained, but the old system of tax farms was abolished. Tax farms and other forms of public income held by private investors represented the enormous public debt left by the Bourbons—over 100 million ducats. The new government sold public assets and expropriated Church assets to put public finances on a healthier footing. Noble and wealthy bourgeois families acquired the lion's share of these assets. By 1813 Murat managed to balance the budget.

In 1809 a wholesale reform of the justice system removed the fragmentation of jurisdictions characteristic of the old regime. Special commissions dealt with the backlog of trials and prisoners that had grown since 1799. Justices of the peace adjudicated small cases at the local level to diminish the work and slowness of tribunals and to bring justice closer to the masses. The Justice Ministry organized the various appeals levels and enacted new judicial procedures. Trials were now public, with open questioning of accusers, defendants, and witnesses. In a major shift from traditional procedure, the police function of investigating crimes and gathering clues was separated from the judicial function of assessing evidence and conducting trials. The Napoleonic Code was enacted in 1809 and a new code of civil procedure, also based on French models, followed in 1812. A remarkable novelty was the introduction of divorce. Only criminal procedure remained different from France, as in Naples there was no trial by jury. Government leaders, with the typical paternalism of the time toward the southern rural masses, believed that, especially in the countryside, widespread illiteracy and profound economic differences and social animosities made the introduction of juries dangerous and unworkable.

Government attention also targeted cultural and intellectual life. At the end of the eighteenth century the royal government had begun promoting geographic research, mostly for military purposes, and produced atlases of the kingdom and its coasts. In 1801 a Mineralogy Museum had opened to foster the economic development of the kingdom's mining resources. The French expanded these beginnings and sponsored a series of research institutions. The government added a new science faculty to the university and increased the number of professorships. In 1811 an engineering school opened, modeled on the Parisian School of Bridges and Roads. In 1806 the Royal Institute for the Encouragement of the Natural Sciences was founded, and in 1810 it gained the right to grant patents; in 1808 the Royal Society began supporting arts, letters, and sciences; in 1809 the Naples Botanical Garden, still today the largest in Italy, opened to the public; in 1813 the Zoological Museum followed; and in 1812 construction began on the Astronomical Observatory in Capodimonte, next to the royal palace. Scientific journals appeared in Naples during the Decennio and foreign scientists visited the city's new research institutions.

In 1806 the Naples conservatories were united into the Royal College of Music. From 1813, following the model of the French Academy's Prix de Rome, government fellowships supported southern artists who studied classical art and architecture in Rome. Beginning in 1809 the government sponsored yearly exhibitions of "National Industry," mainly consisting of applied arts such as cameos, ceramics, furniture, porcelain, and corals. The latter became a Neapolitan specialty after the first factory opened in 1805 in Torre del Greco, just east of Naples, where coral factories still operate. The French also brought modern European style to Naples. Murat and his wife redecorated the royal palaces in Neoclassical style. When the Bourbons returned, King Ferdinand reportedly praised Murat's taste and declared that the latter would have made a fine interior decorator.

Church wealth and powers decreased. The conservative de Nicola lamented that under the French "religion is in Naples manifestly and deplorably despised." The Jesuits were again expelled. About thirteen hundred monasteries and convents in Naples and across the kingdom were closed, their residents distributed to other religious houses, and their buildings put to public secular use as schools, barracks, factories, or offices. Today the state archive, many university institutes, the morgue, and several hospitals and public schools are located in old religious houses in Naples. The monastery of St. Peter Martyr, now the humanities school of the university, housed the state tobacco factory for many decades. Sale of the property of most religious orders and houses helped pay off the public debt. In 1809 the government began collecting data on births, marriages, and deaths, which for centuries had been the sole responsibility of parish churches. Clerics lost their judicial and fiscal privileges. Murat also encouraged the development of public schools, reducing the Church's traditional control of education. Each commune was required to open a primary school, though usually only for boys.

The new government showed concern for groups traditionally relegated to the margins of society. In 1806 a school for the deaf and mute opened in Naples. In 1813 a new asylum for the insane opened in Aversa, near Naples, where, thanks to new humane methods of care, visitors—wrote Pietro Colletta—"marveled at seeing [the inmates] diligent and tranquil in the ordinary occupations of life." Modern practices came in many forms. Marked street names and numbers were introduced in the capital. Naples also got new streets and bridges: a "Corso Napoleone" bridged the valley between the old center and the hill of Capodimonte, and new streets extended the capital's links with its eastern and western peripheries. In 1806 city streets got their first lights. A public postal system began operating within Naples. In 1813 work began on a new public cemetery, which opened in 1838.

The rule of Joseph Bonaparte and Joachim Murat in Naples thus effected revolutionary changes in administration and justice and increased the wealth and status of a powerful bourgeoisie in both cities and rural areas. The French gained the support of most south-

ern elites and managed to contain popular discontent. Military conscription and the presence of French troops remained unpopular,
however. Increasing fiscal pressure to meet Napoleon's requests for
aid in his wars also made it harder to stabilize the new government.
Murat vainly sought to limit French interference and the privileges for
French industry and trade demanded by Napoleon. In 1812 Murat
accompanied his brother-in-law in the fateful invasion of Russia, but
after the defeat he tried to build an autonomous role for himself and
his kingdom. He negotiated with Austria and Britain and in 1814,
after Napoleon's defeat and first exile, sent troops to join Austria in
expelling the French from northern Italy. But Murat was ultimately
unable to protect his crown. When Napoleon returned to France in
March of 1815, Murat, suspicious of the great powers' plans for
Naples, sided with the emperor and tried to rally Italian liberals
under his leadership. Even before Waterloo, Murat was defeated by
Austrian armies, and in late May he left Naples for France and later
Corsica. On June 17 Ferdinand IV again returned to Naples. In October Murat landed in Calabria with a small force, but he was quickly
arrested, tried, and shot on October 17, 1815. At his execution Murat
allegedly shouted to the soldiers, "Aim for the heart, save the face!"
The line remains famous in Italy because it was parodied by the great
Neapolitan comedian Totò, who in one of his films tells his would-
be executioners, "Aim for the feet, save the guts!"

After Napoleon's defeat, the Congress of Vienna, guided by Austrian
Chancellor Metternich, redrew the map of Europe and tried to bring
back political order and international balance of power. Thus began
the Restoration, an age when all European governments feared revolution and sought to prevent it by repression, censorship, and a
renewed alliance between throne and altar. In France the returning
Bourbon king issued a limited charter that allowed for a parliament
elected by a very narrow franchise. But virtually no other continental
monarchy—and the Swiss were the only Europeans who did not live
under a monarchy—embraced the principle of constitutional government. Even the British government and Parliament, dominated by
aristocratic and landowning interests, regarded political innovation
on the continent as a threat. The leading powers opposed nationalist

ideas and movements. Austria, whose empire encompassed multiple religions, languages, and ethnic groups, was especially fearful of nationalism. Austrian forces guaranteed the stability of the Italian states when their various rulers returned to claim their possessions. Austria directly ruled Venice and Milan; princes from its imperial dynasty ruled in Tuscany, Parma, and Modena; and it was the main ally and protector of the pope and the king of Sardinia. Austria adamantly opposed any talk of Italian unity: as Metternich famously put it, Italy was "but a geographic expression"—a statement every Italian schoolchild to this day learns to resent.

Ferdinand IV returned to Naples with the support of both Austria and Britain. The years spent in Sicily had brought the king some unwelcome developments. No sovereign had resided in Sicily in about four centuries. Ferdinand himself had not bothered to be crowned in Palermo until 1806 (there he was Ferdinand III). The island's nobles enjoyed greater freedom from royal interference and more undisputed power, wealth, and prominence than their counter-parts in the continental South. Royal officials were weaker in Sicily; the Sicilian Parliament, dominated by aristocratic interests, contin-ued to meet; feudal rights and powers were larger. Peasant landown-ership was rare and large feudal estates dominated the economy. Intellectual change during the Enlightenment had been limited. Viceroy Caracciolo in the 1780s had observed that Sicily housed only two groups, the oppressors and the oppressed.

The British presence in Sicily during the Napoleonic period influ-enced Sicilian elite leaders, who pressed Ferdinand to accept a limited monarchy based on the British model, with institutions dominated by the nobility. In 1812, prodded by his British protectors, the king agreed to a constitution for his Sicilian kingdom. This posed a prob-lem when Ferdinand returned to Naples, as he had no desire to extend constitutional government to his mainland realm and indeed objected to the limits imposed on his power by the Sicilian constitu-tion. The solution he found was to join his two kingdoms formally into a new entity, which was proclaimed in 1816 as the Kingdom of the Two Sicilies (some earlier rulers had styled themselves kings of the Two Sicilies, but no kingdom by that name had formally existed). The king even renumbered himself as Ferdinand I, leading critics to mock him in a popular doggerel: "You were the fourth, you were the third, / now you call yourself the first. / If you continue with this joke / you'll end up being a zero." As the new ruler of a new kingdom, the king set aside the Sicilian constitution. He abolished differences in the laws of the two kingdoms, centralized the government in Naples, and implemented on the island the system of provincial administration created by the French in the continental kingdom. Palermo even lost its viceroys. These moves left a legacy of bitterness between the monarchy and the Sicilian elites.

The 1815 restoration maintained most of the Decennio's reforms. Across Europe restored monarchs brought back powdered wigs but kept the more efficient fiscal, administrative, and judicial institutions established by the Napoleonic regimes. Ferdinand's government did not restore the feudal system, nor did it do away with new central ministries and tribunals, reformed municipal institutions, tax regimes, or new legal codes, though it immediately abolished divorce. The king recognized noble titles issued by Murat, but by now the nobility had lost its claims to govern either in its lands or in the capital. Noble status heavily depended on proximity to the king, and court ceremony became a powerful tool of royal power. The government restored the Church to its wealth and influence. Monarchy and Church were essential supports for each other. In 1818 a new concordat with the papacy declared Catholicism the only legal religion in the kingdom and returned control of education to the Church. The concordat cut the number of southern dioceses from 130 to 84—eliminating many poor, rural dioceses—and gave the king power to appoint most bishops. Many of the monasteries and convents closed during the Decennio were reopened and their property restored where possible, though few new houses were founded after 1830. Traditional forms of devotion also returned: in 1835 and 1836, after about a century, two new patron saints were added to Naples's rich roster: St. Louis Gonzaga and St. Augustine.

The Church served as a source of stability and political control. The police, censorship, and the armed forces were also deployed to prevent any return of the radical movements that had forced the king to flee twice in seven years. Old policies to indulge the masses of Naples with cheap bread and royal and religious spectacle resumed, accompanied by severe repression of political dissent. Liberals who advocated constitutional government, freedom of conscience, or a free press were exiled, jailed, or executed. It was in the Restoration period that the expression "feast, flour, and gallows," used occasionally in the late eighteenth century by visitors to describe the southern government, became the standard way for liberals to refer to the principles of Bourbon rule.

The Italian situation still reeled from the conflicts of the Napoleonic period. Economic changes exacerbated social tensions. Young military officers who had risen to leadership under the French regimes resented the older men brought back by the Restoration. The reactionary measures of restored rulers and their rejection of all constitutional developments worried even moderate elements of the educated classes. Many Italians resented Austrian influence. Membership in the Carboneria, a secret society dedicated to radical political change, grew among army officers. Radical movements and nationalistic currents spread in Italy as across the Mediterranean. In 1820 news of a revolution and a new constitution in Spain sparked rebellions in several parts of Italy. On July 2 the military garrison of Nola, inland from Naples, rose up in revolt, and soon military officers demanded a constitution. This time revolution did not begin in the capital; instead it reflected the growth and demands of a provincial bourgeoisie and the dissatisfaction of many army leaders. Ferdinand soon issued and swore to observe a constitution. A parliament met in Naples in October of 1820, with most deputies coming from the provincial bourgeoisie.

The usual divisions arose. Sicilians rejected the idea of a single parliament and government. Murat followers and members of revolutionary societies fought over offices and policies. Provincial riots troubled public order. Austria, Prussia, and Russia opposed the new government. Metternich scorned a revolution begun by "a half-barbaric people, of absolute ignorance and limitless superstition, ardent and passionate like Africans, a people who can neither read nor write, and whose last word is the dagger." The great powers summoned Ferdinand to a meeting in Ljubljana, then in the Austrian empire. The king swore to his new parliament that he would defend the constitution, but once out of the kingdom he sought foreign aid against the revolution. In February of 1821 a letter from the king informed the parliament that the great powers demanded an end to the constitution. The parliament prepared for war, and Guglielmo

Pepe (1783–1855)—one of those nineteenth-century liberal figures celebrated for their ardor more than for their successes—led the Neapolitan army to face the Austrians. On March 7 in Rieti, near Rome, the Austrians routed the Neapolitans, and on March 23 Austrian troops entered Naples, while Pepe and others fled into exile.

The constitutional interlude achieved little, though it completed the abolition of the feudal system in Sicily. Southern society did not include cohesive elements that could support liberal ideals of limited government and freedom of press and conscience against the combined strength of monarchy, Church, and foreign opposition to both nationalism and constitutionalism. The southern masses, both urban and rural, remained loyal to the king and suspicious of liberal projects. From 1821 to 1827 thirty to forty thousand Austrian soldiers stationed in the South ensured the stability of the Bourbon monarchy. When Britain's politics veered to more liberal governments, Austria became the main protector of the southern monarchy. Arrests, exiles, and executions followed the king's return, though not on the scale of 1799. In May and June of 1821 the government organized the burning of suspect and foreign books, including works by Voltaire and Rousseau. After 1822 high tariffs made the import of foreign books very costly.

Ferdinand I, the wily survivor of three revolutions, grounded his rule in censorship, police, and royal control of the careers of courtiers and administrators. Uncouth and unenlightened, he however had an earthy charm that seems to have gained him the genuine affection of many Neapolitans, who nicknamed him "King Big Nose" from his most prominent facial feature. He was a man of few illusions and cynical humor: when his grandson asked permission to change the army's uniforms, the old king allegedly replied, "Dress them as you wish, they'll always flee." His son Francis I (ruled 1825–30) increased the bigotry and repression of the regime and allowed corruption to spread: "under this king"—observed an opponent—"everything was sold." Metternich himself deplored the "corruption and venality that reigns among virtually all Neapolitan officials." Francis's son Ferdinand II (ruled 1830–59), pious, austere, and militaristic, changed little of the repressive apparatus of the monarchy. Even the sympathetic historian Raffaele de Cesare noted that this king "had in common with the lowest part of his people his prejudices and fears."

Giuseppe Cammarano, *Crown Prince Francis and His Family Honoring a Bust of Ferdinand I, with a View of Vesuvius* (1820); in 1851 the British visitor Lord Napier described this painting as endowed with "incomparable ugliness"

After Italian unification in 1861, southern patriots vented their loathing for the Bourbons. Niccola Nisco, who was jailed in the 1850s for his political stance, typifies these sentiments. He called the Bourbons "a dynasty inimical to liberty, dishonored by repeated perjury, inglorious in war, loathed for its arbitrary acts, insatiable in revenge," and closed his history of the southern kingdom thus: "the great fault [of the Bourbons] was, by making corruption and espionage into the art of government, by opposing all progress, by maintaining the people in their ignorance, by neglecting all works of public usefulness and economic improvement, to have reduced the greatest state in Italy to despised last."

Yet not everything about the Restoration South was bleak despotism. Naples was still the largest city in Italy. It was the unchallenged center of the South, though Bari and Puglia generally began to grow significantly in population. Naples was home to the South's largest and busiest port, to its only university outside Sicily, to the kingdom's elites, and to communities of foreign merchants, diplomats, and bankers. In 1821 the fifth and final branch of the Rothschild bank opened in Naples, after London, Frankfurt, Paris, and Vienna. The bank operated in Naples until 1864 and became the center of a small Jewish community, which held religious services in private houses. English, Swiss, and German entrepreneurs also settled in Naples; by the late 1820s Protestant services were held in a chapel in the Prussian ambassador's residence. There was also an enclosed Protestant cemetery.

British, French, Swiss, and German entrepreneurs were attracted to the South by the stable political situation after 1821, low labor costs, and the government's protectionist policies, begun in 1823 to encourage industrial growth. By the 1850s foreigners and a few southern entrepreneurs operated factories that produced silk clothes, leather products, tiles, pasta, and tobacco. There were also a few mechanical and chemical industries in a nascent industrial zone east of the capital. As the southern population grew from about 5 to almost 7 million, southern agriculture produced more food staples, owing to the spread—begun in the eighteenth century—of higher-yielding crops including corn, potatoes, and rice. Some areas developed specialized agriculture such as the citrus fruits of Calabria and Sicily, which also supported the manufacture of perfumes and jams.

Social and economic change remained limited, however. The government's efforts focused on the capital. The nationalist Luigi Settembrini wrote in 1847 that "nothing is done for the provinces, nothing for luckless Sicily." The kingdom's exports remained rural: wine, oil, grain, raw silk. Foreign firms dominated profitable exports such as Sicilian sulfur. By the 1850s the economic distance between southern and northern Italy had grown. With few exceptions, the rising southern bourgeoisie consisted of corrupt officials or exploitative landowners, with little interest in manufacturing, trade, or agrarian innovation and investment. The rural masses remained appallingly poor. In 1847 a Sicilian economist wrote that Sicilian peasants "feed upon herbs, clothe themselves in rags, and sleep huddled up together in smoky huts amidst the stench of a dunghill."

The monarchy expanded Naples's diplomatic contacts: Neapolitan consuls resided in Odessa, Constantinople, Buenos Aires, and many other places. Trade agreements were concluded with Britain, France, Russia, and Spain. In 1816 antipiracy pacts with the Barbary states resulted in the return to Naples of almost seven hundred southerners held slaves in Algiers, Tunis, and Tripoli. An American consul was in Naples in 1796. In 1816 President James Madison informed his "Great and Good Friend" the king of the Two Sicilies that he was sending a minister to Naples to negotiate a treaty regarding the confiscation of American ships in Neapolitan waters in earlier years. This was the first formal diplomatic relationship between the United States and any Italian state. In 1831 the United States dispatched its first regular chargé d'affaires to Naples. The 1832 treaty that settled the confiscation issue was the first treaty between the United States and any Italian state. A treaty on commerce and navigation followed in 1845, and another, which also addressed extradition, in 1855. The United States also kept consuls in several southern ports. By the 1830s the kingdom dispatched diplomats to Washington and maintained consuls in several American cities. An amusing international kerfuffle developed in 1831 when a small volcanic island emerged from the sea south of Sicily. The Naples government claimed it and named it "Ferdinandea." Britain and France also claimed it and planted their flags on it, but within a year the islet sank back into the sea; in 2000 it again came close to the surface and Sicilian divers sought to plant the Italian flag on it.

The government continued to support the scientific developments favored by Murat. The Astronomical Observatory at Capodimonte opened in 1819; its long-time director Ernesto Capocci wrote one of Italy's first science-fiction novels, *Report of the First Voyage to the Moon Made by a Woman in the Year of Our Lord 2057* (1857). In 1832 *The Progress of Sciences, Letters, and Arts*, a new journal of moderate opinion advocating cultural openness, began publication. The Vesuvius Observatory opened in 1845 to pursue scientific study of the volcano. That same year the ninth annual congress of Italian scientists met at the Mineralogy Museum in Naples. Ferdinand II in particular was interested in the development of science and technology for military and industrial purposes. The arsenal and shipyards of Naples and nearby towns built ships and weapons. In 1818 the first steamship to be built in Italy—the *Ferdinando I*—came out of the Naples arsenal. In

1825 the new bridge on the Garigliano River was the first suspension bridge in Italy. In 1839 gas-lighting lit the main streets of Naples, and soon gaslights were installed in the San Carlo theater and the royal palace. On October 3, 1839, amidst great fanfare and royal pomp, the first railroad in Italy opened on the Naples-Portici track. In 1841 in Pietrarsa, near Portici, an industrial complex opened to build loco-motives and rail tracks (it now houses a railroad museum). In 1858 submarine cables allowed telegraph communication between Sicily and the continent. All these enterprises received state support, but we should not exaggerate their impact: by 1859 there were only 124 kilo-meters of railroads in the kingdom (none outside of Campania), while Piedmont had 807, Lombardy 200, and Tuscany 308.

Cultural life continued to flourish in Naples and to attract foreign visitors. The San Carlo remained a great center of Italian opera. Polit-ical censorship, however, prevailed in Naples as across Restoration Italy. In the 1830s censorship on moral and religious grounds also became strict because of the influence of Ferdinand II's first wife, the pious Maria Cristina of Savoy, whose delicate sensibility was easily offended by the themes of Romantic art (the dowager queen mother, on the other hand, was rumored to have a weakness for young sol-diers). A British critic noted that "the [Neapolitan] painter, who would indulge the observations of an erotic taste, would probably fall under the notice of the secular or the ghostly guardian of public morals." Romanticism posed special challenges to all Italian censors, who feared what they saw as its moral nihilism. In 1836 one of the San Carlo's censors wrote, "[T]he inclination of most of our modern the-ater writers is to imitate the current bloody school of French theater, which, confusing the true *terrible* with the mere *horrible*, represents human life as a misfortune, vice as a necessity, virtue as a chimera; that school in sum which, putting together into one representation as much as possible of what physical and moral nature have of most depressing and detestable, believes that it moves hearts deeply, whereas it accomplishes nothing but hurting and oppressing them."

Naples remained in any case a lively art center. The city expanded under the Restoration with new neighborhoods and large urban spaces. New broad streets helped develop residential areas both north of the old city, toward the royal palace in Capodimonte, and west of it, where elegant neighborhoods climbed up the adjacent hills. In

1819 a new palace overlooking the harbor—now the town hall—gathered all ministries. The square in front of the royal palace acquired its open, imposing look. Neoclassical villas—such as Villa Pignatelli, now a garden and museum, and Villa Floridiana, named after Ferdinand I's second wife and now home of a museum of porcelain—dotted the new areas.

The capital remained crowded and its masses poor. As late as 1845 almost three-fifths of the population lived in the small area of the old center. Naples never developed much of an industrial sector. In 1824 over one-fourth of the active population worked as servants, usually at extremely low wages, at a time when urban rents grew rapidly. Crowding and poor hygiene proved deadly in 1836–37, when a cholera epidemic killed some fourteen thousand people in Naples, over twenty thousand in Palermo, and a hundred thousand throughout the kingdom. But to the elites the capital offered much in this age of rising bourgeois social life: celebrated cafés, pastry shops, and restaurants; skilled tailors and fashionable clothing stores; numerous magazines; theaters offering everything from opera to circus; beautiful promenades along the sea; and, for the well connected, balls and masquerades at court.

In the 1830s and 1840s excavations at Pompeii and Herculaneum expanded, and mosaics, statues, and paintings from the sites were brought to Naples, where the Royal Bourbon Museum displayed them for locals and foreigners. The Romantic period increased the European fame of the ancient sites near Naples, thanks to works such as Giovanni Pacini's opera *L'ultimo Giorno di Pompei* (The Last Day of Pompeii, 1825) and especially Edward Bulwer-Lytton's novel *The Last Days of Pompeii* (1834). From 1826 a biennial exhibition sponsored by the king displayed the works of modern southern artists. From the 1830s medieval buildings such as the cathedral and the church of San Domenico received elaborate restorations that, though gaudy to modern eyes, reflected prevailing taste. In the same decades Giacinto Gigante (1806–76) and the "Posillipo School" of painters produced images of the city and of the southern landscape that confirmed the South's prominent position in the Romantic aesthetic sensitivity.

Music, archeological sites, Vesuvius, the climate, and the bustle of Naples also continued to attract foreigners. In the Romantic imagination the South became an exaggerated version of Italy: backward, but also natural and picturesque to a fault. One of the most famous Romantic ballets, August Bournonville's *Napoli or the Fisherman and His Bride* (1842), presents all the typical clichés: amorous simple people, superstitious devotions, and baleful landscape. Even natural phenomena took on Romantic aspects, as nineteenth-century visitors saw southern volcanoes as sublime examples of the awesomeness of nature. It was not just ruins and landscape that seemed exotic, but also southern people, especially rural ones. The taste for the picturesque spawned the taste for the folkloric. The primitiveness of the South produced unflattering comparisons to Africa, but it also appealed to Romantic sensitivities. In 1817 Stendhal wrote, "I know perhaps no sight in all the world more picturesque than that of some Calabrian peasant." Shelley deplored the "deformity and degradation of humanity" he found in Naples in 1818, but in a passage that epitomizes Romantic views of southerners, he wrote of the guides who took him to Vesuvius that "nothing, however, can be more picturesque than the gestures and the physiognomies of these savage people. And when, in the darkness of night, they unexpectedly begin to sing in chorus some fragments of their wild but sweet national music, the effect is exceedingly fine." In 1844 Dickens also admired all the "out-door life and stir" but noted "the miserable depravity, degradation, and wretchedness, with which this gay Neapolitan life is inseparably associated."

By 1816 lithographs were produced in Naples; soon prints of scenes from popular life and periodicals containing picturesque images disseminated this charmingly exotic view of southernness. By the 1850s several studios in Naples sold souvenir images in the new medium of photography. Illustrated guidebooks helped visitors in this new age of mass tourism. In the 1850s Francesco de Bourcard edited two volumes on the daily life of Naples, illustrated by lovely prints drawn by local artists to represent local types, meant for visitors interested in the picturesque. The fishermen of Naples—supposedly poor, natural, honest—often embodied the picturesque to foreign visitors, such as the French Romantic writer Alphonse de Lamartine, whose 1849 novel *Graziella* tells the sad story of a young Frenchman's love for a fishing girl of Procida, an island in the Bay of Naples. Neapolitan popular song also was admired as an expression of the local temperament. The early hit "Te voglio bene assaje" (I love you so much) of 1839—still one of the most recognizable Neapolitan tunes—sold 180,000 copies of its printed score to Neapolitans and visitors by 1844; Settembrini wrote in his memoirs that three good things came in 1839: the railroad, gas-lighting in the Naples streets, and "Te voglio bene assaje."

The Romantic image of the Neapolitans developed many of the elements noted by Enlightenment visitors but with a growing notion of the Neapolitans' backwardness and of their childish nature. In 1823 the English traveler Lady Blessington repeated traditional views of the city and its people: "The gaiety of the streets of Naples at night is unparalleled. . . . Neapolitans, like their volcanic country, are never in a state of repose. . . . Nowhere does the stream of life seem to flow as rapidly as here [where it forms] a current that sparkles while hurrying on." The young German Carl August Mayer visited in the mid-1830s. His reactions were typical: he admired Neapolitans for their friendliness, vivacity, hospitality, and philosophical refusal to work too hard. Neapolitans gesticulated ("like our Jews"), their faith was "joyous, ingenuous, rich in fantasy and sensitivity," and "everything among them is public." Above all, "Neapolitans, who possess more than any others the good and bad qualities of Italians, are like big children." The typical Neapolitan "is a simple, natural child, not at all turned or deformed by education." In the same years the novelist Alexandre Dumas called the Neapolitan "the first-born child of nature."

Most observers of nineteenth-century Neapolitans placed at the nucleus of their descriptions a new element that was central to the growing view of Neapolitans as outside the progress of European ideas: Neapolitans believed in *jettatura*, a practice that emerged at the end of the eighteenth century, differed from witchcraft, and had no religious or magical element. Most Neapolitans, not just the uneducated, believed, to the amusement or shock of foreigners, that bad things happened because of the influence of people who had the power to bring harm to others—*jettatori*. The main source of this power was the jettatori's "evil eye": their looks caused illness, misfortune, or even death. Though there were other possible conduits to a *jettatore*'s power, the eyes' dominance is reflected in the still current proverb "eyes are more powerful than gunshots." Jettatori (the term's root is in the verb "to throw," *jettare*) could be unaware of their natural

I MANGIA-MACCARONI

Neapolitan Boys Eating Maccheroni, from Francesco de Bourcard,
Usi e costumi di Napoli (1858)

and involuntary power; they were in a sense its first victims. The only defense was avoiding them altogether, though amulets offered some protection. The most powerful amulets were horns: many Neapolitans to this day wear small coral horns attached to their necks or wrists, and many have large horns in their homes. Dumas claimed that jettatura was an even stronger force in Naples than San Gennaro. Though today belief in the evil eye is found among Mediterranean peasants, the Neapolitan belief in jettatura was mainly urban.

One of the most remarkable Romantic portrayals of this element of Neapolitan life is a short novel by Théophile Gautier entitled simply *Jettatura* (1857). The young Frenchman Paul d'Asprémont comes to Naples to visit his fiancée, the beautiful English lady Alicia Ward, who has come to the South to recover from a mysterious illness. Paul's thin, long nose, his melancholy eyes and close eyebrows, his strong features, and his scanty appetite for local food lead most Neapolitans to fear him instinctively. He causes rain by looking at a cloud, and as soon as he arrives at Alicia's home her hammock breaks and she is hurt. A young Neapolitan count who is wooing Alicia recognizes the threat Paul poses and sends Alicia two large horns. Paul, aware that everyone avoids him, discovers through a book his own nature as a jettatore: he remembers his mother's death in childbirth and the strange deaths of many close friends. He visits Alicia again, and as he gazes on her, she coughs blood. The count challenges Paul to a duel, which they fight in the ruins of Pompeii, both blindfolded lest Paul enjoy an unfair advantage. After killing the count, Paul decides on a drastic remedy. He spends a day looking intently at all that is beautiful around him, including Alicia, and at night he blinds himself with burning coals. His sacrifice is too late: when he returns to Alicia's, he finds her dead. Paul flees to the garden and throws himself into the sea, which welcomes him with a roaring storm.

Amidst its Gothic horrors the novel offers a compendium of European clichés about Naples. The stereotypical English tourists who discover the dead Neapolitan count in Pompeii; the porters and drivers who touch their amulets as they serve Paul; the count who assures Alicia that he "has read Voltaire" but knows that one cannot trifle with jettatura; the beauty of the sea and landscape; the crowded streets—everything fits the image of a wild, exotic land, dangerously fascinating, enormously different from the civilized countries of rational Europe. The beliefs and practices of jettatura appear in all Romantic images of Naples. In Andrea de Jorio's 1832 book about Neapolitan popular culture, the entry for "horns" is by far the largest and mentions the numerous peddlers of horns in Naples. Jettatura was central to a view of southern culture as materialistic and pagan that still marks the European outlook on the South.

Thus, European Romantic culture sustained a contrast between a sentimental view of the South and its people as exotic and charming and a harsher view of them as barbaric and profoundly non-European. By midcentury, as the Romantic movement declined, industrial growth and scientific advances led educated western Europeans to discard Romantic idealism in favor of more material, practical approaches and values. In this new framework, the negative elements of the characterization of the Italian South became prevalent, and they still shape an image of the South as antimodern, savage, corrupt, and no longer charming. The events and effects of 1848 accelerated this development.

In the 1840s liberal and nationalist ideals inspired many young Italians to work for political freedom and national unity. A few groups attempted to spark revolts: in June 1844 the Bandiera brothers, members of a revolutionary republican movement, tried to set off a rebellion in Calabria that was easily repressed by royal troops. Across Europe the urban bourgeoisie and the rising working classes advocated a broader franchise and more equitable society. In the early months of 1848, the Springtime of the Peoples, crowds of workers, students, artisans, intellectuals, traders, and professionals demonstrated against oppressive governments in most of the continent's large cities. In February in Paris a revolution pushed King Louis-Philippe into exile and established a republic that promised work to all and full adult male suffrage. By March the king of Prussia and the emperor of Austria were forced to dismiss their governments and issue constitutions. Nationalist movements in German territories and principalities obtained the summoning of a German parliament in Frankfurt, charged with creating a united German state. In Budapest, Prague, and other cities of the Austrian empire, movements for autonomy threatened the unity of the Habsburg lands. Nationalism and constitutional principles seemed unstoppable.

Events in Sicily preceded even those in Paris. On January 12 a riot in Palermo produced revolutionary committees calling for a return to the 1812 constitution. Three days later troops bombarded the city from the royal fortress, earning Ferdinand II his nickname "King Bomb." Foreign consuls protested the bombing, and royal forces failed to stop the revolution's advance. By early February the entire island was under rebel control. Agitation and liberal pressure grew in Naples as well. On January 29 the king promised a limited constitution with a narrow franchise, no religious tolerance, and royal control over the armed forces. It was issued on February 10, and on February 24 the king—like his grandfather twenty-eight years earlier—swore to observe it. The new government adopted the tricolor flag of Italian nationalism. By March, rebellions in Venice and Milan against Austrian rule threatened Ferdinand's hope of receiving aid from his family's old protector. All Italian rulers, including Pope Pius IX, were forced to issue constitutions. On March 30 southern volunteers left to join the fight against Austria.

As events unfolded, however, the same political and social divisions that weakened the revolution in northern and central Europe affected Italian developments. The Sicilians refused to accept the king's constitution. On April 13 the new Sicilian Parliament deposed the Bourbons and declared it would seek a new king and independence for the island. Radical excesses in Naples—and peasant takeovers of land in Sicily and elsewhere—worried the elites. By April, war flared in Lombardy, where rebels, volunteers from across Italy, and the forces of the Kingdom of Sardinia fought against Austria to achieve national unity and freedom. General Pepe, back from decades of exile, led an official Neapolitan contingent to join this fight. But on May 15, as the new Naples Parliament was about to convene, political disagreements and street riots degenerated into urban warfare between rebels and royal troops. Up to five hundred people were killed and a thousand taken prisoner. Unlike in 1820, the army leadership remained loyal to the king, and large contingents of Swiss mercenaries strengthened royal forces. Ferdinand II suspended parliament, abolished freedom of the press, and went to thank the Madonna of the Carmine, surrounded by white Bourbon flags and amidst the joyful crowds of the poorer neighborhoods. He also called back the troops fighting in northern Italy.

Neither the Sicilian nor the Neapolitan revolution was democratic: the franchise in Sicily excluded the illiterate (about nine-tenths of the population), and in Naples it was limited by income. Overall, the revolutionaries offered little to southern masses, especially to the rural poor. Once his forces controlled Naples, therefore, the king had the upper hand. As Austria's forces gathered strength in the Lombardy war, repression advanced in the South. By September royal troops took Messina and began to march toward Palermo, while the Sicilian Parliament failed to find a suitable and willing candidate for the island's crown. A truce in Sicily, mediated by France and Britain, and the king's worries about radical developments in Rome and elsewhere in Italy slowed the repression. But in March 1849 Ferdinand dismissed the Naples Parliament he had permitted to convene a month earlier, and on May 15 royal troops entered Palermo. The constitution was not formally revoked, but the king simply ignored it. Reprisals began in earnest: hundreds were exiled or jailed, police and clerical control of public life intensified, and the bureaucracy was purged of anyone who had shown sympathy for rebellion.

Although the monarchy survived with its power undiminished, 1848 marked a transition in its status within and outside the kingdom. Ferdinand II viewed Austrian support, clerical power, and the armed forces as essential to maintaining his regime, and political and intellectual life became even more constricted than before. The king expanded the army from sixty thousand to almost a hundred thousand men and spent almost half his revenues on it, but aimed it primarily at the domestic defense of his throne. He believed his kingdom safe from outside threats, protected—as the king allegedly put it—between salt water and holy water. The moderate middle classes long supported the Bourbons and profited from the economic changes of the first half of the century, but even they found the monarchy's despotism increasingly unacceptable. Anyone who desired greater integration between the Italian states saw the Bourbons as the greatest obstacle to the achievement of any nationalist aspiration. The fact that Sardinia kept its constitutional government in spite of its defeat by Austria led nationalists—from conservatives to republicans, and including southerners—to accept Sardinian leadership for any initiative that would lead to greater unity on the peninsula.

In the 1850s, moreover, western European attitudes toward political repression became more critical. The Naples government appeared ever more out of step with the standards of modern life. Raffaele de Cesare noted that "in the last years of Ferdinand II Naples presented more markedly the appearance of a city subjugated by fear." Ferdinand's moralism and bigotry grew: he ordered that veils cover "the nudity of statues in museums" and that "ballerinas in the theater be covered by long garments, in colors least apt to excite the senses" (alas, de Cesare did not specify the acceptable colors). Yet the king did little to combat corruption and regarded personal honesty in his officials as secondary to political submission. The United States minister to Naples observed in 1853 that "except in Turkey and Spain there is not probably to be found a more corrupt body of public officers than those of the Kingdom of Naples." In December 1856 a soldier failed in an attempt to assassinate the king. In June 1857 Carlo Pisacane, a republican nationalist, landed with other rebels near Sapri, south of Salerno. Their naive hopes to rouse the rural masses miscarried tragically, as peasants mistook them for bandits and killed many of them; the latter event provoked the feeble muse of Luigi Mercantini, whose maudlin poem "La spigolatrice di Sapri" (The Harvest Girl of Sapri)—with its dreary refrain "They were three hundred, they were young and strong / and they are dead"—is still inflicted on Italian schoolchildren. After these episodes, repression and fear grew even greater in the kingdom.

The oppression and corruption of the Bourbon government affected the image of the South in western Europe. In 1850–51 William Gladstone, already a rising politician, visited Naples, met jailed patriots, and was horrified by the political situation. The pamphlet he wrote to denounce Ferdinand's government appeared in eleven English editions in 1851 alone, plus translations into Italian and French, and caused European revulsion against the southern monarchy. Gladstone declared the Naples government "an outrage upon religion, upon civilization, upon humanity and upon decency" and famously called it "the negation of God erected into a system of government."

Gladstone's comments shaped impressions of the South across the globe. In April of 1852, the New York *Daily Times* wrote, "The King of Naples . . . represents to the reflective mind murder enthroned and crowned, the incarnated evil, the final result of diabolical malice as practised upon humanity. Naples is the prey of the foulest and fiercest misrule that ever trampled a nation to dust." In 1853 the United States minister to Naples deplored the government's "unlimited despotism" and noted that "a deep and sullen hatred and desire for vengeance has been implanted in the popular heart."

Revulsion at the government accompanied negative views of Naples and southerners. Nassau William Senior, who traveled with Gladstone, reversed the eighteenth-century admiration for the bustle of Naples: "The disgusting population of Naples was all abroad—basking, quarrelling, gambling, and begging over the whole road. In cold countries the debased classes keep at home; here they live in the streets . . . you are never free from the sight, or, indeed, from the contact, of loathsome degradation. I never saw so hateful a people; they look as wicked as they are squalid and unhealthy." In the Sicilians he found "a perverseness, a rashness, and a childishness which are not European, and can be accounted for only by the mixture of Saracenic blood." In 1850 the French scholar Ernest Renan found in the Neapolitans "the total extinction of all moral sentiment . . . they are brutes, among whom you'll search in vain for some trace of that which constitutes human nobility." In 1853 the German historian Ferdinand Gregorovius found "something repulsive about Naples, with its chaos of Baroque buildings reaching up into the sky, with the heat, the dust on the streets, and the deafening confusion." What Goethe and Stendhal had found exhilarating now appeared disgusting. In 1854 the French journalist Alfred Maury drew a similar picture of distance from Europe, describing travel southward into Italy as travel backward in time: "In Milan, in Turin, one finds modern society. . . . In Rome you are immersed in the Middle Ages. . . . In Naples, we re-enter full paganism," and further South one finds "ancient times."

The anti-Bourbon campaigns of Italian nationalists added to the European perception of southerners as barbaric savages, unworthy of modern Europe. Settembrini, who had denounced Bourbon government already in an 1847 essay, decried this negative effect: "we have cried all across the world that the Bourbons had turned us into barbarians and beasts; and everybody believed that we were barbarians and beasts." Another epidemic of cholera in 1854 killed about eighty-five hundred people in Naples and added to this image of a blighted land, as did a major earthquake in 1857 that killed ten thousand in Basilicata alone. An agrarian crisis in the late 1850s further weakened the kingdom. In 1856 the French and British governments urged Ferdinand II to free political prisoners and alleviate repression. When the king haughtily rejected any foreign interference in his kingdom (not unreasonably pointing to British policy in Ireland), France and Britain recalled their ambassadors from Naples and expelled Ferdinand's envoys. The kingdom became a pariah in western Europe.

Early in 1859 the Naples court traveled to Puglia to welcome Maria Sofia of Bavaria, sister of the empress of Austria and bride of Francis of Bourbon, heir to the southern throne. While in Puglia Ferdinand II became gravely ill. The court returned to the palace at Caserta—Ferdinand's favorite residence—where relics and holy images in his bedroom did not slow the king's decline. In April came disturbing news of a new war between Austria and Sardinia, the latter this time aided by France. Ferdinand lived long enough to learn of Austria's danger and of nationalist movements in Tuscany and across central Italy. He died on May 22.

The epilogue came quickly. Francis II was twenty-three years old, conscientious and likable, but not endowed with a forceful personality. His imperious father called him "Lasagna" after the prince's favorite dish. Neapolitans still refer to their last king as "Franceschiello" (Li'l Francis). Nonetheless, a new reign always brought hope for change, and Britain and France restored diplomatic relations. But events in northern Italy demanded an experienced hand and a daring mind, both of which Francis II lacked. Riots occurred in Sicily in April of 1860. In May Giuseppe Garibaldi, a popular hero of liberation struggles from Italy to Latin America, sailed to Sicily from Genoa with a thousand young rebels. The Mille (Thousand) reached western Sicily on May 11 and gained control of the area. The Sardinian government, whose recent annexation of much of central Italy worried European powers, feared alienating France and Britain if it pursued war and threatened the pope's rule over Rome. The relationship between the government of Sardinia and Garibaldi remained ambiguous, and the expedition to Sicily was mainly Garibaldi's initiative. However, the Sardinian government did nothing to discourage his plans and stood ready to take advantage of any promising development.

The southern state collapsed. Sicilian elites quickly abandoned a dynasty that had repeatedly stifled the island's desire for autonomy. Francis II had already dismissed his Swiss regiments after a mutiny. The rest of the Bourbon armed forces proved inefficient and badly commanded. Garibaldi advanced to Palermo and Messina. France advised Francis II to negotiate with Sardinia and liberalize his government. On June 25 the king offered autonomy to Sicily and an amnesty to all political prisoners, restored the 1848 constitution, and accepted the tricolor flag. But these moves did not receive the enthusiastic response of 1848. Confidence in the monarchy had waned. By the end of July, royal troops left Sicily. Military and civilian officials and even members of the royal family abandoned Francis. On August 20 Garibaldi landed in Calabria while nationalist rebels took control of many provinces. On September 6 Francis II and his wife left Naples for the fortress at Gaeta, and the next day Garibaldi entered Naples, after a triumphal march through the kingdom. Bourbon forces resisted valiantly at Gaeta. But on October 21, in a hastily arranged plebiscite, the southern population overwhelming voted to join the nascent Kingdom of Italy (the official tally yielded about 1.7 million yes votes and 10,000 no votes). On November 7 King Victor Emanuel II of Sardinia entered Naples amidst cheering crowds. Francis II surrendered Gaeta on February 13, 1861, and he and his wife left for exile in Rome and later Paris.* On March 12 and 20 the fortresses of Messina and Civitella were the last to lower the Bourbon flag. After seven centuries, the southern kingdom was no more.

*The court resided in the Farnese Palace in Rome until Italy took Rome from the pope in 1870. Until 1866, when he lost the recognition of all European powers except the papacy, Francis II kept a diplomatic corps and a council of ministers. The king died in 1894; Queen Maria Sofia lived until 1925 and appears as a character in a poignant scene in Proust's *Recherche*. In 1984 their remains were brought to Naples and buried in the Bourbon chapel in the church of Santa Chiara.

The South as Part of
the Italian Nation

America costs us tears, to us Neapolitans. For us, who cry for the
sky of Naples, how bitter is this bread. . . . What, what is money?
For he who cries for his fatherland it is nothing. Now I have a few
dollars and yet I have never felt so poor. . . . I, who have lost country, family, and honor, I am meat for the slaughter, I am an
emigrant.

"Lacreme Napuletane" (Neapolitan Tears,
Neapolitan song, 1925)

The Sicilian town of Bronte plays an unlikely role in British literature. It was the center of the estates bestowed after 1799 by the
grateful Bourbons on Horatio Nelson, who received the title of duke
of Bronte and the attendant eighteen thousand ducats in annual
income. The town was named after a mythical Cyclops from nearby
Mount Aetna and thus seemed especially suited to the one-eyed
admiral. A Yorkshire minister who greatly admired Nelson was so
taken by this title that he altered his own last name to match the
duchy's. His daughters' literary talents made the name dear to readers
around the world who have no knowledge of its Sicilian roots. The
town has a more prominent and sadder part in the history of the
South.

Garibaldi, though originally a radical republican, eventually accepted
royal leadership for the unification of Italy that followed his conquest
in the South. However, when his forces advanced into Sicily on their
way to the mainland and Naples, the message that resonated with the
island's rural masses was one of freedom, and they took this to mean
freedom from their oppressive landlords. In early August of 1860 the
peasants of Bronte, like those of many other estates, rebelled against

their distant English masters and the local elites who controlled most of the land. In Bronte the rebels looted the homes of wealthy locals, killed one of the town guards and several residents, and set the local theater, the town archive, and several elite residences on fire.

These events deeply troubled Garibaldi. Sicilian elites were by then rallying to his cause and abandoning their king. Northern radicals had no idea of the actual conditions of the southern peasantry and no appreciation of its plight and of its hatred for its exploiters. The peasants of Bronte seemed savages who endangered victory and unification. The British consuls in Sicily urged Garibaldi to intervene. On August 6 Nino Bixio, one of Garibaldi's lieutenants, arrived in Bronte and declared a state of siege. Bixio's troops imposed order, and on August 9 he issued a warning to the local population: "either you remain calm, or we, as friends of the fatherland, will destroy you as enemies of mankind." On August 10 Bixio had several peasants shot, without any judicial inquiry into their individual responsibility for the violent events. Numerous other executions that summer helped restore order in the Sicilian countryside. The suppression of the rebellions in Bronte and elsewhere sealed the support of Sicilian landlords for unification.

The Bronte events reveal the major themes of southern history after unification: rural exploitation, ignorance, and poverty; the disenfranchisement of southern masses; and the prevalence of elite and northern interests. Italian unification brought no real social or economic change. None of its leaders wanted a revolution in that sense. In their struggle for unification, northern Italian nationalists had embraced a view of the South as backward and of its government as the antithesis of all that modern Europe cherished. Northern Italians made themselves look both modern and European by denouncing the conditions and character of the South. This was not a recipe for careful analysis of the deep causes and features of southern problems. Thus, when unification came, the leaders of the new Italian kingdom had no clear understanding of southern circumstances, let alone an effective plan to alleviate them.

Northerners who visited the South were shocked by what they saw: violence, poverty, superstition, corruption. Illiteracy was above 80 percent across the South. It proved difficult even to see southerners as Italians. Shortly after entering Naples, Bixio himself wrote to Prime Minister Cavour that "Neapolitans are a bunch of Orientals—they understand nothing but force." In October 1860 Luigi Carlo Farini, one of Cavour's agents in the South, wrote the prime minister, "What lands are these, Molise and the South! What barbarism! This is not Italy! This is Africa: compared to these peasants the Bedouins are the pinnacle of civilization." Here was an alien population, wretched and uncivilized after decades of misrule, lazy and largely unworthy of the benefits of culture and progress that unification would undoubtedly bring.

The violent rural events that accompanied the conquest proved only the first evidence that something was terribly wrong in and with the South. Unification was followed by protracted rural warfare, which caused more deaths than all the independence struggles between 1848 and 1861 combined. Bands of rural brigands fought against the national armed forces, and areas of the countryside remained outside government control until the late 1860s. The government suspected the clergy and the Bourbon court in exile in Rome of supporting the insurgency. Dynastic loyalty and hostility to the secular policies of northern leaders indeed played a role in the first year or so after the conquest, when Bourbon supporters led armed bands to take over several villages and towns and raise the Bourbon flag. This early phase saw the participation of many soldiers and officers of the disbanded Bourbon army, who found no alternative employment. The scale of the insurgency led the government to speed up administrative centralization and quickly to impose northern laws, institutions, and practices on the South.

At the end of 1861 an amnesty led over twenty thousand former soldiers to abandon their struggle against the new government. But rural brigandage remained active, as its wellsprings were the abject poverty of rural people, their long-standing hostility to urban and central forces, and their resistance to conscription and new heavier taxation. Brigands kidnapped travelers for ransom, sacked farms and villages, assaulted coaches, damaged crops, and killed livestock. Land travel in the South and Sicily became virtually impossible. In August 1863 the parliament passed a severe law that placed almost the entire South under military law. Summary executions and arbitrary arrests ensued. By late in 1863 about a hundred thousand soldiers were fighting to restore order in the South. Thousands were arrested and thousands killed; the victims of brigands were also numerous, though we have no reliable figures. By the end of 1865 the number of soldiers involved in the repression was down to about forty thousand, and military government expired after that year. But rural violence continued, and bands of brigands operated in mountainous and wooded areas for the rest of the decade.

The fight against brigandage in the 1860s confirmed the image of southerners as alien to civilization and fundamentally foreign to Italian and European identity. Repression was based on a view of bandits as subhuman: "this rabble of fearsome beasts whose only human characteristic is their bodily form" is how an army lieutenant described them in 1865. The severity of punishments also expressed the old stereotype of southerners as easily swayed and in need of determined guidance.

In Sicily in particular, the violence of the 1860s, which included a revolt in Palermo in 1866, was blamed by authorities on the mafia. The term "mafia" had existed since the seventeenth century and referred to various types of criminal activities. By the early nineteenth century, criminal networks existed in numerous parts of Sicily, often allied with local notables to resist outside powers. But sheer rural poverty and resistance to taxes and conscription were much more significant factors in the violence of the 1860s than the mafia. By blaming the mafia for the turmoil, the government conveniently blurred these distinctions, but dangerously increased the mafia's notoriety. After unification, as traditional elites continued to dominate the island's society and to resent outside interference, the mafia grew as an illegal organization linked to crime, protection rackets, and political corruption.

The brutal war against the brigands increased the fear and disgust governing elites felt for the southern masses. The institutions of the new Italian state added to the alienation between the government and the governed. Italy's franchise was one of Europe's most limited: age, literacy, and income requirements ensured that only about 2 percent of the population (or 8 percent of adult men) had the right to vote; the rate was lowest in the poorer, less educated South. Reform in 1882 raised the percentage of voters to about 7 percent of the population, 8.2 percent in the North and 5.5 percent in the South. Only in 1912 would most Italian men receive the right to vote, though the voting age for the illiterate (thirty) remained higher than for the literate (twenty-one); since over 60 percent of Italy's voters were then illiterate, this was not a minor difference. Most southerners thus remained outside the political system. Equal universal male suffrage only came in 1919 (and female suffrage in 1946). Restricted suffrage meant that, as the politician Sidney Sonnino put it in 1881, "the vast majority of the people . . . feel estranged from our institutions; they see themselves as subjects of the State."

Italian public education developed later than in other western European countries and only very slowly spread literacy among the southern masses. In 1911, 58 percent of the people in Sicily, 70 percent in Calabria, and 65 percent in Basilicata were illiterate, far higher percentages than in most of western Europe by then. The fiscal system of the new state also maintained the South in a dependent position. Taxes that bore heavily on agriculture (and thus on southerners) helped finance investment in infrastructure and industrialization in the more prosperous and urbanized North. Southern taxes also paid off Italy's public debt, whereas the old southern kingdom had been virtually debt-free. Early on, government free-market policies damaged what little industry had grown in the South under the protection of Bourbon high tariffs. Overall, Italian policies reflected the political alliance of southern landed elites with northern industrial interests, a compromise not unlike the situation in the United States after the end of Reconstruction in 1877.

The result was to perpetuate southern poverty. The economic circumstances of the southern rural population—and of the urban poor of Naples—remained miserable. The expropriation of some Church land in the 1860s only strengthened the traditional southern *latifondi*, large estates that employed landless laborers in conditions that had changed little since feudal times. The large-scale sale of public and Church land to private owners in the decades after unification increased the pace of deforestation, with tragic results in terms of peasant life, especially more frequent landslides and the greater spread of malaria. In the 1880s an agrarian crisis across Europe, due to easier maritime transport and the resulting availability of cheap Russian and American grain, brought debt and decline to many southern aristocratic families and further diminished the economic prospects of southern peasants. In the 1880s in Basilicata fewer than half the children lived past the age of fifteen. Peasant misery fed turmoil in Sicily in 1893–94, led by a local Socialist movement. The government responded to the agitation by declaring a state of siege and by military repression that took the lives of about one hundred Sicilian peasants.

Persistent rural poverty and the suppression of brigandage were among the causes of large-scale rural emigration. Starting in the 1870s, and in growing numbers between the 1880s and World War I, southern Italians began leaving their villages and seeking their livelihood abroad. The southern scholar and politician Francesco Saverio Nitti noted that many southerners fell under "a sad and fatal law: either emigrants or brigands." Between 1901 and 1913 about 200,000 southerners left Italy every year, 90 percent of them leaving Europe altogether. They included 1 million Sicilians, out of an island population of about 3.5 million. Emigrant remittances to the families they had left behind became a major element in the southern economy. World War I abruptly interrupted this mass movement.

The phenomenon of emigration was not limited to southern Italians: between 1876 and 1914, approximately 14 million Italians left Italy, about one-fifth of them women and one-third southerners (half returned at various times). But the patterns and destinations of emigration differed for southerners. About 6 million Italian emigrants went to various European countries, while close to 5 million went to the United States, and the rest primarily to South America. Yet three out of four of the Italians who emigrated to the United States came from the South, and southern emigrants were almost exclusively rural: although the great majority left from Naples, very few had lived in the city itself. Emigration became the main motor of the economy of Naples: by 1910 its harbor was the largest in Italy and the fifth in Europe by tonnage, and the first in the continent in number of passengers. Emigration emptied rural provinces, such as Basilicata, where in 1905 women formed about two-thirds of the remaining population.

The peasants who passed through Naples to go to America were destitute and desperate. In 1888 the United States consul in Naples wrote that "the persons emigrated from this country to the United States during the last two years belong to the poorest and most ignorant classes; they are without any school education and with few exceptions are unable to write their names; they have no conception of our institutions and form of Government. . . . Their sole aim is the amelioration of their pecuniary condition. . . . Of the persons emigrating to the United States from here 85 or 90 per cent are farm hands." These trends in Italian emigration confirmed the common notion that northern Italians were more European than southerners. They also formed the American image of Italian immigrants as rural and southern and have shaped Italian-American culture and identity to this day. By 1910 there were about six hundred thousand Italians in New York City, about as many as in any Italian city at the time.

Emigrants sought abroad fortunes that seemed unreachable at home. The South remained poor and heavily rural through the mid-twentieth century. Railroad and road networks expanded in the half-century after unification (they were minimal in 1860), and maritime traffic in southern ports grew. Small industrial areas developed around Naples and later Bari and a few other cities. But the economy remained weak and marginal to advances in the North. The South, as always, was also hit by natural disasters. In 1883 an earthquake killed over two thousand people in Ischia. In 1906 an eruption of Vesuvius killed over two hundred. In 1908 Italy's most deadly modern tremor destroyed most of Messina and much of Reggio Calabria, across the strait, killing up to a hundred thousand people. In 1915 another earthquake centered in Avezzano in Abruzzo left about thirty thousand dead.

After unification the circumstances of the city of Naples changed perhaps even more than those of the rest of the South. It was still by far the largest city in the new kingdom (and the fifth largest in Europe); Milan only surpassed it around 1920 and Rome sometime later. But Naples lost its position as the capital of the peninsula's largest state, which it had enjoyed for almost six centuries. This meant the loss of the royal court with its attendant economic and social benefits, and forced Neapolitan elites to look outside the South for patronage, prestige, and traditional forms of employment such as diplomacy or the military. The city lost the tax income that used to flow into it from southern provinces, and its status as the South's main marketplace slowly diminished.

The city also suffered from an especially poor image in the eyes of its new masters: northerners might excuse the general savagery of southerners with the ignorance and poverty in which Bourbon misrule had allegedly kept the South, but most visitors were simply appalled by Naples. With the typical scientific rhetoric of the mid-nineteenth century, northerners saw Naples as diseased, both physically and morally, almost beyond remedy. Soon after unification, Massimo d'Azeglio, an aristocratic politician, wrote that "fusion with the Neapolitans" was "like going to bed with someone who has smallpox" and described the city as "an ulcer that gnaws at us." Chaos and dirt shocked visitors, but they perceived physical degradation and moral corruption as still deeper dangers. Giuseppe La Farina, a Sicilian returning from exile, wrote to Cavour about "theft in public offices" that "it will take fire and iron to extirpate this gangrene." Farini combined the crowdedness and the degradation in writing to Cavour: "the multitudes teem like worms in the rotted-out body of the state."

The city presented in extreme fashion the problems of all nineteenth-century urban centers. The poorer classes lived in appalling conditions of hygiene and congestion. The 1881 census revealed that in poor neighborhoods there were three Neapolitans for every available room. The Swedish doctor Axel Munthe (1857–1949), who later lived in Capri, where his beautiful home is now a museum, described the hovels of Naples's old center as "the most ghastly human habitations on the face of the earth." Average rents more than doubled between 1860 and 1885, rising much faster than average salaries and adding to popular misery. There were more Neapolitans in the 1880s than in 1860, and yet the city consumed less and worse food. The camorra network of organized crime grew in strength and complexity: by the end of the century it controlled the wholesale food market, ran smuggling rings in various goods, and extorted protection money from many shops and businesses. Poor residents, perennially short of life's necessities, found limited help in the numerous pawnshops and often became the victims of a vast number of usurers. Corruption and bribery prevailed in business and public life: for most Neapolitans contact with public institutions occurred primarily through the mediation of personal recommendations and contacts—what Neapolitans still call having a saint in paradise.

Traditional devotions continued: the city added three more patron saints in 1895–1904 and two in 1927–28, and San Gennaro was as popular as ever. Another potential source of aid was the lotto: with its promise of quick riches, it enjoyed enormous popularity in Naples. Neapolitans of all social classes pursued its dream of easy money, just as all of them had always sought aid in saints' relics and miracles. The lotto continued to generate for the Italian government the substantial revenue it had produced for the Bourbons, and it continued—as an American diplomat put it in 1853—to exert "a most deleterious influence upon the habits and morals of the lower classes." The writer and journalist Matilde Serao (1856–1927) described the lotto as "the liquor of Naples," and in 1892 the French consul called it "the scourge, the tapeworm of the Neapolitan people." The old Neapolitan *Smorfia* grew in the late nineteenth century into an elaborate system: numerous books detailed how to interpret dreams and events to predict upcoming lotto numbers, so bettors could increase their chances. The camorra also ran a clandestine lotto circuit. Like the belief in jettatura, hope in the lotto not only cut through class divisions but to this day flourishes in the city.

Yet there were some bright spots. The beautiful location and the surrounding archeological sites continued to attract to Naples even visitors wary of the city's problems. In 1884, Cook's tour guide described it thus: "Naples is an ill-built, ill-paved, ill-lighted, ill-drained, ill-watched, ill-governed, and ill-ventilated city," but also "perhaps the loveliest spot in Europe." New luxury hotels opened along the hills west of the old center and along the renovated coastline in the Santa Lucia area, where lovers of the picturesque deplored the decline of the old fishing population. By the end of the century seventy thousand tourists visited the city each year, and the archeological museum had fifty thousand visitors annually. Naples also continued to be a significant cultural and artistic center.

Until the 1920s Naples had the only university in the continental South (Sicily had three small universities in Palermo, Catania, and Messina); indeed in the 1880s, with its ten thousand students, the university was the third largest in Europe after those in Berlin and Vienna. In 1860 Garibaldi placed Francesco De Sanctis (1817–83), another returning exile and one of Italy's greatest intellectuals at the time, in charge of reforming the university. De Sanctis purged the faculty of conservative Bourbon supporters and appointed some of the major figures of the time to new chairs. Darwinism, Hegelianism, historicism, and other recent intellectual trends arrived in Naples through the university, and interest in the physical sciences expanded. New schools opened in pharmacology (1865), applied mechanics (1869), and agriculture (1872). Scientific journals and societies also proliferated.

One of the most interesting new scientific institutions developed separately from the university. The German biologist Anton Dohrn (1840–1909) decided that Naples, with its large population, maritime location, and tourist attractions, would be the ideal place to establish a new zoological station for the study of aquatic creatures. In 1873 Dohrn's plan came to fruition with the opening of an aquarium in the public gardens, in a large new building decorated with remarkable frescoes depicting sea life. Dohrn aimed not only to display a significant collection of aquatic species, but to sponsor research that would buttress the new Darwinian ideas. Darwin himself sent books and one hundred pounds to help launch the new institution, which quickly became well known across Europe. Eighteen Nobel Prize winners have studied at the Naples aquarium. It still operates in its original building, where its large tanks and darkened rooms have frightened generations of Neapolitan children.

The fall of the Bourbon monarchy more generally allowed the growth of public opinion and of social and cultural life in the city. Religious minorities finally achieved legal equality: Garibaldi himself granted land to the Anglican community to build the first Protestant church in Naples. The libraries in Naples were among the most heavily used in Italy. Eighty new periodicals appeared between 1860 and 1880, including a dozen new dailies. In 1892 Serao and her husband founded *Il Mattino*, today Naples's main daily; that year *Napoli Nobilissima*, a journal devoted to celebrating the city's history, art, and culture, also began publication. The publishing business grew and produced novels and poetry in addition to scholarly works. New circles and associations—social, cultural, charitable—formed bonds among the elites and middle classes of the city, which also socialized in elegant new cafés and restaurants. In 1875 the Neapolitan Society for Local History was founded, and public archives, both state and municipal, expanded. The repertory at San Carlo finally reached beyond traditional Italian opera: by the 1880s and 1890s, French opera, Wagner, and Russian opera appeared on the Naples stage. In 1912 Richard Strauss conducted the Naples premiere of his *Salome*.

More popular forms of entertainment and culture also flourished, to satisfy the needs of the city's growing middle-class public. These more "middle-brow" forms—in theater, literature, music—celebrated *napoletanità* (Neapolitanness) as a strong regional identity within Italian nationalism. As happened elsewhere in Europe in the late nineteenth century, these cultural forms extolled local color and character traits, with the added element of the prevalence of dialect. In fact, late in the century comic theater in Neapolitan dialect produced some of its greatest actors and works. In particular, works and performances by Eduardo Scarpetta (1853–1925) achieved national success. His comedies in dialect mixed elements of farce and vaudeville. His signature role as Don Felice Sciosciammocca replaced Pulcinella as Naples's most famous theatrical figure. Don Felice, perennially hungry and plagued by misfortunes of all sorts, spread a somewhat buffoonish image of the Neapolitan that continues to this day. After 1900, silent movies added to this image of Naples, which became one of the main production centers of early Italian cinema.

Numerous new magazines and newspapers published poems, short stories, and serialized novels that further developed the picturesque view of the city and its people. Serao and others produced tale upon tale that presented Naples's life, especially among the lower classes, as collective and theatrical, always judged by meddlesome neighbors. These sentimentalized stories offered contrasts between honor and shame, devotion and sensuality. A particular theme was the danger and pain caused by sexual misbehavior, especially on the part of women: self-sacrificing mothers suffered and interfered as restless, unfaithful wives brought sorrow to men and forced many to resort to crimes of honor. The shameful threat of *corna* (the cuckold's horns) led men to murder or *sfregio*, the scarring of a guilty woman's face that marked her as unworthy and made her less attractive to lurking suitors.

The poems, stories, and plays of Salvatore Di Giacomo (1860–1934) offer some of the best examples of these themes. His famous story

"Assunta Spina" (1888) tells the tale of a married woman who, when abandoned by her lover, reveals their affair to her husband. The husband understands his public shame and rages: "I walk by and people laugh in my face. Our shame is known to all." Through her jealousy, Assunta provokes her husband, who stabs her former lover to death. In the end, though, as her husband flees, she takes the blame for the crime. In "Without Seeing Him" (1887) Carmela, the widow of a street sweeper, places her older son in the poorhouse because of her poverty. On a cold winter day, with her daughter and her infant son, Carmela climbs the long staircase of the poorhouse to visit her son and bring him three apples. The secretary realizes that Carmela's son is dead but lacks the courage to tell her and to acknowledge that the institution never alerted her to his illness. He tells Carmela that the children are in class and that she must return on another day. The story ends with the poor woman leaving, having entrusted the three apples to the secretary. These two stories were so successful that Di Giacomo adapted them for the dialect stage, in powerful melodramas that greatly expanded their essential plots (a film of "Assunta Spina" appeared in 1915).

Even more effectively than theater or literature, popular music spread this image of napoletanità beyond Naples. In the Romantic period Neapolitan songs had by and large spread informally. In 1877 an annual contest for Neapolitan songs began in conjunction with the festival of the Madonna of Piedigrotta. In 1880, as an advertisement for the newly opened funicular that ascended Vesuvius, Luigi Denza and Peppino Turco wrote "Funiculì, Funiculà," destined to become one of Naples's most popular songs (outliving the funicular, which ceased operating after the 1944 eruption). Giovanni Capurro's " 'O sole mio" came in 1898. The golden age of the Neapolitan song had begun. Di Giacomo and other local poets wrote hundreds of songs. Street musicians throughout the city popularized them. Emigration, the phonograph, and then radio spread them across the world. Enrico Caruso (1873–1921) got his start singing the songs of his native city, and even after his career took him to the great opera houses of Europe and America, he recorded and made famous many Neapolitan songs.

The exaggerated love and sentimentalized emotions of songs also populated the *sceneggiata*, an overwrought melodrama accompanied by songs and set amidst poor—but honorable—people, which spread at the start of the twentieth century and is still popular in Naples. Perhaps the most famous example is *Zappatore* (The Tiller, 1926, by Libero Bovio and Ferdinando Albano), in which an aged peasant bursts in upon an elegant ball in the fancy house of a Naples lawyer. It is later revealed that the peasant is the lawyer's father, who has come to urge the son's presence at his mother's deathbed, and that the son has long forsaken his humble origins. At the end the father bitterly remarks that "it would have been better to raise you a tiller, because a tiller does not forget his mother." As the lawyer cries in shame, the show ends with the father's imperious command: "kneel, and kiss these hands of mine." The prevalence of dialect in these cultural forms both reflected and contributed to the use of Neapolitan as a spoken language; still today dialect is spoken more commonly in Naples than in other Italian cities.

A final element of Neapolitan identity that began its global ascendancy in the late nineteenth century was pizza. Neapolitans had eaten this local version of fast food since the seventeenth century, but it achieved Italian fame in the decades after unification. "Pizza Margherita," created by a famous Naples pizza-maker and named after Italy's first queen, added mozzarella (a regional specialty) and basil to the traditional tomato pizza. Pizza thus offered the red, white, and green colors of the new national flag, and such clever marketing aided its rise to world popularity. Emigration spread pizza—and other southern foods—to new lands around the world.

Naples remained not only a lively cultural center, but also by far the largest city in the South. In 1861 its population was more than ten times that of Bari, the second largest southern city outside of Sicily. Naples's appearance also changed considerably. In 1866 the government closed many monasteries and sold ecclesiastic real estate to secular owners; many monasteries also were used to house secular institutions. In the 1860s a railroad station opened (it was demolished in 1954 to make way for a larger one). Broader streets were built in the old center. Refurbished or new broad streets built on landfill lined the sea from the old center westward all along the public gardens, giving the city an elegant promenade with spectacular views, though depriving Neapolitans of many of their old beaches.

From the 1880s on, new neighborhoods appeared: in areas east of the old center, lower-class housing prevailed, while a new western neighborhood, inland from the public gardens, attracted a growing bourgeoisie of professionals, businessmen, and building speculators. This area, graced by Art Nouveau buildings and fine shops, is still the most elegant in Naples. New tunnels linked the various parts of the city more effectively, as did new trolley service (a subway line was planned, but did not open until 1925). In 1884 a new tunnel led gradually to the development of Fuorigrotta ("outside the grotto"), a large new area farther west, toward Pozzuoli. Beginning in 1885 another entire new neighborhood, the Vomero, grew on the hills below the old castle of Sant'Elmo, and soon two new funiculars eased travel between the Vomero and downtown.

Yet for all these improvements the majority of Neapolitans remained desperately poor and the city's congestion persisted. The gap between the lives of the rich and the poor widened. Bourgeois neighborhoods acquired amenities while poor ones suffered from neglect and lack of services. As late as 1900, 89 percent of Neapolitans owned no net assets at their death. The city's population density was twice that of Paris or Rome and almost five times that of London. Water and sewer systems remained inadequate; waste flowed into the bay, poisoning beaches and the seafood many Neapolitans ate. In 1884 Serao described a typical street of the poor center:

> It may be four meters wide, so that coaches cannot pass, and it is windy, it turns like a gut: very high houses submerge it, on the most beautiful of days, in a dead and pale light: in the middle of the street runs a black, fetid, stagnant, swampy stream, made up of suds and lurid soap, of water from cooking pasta or soup, a dirty mixture that rots. In the street . . . one finds everything: dark shops, in which shadows move, selling anything, pawnshops, lotto offices; every now and then a dark door, or a muddy alley, every now and then a frying shop, from which comes the smell of bad oil, or a grocer, from whose shop comes the stink of fermented cheese or rotten lard.

Serao was keen to stress that the people who lived thus were no different from their more comfortable neighbors: "this is not a bestial, savage, lazy people; they are not lost to faith, darkened by vice, or angry in their misfortune." But bad hygiene and deep poverty were undeniable and had dramatic effects.

In 1884 cholera hit Naples, infecting at least twenty thousand people and killing over seven thousand, especially in the poorest central neighborhoods. The epidemic—the eighth in the city since 1835—shocked Italian and European public opinion. It was then that Serao wrote *The Bowels of Naples* with its poignant descriptions of the life of the urban poor (the title refers to a statement by the prime minister after the epidemic that it was necessary to "disembowel Naples"). After the immediate crisis was over, the national and municipal governments responded with a major plan for restructuring the city, soon called—with another medical metaphor—the Risanamento (Healing). In 1885 a new aqueduct alleviated the city's water needs. Large-scale work began in 1889 and lasted until World War I. Entire areas were gutted and a broad new street cut through the old center, linking the harbor with the new railroad station. The aims were to destroy the worst housing, bring air and light to poor areas, and elevate streets above stagnant groundwaters. In 1894 the Corso Umberto, named for Italy's king, formally opened. Imposing buildings, including in 1908 new headquarters for the university, lined this straight, broad boulevard. A nearby project resulted in the opening in 1892 of the Galleria Umberto, a domed, covered gallery for shops and offices

Piazza della Borsa and Corso Umberto, Naples,
nineteenth-century photograph

The Galleria Umberto, Naples, nineteenth-century photograph

and Naples's most remarkable Art Nouveau building. All this construction, while at times impressive and helpful in fighting filth and disease, also produced wild financial speculation and unchecked growth, as no serious effort was made to regulate the city's expansion. The rebuilding program also failed in its intent to preserve the city from disease: in 1910–11 another epidemic of cholera killed about twenty-five hundred people in Naples.

By the time of the 1884 cholera epidemic, Italian educated opinion had begun to realize the facts of southern poverty. In 1876 a national political realignment had brought to government a new coalition that included most southern deputies. In 1875 Pasquale Villari's *Southern Letters* revealed in stark language, and with solid evidence, the miserable conditions of southern society and economy, particularly in the rural world. Soon, other social scientists and southern advocates published the shocking results of inquiries into southern life. These authors were inspired by, and contributed to, the general development of the social sciences in late-nineteenth-century Europe. Their works began what Italians still call the *questione meridionale* (southern question) and formed the intellectual movement known as *meridionalismo*: the effort to dispel traditional views of the South as fertile and prosperous and replace them with a serious understanding of southern realities, in order to produce reform initiatives ("Meridione" or "Mezzogiorno"—literally "midday"—indicate the South, just as "Midi" does in French). Villari captured the movement's aim when he wrote that "it is useful to enlighten public opinion, revealing our wounds and our shames, without fear of ridicule or discredit."

Villari stressed the dramatic poverty of the southern masses, their alienation from state institutions and governing classes, and the strength of organized crime networks in Sicily, Naples, and across the South. His work placed the southern situation at the center of Italian politics and analysis, as the crucial issue left unresolved by national unification. The next year two Tuscan landowners, Leopoldo Franchetti and Sidney Sonnino, published the results of their inquiries into Sicilian conditions. Like Villari, they were motivated by fear of the spread of Socialism among the southern masses. They went further than Villari in analyzing the exploitative economic relationships that prevailed in the southern countryside and in regarding land as the essential issue of southern life. "The abolition by law of the feudal system produced no social revolution," Sonnino wrote, and southern peasants "were reduced in fact to greater servitude than before because of their poverty." Worse, he argued, Italy's institutions "have provided the oppressor class [of Sicilian landowners] with the means better to cloak with legal appearances the oppression that already existed in reality."

The last main figure in the emergence of meridionalismo was Giustino Fortunato (1848–1932), one of the greatest southern intellectuals of the time. Beginning in 1878 he published thorough analyses of the resources and economic structures of the entire South, shattering remaining illusions about southern prosperity and fertility. Fortunato also severely criticized southern elites, both landowners and the wealthy and educated classes of Naples, describing the latter as "lazy, fragmented, indifferent, gossipy, suspicious . . . without faith or character."

At the end of the century, when across Europe the positivist movement urged scientific analyses of and remedies to social problems, negative views of southerners were shaped by Italy's imperialist adventures in East Africa. A colonial rhetoric grounded in dubious racial science began to appear in discussions of the South. The sociologist Alfredo Niceforo argued that southern and northern Italians were, in fact, two separate ethnic groups, characterized by different skull and chest sizes: northerners were Aryan and shared the physical and moral traits of civic-minded and masculine northern Europeans, while southerners were Mediterranean and thus weak, individualistic, and more inclined to immoral and criminal behavior. Niceforo framed the relationship between the two areas in clear terms: "[h]ere modern Italy has a lofty mission to accomplish and a great colony to civilize." The Sicilian writer Napoleone Colajanni countered that poverty and illiteracy were the true causes of southern problems and denounced racist views: "[o]ur northern brothers have attended to the economic ills of the South and Sicily by regarding these regions as a colony peopled by barbarians."

The writers of meridionalismo continued to insist that southern problems could be solved through economic investment and new fiscal policies, though their optimism about government intervention waned over time. In his *North and South* (1900) Nitti proved that the South contributed more than its share of the Italian fiscal burden while receiving less in state services and investments. Indeed, the agrarian crisis of the 1880s and the ensuing protectionist policies of the Italian government—as of most European governments at the time—to stimulate northern industry further weakened the southern economy at the end of the century. In 1902 Giuseppe Zanardelli was the first prime minister to visit a southern region, Basilicata. Several parliamentary inquiries into the conditions of Naples and the South produced grim reports but few effective remedies. Northern industry remained the primary concern of Italian governments, and the southern economy continued to be dominated by the interests of all-powerful landowners. In 1904 parliament passed the first Special Law for Naples; as with later similar initiatives, it sought to direct industrial investment to southern areas by offering fiscal and other advantages. A few major factories opened near Naples and employed a few thousand Neapolitans, but the effects remained limited and poverty widespread.

Meridionalismo tried to counter the negative image of southerners that prevailed among Italians in the decades after unification. The literary movement known as *verismo* (Realism), closely connected with meridionalismo in its origins, added to these shifts in perception. Like their European counterparts, verismo authors strived in their novels, stories, and plays to present objective images of ordinary reality—what French authors called slices of life. The Italian movement focused much of its attention on the South and produced works that depicted the miserable conditions of southern peasants and cities. The main authors of Italian verismo were Sicilian by birth or origin, but their works, though steeped in Sicilian reality, transcend their context and have gained readers across the world. Unlike the Neapolitan literature in which local color is primarily decorative, in verismo works southern realities are used to address larger moral and spiritual questions of modern life.

Giovanni Verga (1840–1922), the greatest verismo writer, left his native Sicily and began his career with sentimental romances. In 1874 he wrote "Nedda," the story of a Sicilian olive picker and the first of Verga's stories to be set in rural Sicily. It met with great success. Verga then read and met the meridionalismo authors and shifted his aesthetic focus. The story "Rosso Malpelo" (1878) marked his abandonment of picturesque, quaint elements in his depiction of Sicilian life. This tale of a destitute boy who labors in a mine and spends virtually his entire life underground is unremittingly grim. Rosso's nastiness prevents any sentimental reaction to the plot, and the boy's death—lost in an underground maze—comes as simply a liberation from a brutal life, unloved and unlovable.

Verga went on to the stories collected in *Country Life* (1880) and two masterful novels, *I Malavoglia* (1881) and *Mastro-Don Gesualdo* (1888). In the stories, Verga describes the harrowing poverty of Sicilian miners, peasants, and workers; he turned some of them into plays, none more famously than *Cavalleria rusticana* (Rural Chivalry), which in 1890 Pietro Mascagni made into one of the world's most popular operas. The two novels center, respectively, on the desperate members of the Malavoglia family of fishermen and on Gesualdo, an enriched farmer whose money brings him both flattery and secret contempt from his social betters and whose only daughter reviles him for his uncouthness. When Gesualdo dies, alone in his nobly married daughter's palace, servants gather and the novel ends with their banter:

> "Well," said the concierge, "should I go down and close the front door?"
>
> "Yes, sure! He's family stuff. Now we must alert the duchess's maid."

Verga's works present human frailties and miseries in a cold and yet affecting manner. Their effect is strengthened by his linguistic ability: his characters do not speak strict dialect, but he manages to convey the linguistic layers and barriers created by regional and social identities. Verga's fiction influenced another great Sicilian writer, Luigi Pirandello (1867–1936). Pirandello lived most of his life in Rome and acquired global fame with the plays he began writing in the 1910s, which gained him the Nobel Prize in 1934. But Pirandello began his writing career in the 1890s with many short stories, most of which follow the themes of verismo in their focus on Sicilian situations and characters.

Verga planned but never finished additional novels on the Sicilian upper classes. Federico De Roberto (1861–1927) in *The Viceroys* (1894) presents the story of the Uzeda noble clan in the generations before and after Italian unification. It is a devastating portrayal of weakness and cruelty, of greed and ambition, with rich characterizations and a sober analysis of the unlikeliness of improvement in Sicily's woes. The novel closes with the young Duke Consalvo, newly elected to the Italian Parliament, defending to his bitter old aunt Ferdinanda what in her eyes is Consalvo's betrayal of the family's ties to the old Bourbons: "Once the power of our family came from the kings; now it comes from the people. . . . The difference is more apparent than real. . . . The first person elected by almost universal suffrage is neither a man of the people, nor a bourgeois, nor a democrat: it is I, because I am the prince of Francalanza. . . . Our duty, instead of despising the new laws, seems to me to use them! . . . No, our race is not degenerate: it is always the same."

World War I and the crises that followed it affected the South like the rest of Italy: southerners fought and died at the front and turmoil riled Naples and other cities in 1919–22. Unemployment, acute social strife, fear of Communism, political fragmentation, and nationalistic disappointment with the peace settlement opened the way to Fascism, which originated in northern Italy. The Fascist years (1922–43) did little to alleviate southern problems. The regime frowned upon emigration, which it regarded as a symptom of national weakness, and moved to limit it. This approach coincided with decisions in the early 1920s by the United States government to limit immigration. The Fascist government expanded previous policies of supporting industrial investment in the South, and state ownership and management of Italy's industries grew generally under the regime. This led to new factories in the Naples area in particular, though the proportion of industrial workers never rose above 20 percent of the Naples workforce. The regime's emphasis on Italy's self-sufficiency in grain production forced southern agriculture away from more lucrative crops, thus increasing rural poverty in the South, where still in 1936 almost 60 percent of the population consisted of peasants. Limits on emigration, which reduced remittances and boosted unemployment, added to rural misery. As late as 1951 one in four southerners remained illiterate.

In 1925–29 the government conducted a repressive operation against the mafia, to strengthen the regime's support in Sicily. Several thousand people were arrested. The government purged the island's bureaucracy, staged military operations to arrest rural bandits, and launched public works programs to employ urban Sicilians. But the basic inequalities of Sicilian society and the deep poverty of rural areas remained untouched, and the campaign did not diminish the long-standing hostility of Sicilians to the Italian state, or local crime levels. The only other significant Fascist initiative in the rural South—a draining program aimed at diminishing malaria and increasing cultivation—also bore limited results.

Censorship was, of course, a major component of Fascist rule, and among its targets was meridionalismo, with its criticism of government policies. New reflection on southern issues came from proscribed opponents of the regime. The Sardinian Antonio Gramsci (1891–1937), founder in 1921 of the Italian Communist Party and Italy's greatest Marxist intellectual, was jailed in 1926 and only released days before his early death. In the year of his imprisonment, Gramsci wrote an essay on the southern question in which he argued that the national capitalist system oppressed northern workers and southern peasants alike, necessitating a united resistance. Unlike more orthodox Communist thinkers, Gramsci envisioned peasants as an essential element in revolutionary struggles, but he noted that the South presented "an extreme social disintegration" and that its peasants were "incapable of giving a unified expression to their aspirations and their needs." Their alliance with northern workers would bring to power the proletariat, which then would "direct the enormous power of state organization to support the peasants in their struggle against the landowners, against nature, against poverty."

The Fascist regime also objected to negative depictions of Italian realities in cultural forms, so actual southern conditions are largely absent from the literature, art, and film of the interwar years. Powerful descriptions of peasant life and society in Abruzzo appear in Ignazio Silone's novels—*Fontamara* (1933) and *Bread and Wine* (1936)—but Silone (1900–1978) was in exile in Switzerland during the 1930s and his two novels first appeared in German and were not published in Italian until after World War II. Another affecting depiction of southern life to appear after the war was the product of the Fascist practice of sending opponents to the South for internal exile: Carlo Levi's *Christ Stopped at Eboli* (1945).

Because of his anti-Fascist activities, Levi (1902–75), a painter from Turin, was sent to Aliano, a small village in Basilicata, in 1935–36. From his experiences Levi drew a moving portrait of southern conditions and characters. The peasants among whom he lived emerge from his book as shaped by the primitive circumstances of their life and work, but also as profoundly human. Levi saw the rural world, especially the remote villages of mountainous areas, as deeply different even from the urban, more modern South embodied by Eboli, the large town in the plains where his train dropped him as he made his way to the village (renamed Gagliano in the book). Levi presents the world of the villagers as a timeless one, which neither the culture nor the institutions of the outside world can reach: "No one has touched this land except as a conqueror or an enemy or an undiscerning visitor . . . no human or divine message has addressed itself to this resisting poverty . . . to this dark land, without sin and without redemption, where evil is not moral, but is an earthly pain, forever residing in things, Christ did not descend. Christ stopped at Eboli." Levi reflected on the enormous distance between the villagers and the government, any government: "To the peasants, the State is farther than the sky, and more malignant, because it is always on the other side. . . . The only possible defense, against the State and against propaganda, is resignation. . . . For the people of [Basilicata], Rome is nothing: it is the capital of gentlemen, the center of a foreign and malevolent State. . . . Not Rome or Naples, but New York would be the true capital of the peasants of [Basilicata], if ever these stateless men could have one."

One of Levi's most famous pages describes his sister's visit to the "Sassi" of Matera, the provincial capital. These poor neighborhoods, excavated in the steeply declining rock under the cathedral, face "a bald mountain, of an ugly greyish color, without sign of cultivation, or even a single tree." Lodgings were part of the rock, caves really, "which receive no light or air except through their door. . . . Inside those black holes, with dirt walls, I saw beds, miserable furniture, hanging rags. On the floor lay dogs, sheep, goats, pigs. Each family generally lives in only one of those caves, and all sleep there together, men, women, children, animals. So live twenty thousand people." Levi poignantly contrasted such hopeless poverty with Fascism's empty promises of Italy's imperial glories.

The regime was largely successful in its political repression and cultural control. Naples had the distinction of housing one of the few opposition voices that managed to speak out throughout the Fascist period. Benedetto Croce (1866–1952) began his intellectual career in the 1890s with literary criticism, essays on local history, and works of philosophy. Independently wealthy, Croce remained outside the formal institutions of intellectual life: though he gathered followers in his aristocratic residence and library and participated in numerous journals and local societies, he never occupied any position at the university. By the 1920s he was Italy's most prominent intellectual. Croce's works gained a broad readership in Italy and abroad. He was conservative in his philosophy and politics and initially saw Fascism as useful to remedy Italy's political instability. But he quickly grew disillusioned with the regime and expressed his opposition—and his confidence in the future freedom of Italy—in numerous books published by the courageous Laterza of Bari. My grandfather owned them all and filled their margins with comments about the comfort he found in Croce's liberal hopes. Such was Croce's international prestige that he was able to live quietly in Naples and to continue publishing throughout the Fascist era.

The Fascist regime eventually led Italy into war. World War II devastated the South. Sicily suffered terribly through the Anglo-American conquest, which in July and August of 1943 involved almost nine hundred thousand soldiers fighting over the island. Because of the importance of its port, Naples underwent heavy bombardments both from Allied forces and later—when the front was stuck at Cassino, halfway between Naples and Rome, until May of 1944—from German ones. In late September, Neapolitans rose against the Germans in the "Four Days," which left hundreds dead and helped force the Germans out. Because of the Allied conquest, the South took limited part in the Resistance that took place in the North in 1944–45 and so did not fully share in the founding political experience of modern Italy. Naples's Four Days thus played a prominent role in shaping southern identity in the immediate postwar climate. The South also played virtually no role in the Holocaust, as deportations of Jews from Italy largely began after the Allied arrival in the South and most Italian Jews lived in the North.

Soon after the Four Days, on October 1, 1943, Neapolitans warmly welcomed the Allied forces, which included many whose ancestors had emigrated to the United States from Naples. The German bombardments continued. The prolonged presence of American and British soldiers in the city left its mark both on the Neapolitan imagination and in the city's newborn population. For many months Neapolitans lived under constant threat from the air and with grave hunger and shortages of all goods. Over two hundred thousand people were homeless, water was scarce, and sewers did not work. In March of 1944 Vesuvius added to the chaos with a major eruption that spewed lava and rained ash on the city (since then Vesuvius has been largely dormant, and volcanologists worry that its next activity will be all the more cataclysmic because of this long quiet). The Allied occupation of Naples lasted until December of 1944.

The Allies reached Naples at one of the lowest points in its history. A British soldier remembered entering the city: "The animal struggle for survival governed everything. Food. That was the only thing that mattered. Food for the children. Food for yourself. Food at the cost of any debasement and depravity." Another wrote of "this city so shattered, so starved, so deprived of all things that justify a city's existence." The writer and journalist Curzio Malaparte (1898–1957) offered a shocking account of the moral and social degradation in Naples during the war in his novel *The Skin* (1949). He also ironically depicted the Neapolitans' embrace of the liberating forces: "The people had immediately loved those magnificent soldiers, so young, so handsome, so well combed, with such white teeth and such red lips. In so many centuries of invasions, of wars won and lost, Europe had never seen soldiers this elegant, clean, courteous, always freshly shaven, in impeccable uniforms."

The fall of the Fascist regime liberated Italian culture to explore the country's dramatic realities. The impact of the war and the degradation—economic, social, cultural—of the South became one of the first topics of reflection. As with verismo in the late nineteenth century, the South featured prominently in the aesthetic and intellectual concerns of Italian Neorealism, a movement that achieved its greatest expression in film and its broadest impact outside Italy. The frothy romances and nationalist epics of the Fascist period gave way to stark renditions of Italy's desperate conditions. Roberto Rossellini's *Paisà* (1946), one of the greatest Neorealist films, depicts six episodes during the liberation of Italy: the second one portrays an African-American soldier following a Neapolitan street urchin who has taken the soldier's shoes. The boy leads the soldier to an overcrowded cave, and its residents' abject misery moves the soldier to forgive the little thief. Luchino Visconti's *La terra trema* (The Earth Trembles, 1948) presents the life of Sicilian fishermen through an adaptation of Verga's *Malavoglia* that employs dialect and local people as actors. The link between southern problems and the Neorealist approach emerged in several works of the ensuing decades, down to the films of Gianni Amelio, whose *Ladro di bambini* (Stolen Children, 1992) sets much of its grim story of broken families and child prostitution in a southern landscape of economic and moral decay.

The depiction of southern problems in Neorealist film and literature coexisted uneasily in the 1950s with other images of the South. Perhaps the most famous postwar text portraying the South was *The Leopard*, by the Sicilian aristocrat Giuseppe Tomasi di Lampedusa (1896–1957). This novel ran so contrary to the then prevailing literary realism that various publishers rejected it as old-fashioned, and it only appeared posthumously in 1959. Lampedusa centered his Sicilian story around the 1860 campaign, offering a skeptical interpretation of the creation of the Italian state. He presents an image of an unchanging, fascinating land that echoes both Romantic views of the South and the gloom of verismo, tinged with a sad, ironic nostalgia. The grand, if fading, noble family at the center of the story weathers the stormy times by allying itself with newly enriched commoners and by relying on the deep resistance to, and skepticism toward, change that the author sees entrenched in the Sicilian character. In one of the book's most famous scenes the prince of Salina turns down a visiting northern dignitary's offer of a seat in the new Italian Senate with words that recall many nineteenth-century ideas about the South: "We are old, Chevalley, very old. For at least twenty-five centuries we have been carrying on our shoulders the weight of magnificent, heterogeneous civilizations, all come from outside, none produced by ourselves, none started by us. We are as white as you are, Chevalley, as the Queen of England; and yet since twenty-five hundred years we are a colony. I do not say this to complain: it is our fault. But even so we are tired and worn out."

The popular tradition and image of napoletanità also flourished in the postwar decades, at times as a protest against Neorealist perceptions. Theater and film expressed this popular celebration of the Neapolitan temperament. Neapolitans still love to recount favorite moments in the countless films of the comic Totò (Antonio de Curtis, 1898–1967), whose sad and expressive face became an icon of both comedy and pathos across postwar Italy. *L'oro di Napoli* (The Gold of Naples, 1954) by Vittorio de Sica is the best known of a number of 1950s film comedies offering a colorful picture of the city and its inhabitants (like many others, it starred local glory Sophia Loren). Eduardo De Filippo (1900–1984) was for five decades the greatest Neapolitan playwright and is the main Italian modern author to write primarily in dialect. He and his brother Peppino (1903–80) and sister Titina (1898–1965)—the children of Eduardo Scarpetta, they came to theater from birth—were also acclaimed actors across Italy. De Filippo's plays are comedies, but they often deal with serious issues, none more than *Napoli milionaria* (Millionaire Naples, 1945), which ends with worried parents hoping for the recovery of their ill daughter, a poignant metaphor for the city's dubious survival after the war. Many of his works have been filmed, and also staged in Italy and abroad.

Just as verismo had accompanied early analyses of the southern question, Neorealism coincided with a revived effort to study and remedy southern problems. In 1946 the first Italian vote with universal male and female suffrage established the new Italian Republic—in a referendum in which 60 percent of southern voters preferred the monarchy—and elected its first parliament. Reconstruction was high on the new government's agenda, and with it came alleviation of southern conditions. In 1946 in Rome a group of economists and entrepreneurs formed a private association called SVIMEZ devoted to studying the economy of the South. The dominant approach centered on the notion of southern delay: the South needed to transform its economy into a modern industrial one. The writings of Carlo Levi and others describing a timeless rural culture came under attack as celebrating an obstacle to southern progress. Social scientists critiqued southern peasant culture as backward, amoral, and unable to effect improvement or to act for the common good. This view was brought to an international public in 1958 by *The Moral Basis of a Backward Society*, a study of a remote southern village by the American sociologist Edward Banfield.

In 1950 the government founded the Cassa per il Mezzogiorno (Fund for the South), which—thanks also to American aid through the Marshall Plan—invested heavily in southern infrastructure and later in industrialization. Since the Fascist period, public ownership of industrial enterprises has been widespread in Italy, and several laws in the 1950s to 1970s required these enterprises to place substantial percentages of their investments in the South. The Cassa also offered incentives for private firms to invest there. Chemical, oil, automobile, and other plants opened across the region, where they often bore no connection to local conditions—thus earning from critics of such programs the name "cathedrals in the desert." The Cassa, originally planned for ten years, was repeatedly renewed and did not fully cease operating until 1992.

These projects largely coincided with Italy's so-called economic miracle of the 1950s and 1960s. Southern circumstances underwent remarkable transformations, especially in the countryside. The war had left dreadful conditions: in 1950 per capita income in the South reached only 60 percent of its 1924 level. In 1949–50 peasants across Italy occupied estates and demanded land reform, particularly in the South, where most peasants were landless laborers. The government responded not only with repression that resulted in several casualties, but also with a plan to expropriate underutilized estates and distribute them to peasants, though implementation of this plan was slow and partial.

Rural change also came in other ways. On the one hand, the draining of swamps and advances in medicine meant that drought and malaria ceased to afflict southern peasants. On the other, deforestation, soil erosion, and market integration emptied many mountain villages, where today much of the population is elderly and underemployed. Furthermore, irrigation and increased agricultural mechanization and productivity made many rural laborers unnecessary, leading to a massive migration. Poor Italians—mostly rural, as had been the case around 1900—migrated to Germany, Switzerland, and other countries, attracted by employment opportunities in a growing western European economy. About 4 million southerners (one-third of them women) left Italy in the 1950s and 1960s, out of a southern population of about 17 million in 1951. Southerners made up just over half of this new wave of Italian emigration; this time only about 13 percent went to North America, while over two-thirds went to western Europe. Millions more left for temporary or permanent employment in northern Italy: by 1970 Turin's southern population was smaller only than Naples's and Palermo's.

Peasants also moved to growing southern cities. In particular, the population of the Adriatic region of Puglia grew to rival the Naples area: Bari, Puglia's capital, which in 1861 had 34,000 inhabitants, or less than one-tenth the population of Naples, by 1991 reached almost 350,000, or roughly one-third the size of Naples. The University of Bari, founded in 1924, was the first university in the continental South outside of Naples; today a network of universities operates across the South. Southern cities grew generally as centers of administration and services much more than as industrial centers, though Taranto in Puglia became an industrial hub.

Economic change advanced faster than political reform. Southern political culture remained mired in traditional networks of patronage and nepotism. Poverty and low education levels, a weak democratic tradition, and entrenched—often corrupt—social and political elites kept the southern electorate compliant and resigned. Given the scarcity of viable industries, many urban jobs depended on public patronage and employment, and to this day public institutions in the South are bloated by hires resulting from clientage systems. The centrist Christian Democrats, Italy's dominant political party from the time of liberation until the 1990s, maintained a close lock on southern politics by relying heavily on such patronage networks. In Naples the number of municipal employees quadrupled between 1953 and 1968, and in Palermo in 1976 public employees formed 36 percent of the labor force.

The building speculation that accompanied the rapid growth of cities also afforded political leaders opportunities for financial gain. Many southern cities expanded without any regulation; the camorra in Naples, the mafia in Sicily, the 'ndrangheta in Calabria enjoyed large shares of the resulting wealth and of the government money poured into public works. Ugly modern buildings went up close to the Greek temples of Agrigento in southern Sicily. In Naples these trends were at their worst in the 1950s under Mayor Achille Lauro (1887–1982), a shipbuilding entrepreneur—and expert vote-buyer—allied with the monarchist movement and later with the Neofascists (his name lives on beyond Naples for the 1985 terrorist hijacking of a passenger ship named after him). Francesco Rosi's film *Mani sulla città* (Hands on the City, 1963)—an indictment of the Lauro regime—was one of several 1960s films addressing the corruption that accompanied Italy's economic boom.

Sicily's postwar political and social struggles were especially grave.

The Allied invasion in July of 1943 was probably facilitated by contacts between the Allies and both the American and the Sicilian mafia. The Allied administration replaced many Fascist local leaders with men close to the criminal world, often the only available substitutes. Criminal networks controlled the island's active black market. An American report in October 1943 expressed concern about the revival in the mafia's fortunes: "the mafia, in a sense, more than an association is a real social system, a way of life, a profession." Moreover, even before the war ended, large-scale peasant agitation convulsed the island, and a separatist movement—supported especially by landowners and the mafia—added to the tensions.

In 1945–46 a separatist insurrection extended armed conflict in Sicily. The new Italian government fought the armed revolt with more moderation than in previous struggles on the island, and in 1947 it granted Sicily (and Sardinia and three border regions) special status as an autonomous region with a local parliament and government (in 1970 all twenty Italian regions received greater administrative autonomy). But struggles between peasants and landowners continued, and criminal bands operated with near impunity across the island, most infamously one headed by Salvatore Giuliano. The struggles pitted mafia and landowning interests against peasant and leftist agitation. Between November 1946 and April 1948 twenty-eight Sicilian leftist politicians and union leaders were murdered. Local elections in April 1947 gave leftist parties a plurality and weakened Sicily's Christian Democrats just as cold war tensions intensified nationally and internationally. On May 1—Labor Day—about fifteen hundred people gathered for a leftist celebration at Portella della Ginestra, outside Palermo. Giuliano and his band fired upon the crowd, killing eleven and wounding sixty-five. Strong suspicions about political and mafia involvement remain.

This dramatic episode contributed to the breakdown of the national governing coalition that united the Christian Democrats and the Communists; a center-right alliance soon came to power. For decades social and political change remained very slow in Sicily, though in the 1950s limited agrarian reform and the discovery of oil and gas deposits in southeastern Sicily boosted the island's economy. Sicily's struggles of the 1950s and 1960s are beautifully explored in the novels and essays of Leonardo Sciascia (1921–89).

An observer of the Italian South in the 1950s could easily note that much had not changed since unification: one still found widespread rural poverty and ignorance, actual if not legal disenfranchisement, an authoritarian government and police intervention in social conflicts, economic backwardness linked to northern advantage, emigration, political corruption, and disease in overcrowded cities. As late as 1968, in an incident eerily reminiscent of the Bronte events of 1860, the police killed two striking peasants in the eastern Sicilian village of Avola—though this time the episode aroused national indignation. That same year an earthquake in the Belice valley in southwestern Sicily killed five hundred people and left a hundred thousand homeless. Nine years later—due to bureaucratic delay, incompetence, and corruption—sixty thousand still lived in temporary structures. In 1970 Catanzaro became the regional capital for Calabria; this loss of patronage and employment opportunities to a rival city caused rioting in Reggio, one of Italy's poorest cities, that left three dead, over two hundred wounded, and substantial economic damage.

But by the end of the 1960s remarkable changes had improved the lives of southern Italians. In the 1950s and 1960s all of southern Europe enjoyed an economic expansion based on control of malaria, renewed emigration, cheaper energy (with Near East oil replacing coal), and American aid through the Marshall Plan. In the Italian South illiteracy, child mortality, and the birthrate declined, while education levels and health indicators rose. In 1976 the proportion of southerners working in agriculture stood at 27 percent, less than half the 57 percent of 1951 (it is now 8 percent). The most remarkable change has probably come in food consumption: after decades of shortages and poor diet, and severe hunger during and soon after the war, by the 1960s most Italians began to have access to plentiful and varied food.

The European economic depression of the 1970s slowed economic growth, but the modern South participates in an advanced consumer economy. Most economic indicators remain lower than those for northern Italy, and unemployment, especially among the young, is a particular concern. Southern levels of consumption, production, and income are still about three-fifths of the national averages, though this means that the percentage gap with northern levels has not increased. Economists have described the southern situation as modernization without development, in that standards of living are more advanced than either productive forces or civic institutions. A large underground economy and a substantial infusion of government subsidies in the form of welfare payments (a major component of political patronage) are troubling elements of southern prosperity. But it remains noteworthy that the great majority of contemporary southerners live in material comfort and security that would amaze their grandparents. Even the Sassi of Matera, the poor residents of which were moved to healthier suburbs in the 1950s and 1960s, are today a tourist attraction dotted with craft shops and charming restaurants. Since the 1980s, southern Italy—for so long a land of desperate emigrants—has attracted immigrants from Africa, Asia, the Caribbean, and most recently Eastern Europe and the Balkans.

The 1990s brought new challenges. The end of the cold war and the "Clean Hands" inquiry into political corruption undermined the traditional balance of power at the national level (the investigation also proved that corruption was far from a solely southern problem). The Christian Democrats had based their national predominance on their electoral domination in the South, where their patronage system spread welfare and subsidies and their ties with crime networks preserved traditional power structures. In the late 1980s to early 1990s, however, northern hostility to public funds for the South grew, just as the stringent requirements of membership in the new European monetary system necessitated cuts in Italy's public debt and budget deficit. The Northern League, a new northern political movement aggressively opposed to national taxation and advocating a foggy federalist or separatist agenda, deployed a stunningly racist rhetoric against both non-European recent immigrants and the *terroni* ("dirt people," a derogatory term for southerners) who had long lived in the North. The position of the South in national politics is now probably weaker than at any time since 1945.

Naples and Palermo, the South's two traditional capitals, also have faced difficult times in recent decades. The 1971 census found that 47 percent of dwellings in Naples had no shower or bath. In 1973 pollution in the bay brought a brief epidemic of cholera to Naples, killing about thirty people and shocking Italian public opinion, which believed cholera eradicated in the developed world. A 1980 earthquake in the area of Avellino, near Naples, killed over three thousand people; public reconstruction funds were misspent or ended in criminal hands. Through the 1980s organized crime networks operated largely unchecked and profited from an expanding trade in hard drugs. Unemployment and urban degradation were high, and local administration rife with corruption. In 1982 there were 284 killings among the criminal networks in Campania. In the 1970s and 1980s the mafia was especially powerful and fully integrated in the Christian Democratic power structure in Sicily. In 1982 the general commanding anti-mafia operations on the island was killed in Palermo. Even as recently as 1992 the mafia killed two prominent antimafia judges in brazen attacks.

By then, however, positive factors had begun to work as well, and the last ten years or so have brought improvements to the two cities. A major new neighborhood—the "Centro Direzionale"—revived a blighted area of Naples with remarkable modern buildings planned for both residences and new public offices. A long-awaited second subway line, though still unfinished, is finally operating in Naples, linking old and new neighborhoods more effectively than ever before. A new system for the direct popular election of mayors allowed reformists in Naples, Palermo, and other cities both to win elections and to implement their agendas more forcefully than in the past, producing better and more stable local governments. In 1994 Naples hosted the meeting of the seven most industrialized countries, and the occasion brought significant government investment in infrastructure and tourism. It was Naples's good fortune that these investments came at the high point of the Clean Hands investigation, when press and judicial scrutiny over the proper use of public funds was especially sharp. The effect was that these funds produced real results for the city and the meeting turned into a major—and global—success for Naples's image.

The years since have not resolved all southern problems. Naples, which with its periphery is home to about three million people, remains crowded and dirty. Many outlying neighborhoods have active crime and drug networks and offer little hope and few services to their residents. Unregulated building continues to endanger both landscape and inhabitants. Campania is still the most densely populated region in Italy. Organized crime is far from defeated, in Naples, Sicily, or elsewhere. The exploitation of new immigrant workers, the most desperate of whom work as underpaid farm hands or in prostitution, poses new challenges, both economic and moral. But the last forty years or so have brought previously unimaginable levels of prosperity and education to the South, and recently the entire region has again become a destination for international tourism. Naples itself has a dynamic cultural life and is once more fashionable among European tourists, who are rediscovering and reembracing both its sights and its color and character. One can hope that these positive trends will take root so in the future there will no longer be room to doubt that this ancient land is indeed fully part of an integrated Europe.

Population Charts

Kingdom of Naples

YEAR	NO. OF HOUSEHOLDS	NO. OF PEOPLE (ESTIMATE)
ca. 1300		2,500,000
ca. 1400		1,500,000
1505	254,823	1,146,703
1532	315,990	1,421,955
1545	422,030	1,899,135
1561	481,345	2,166,052
1595	540,090	2,430,405
1648	500,202	2,250,909
1669	394,721	1,776,244
1734		3,000,000
1765		4,000,000
1791		5,000,000
1828		5,800,000
1861		6,900,000
1901		8,650,000
1951		12,300,000
2001		14,300,000

NOTE: The figures for the sixteenth and seventeenth centuries come from the censuses conducted in those years. Historians generally agree that the censuses of 1648 and 1669 underreported the kingdom's population. The censuses give the number of households. Since most historians place the average number of people per household in early modern Europe between 4 and 5, I multiplied the number of households by 4.5 to arrive at estimates of the total population. The figures for other centuries are estimates from various scholars. Until 1734 the data do not include the city of Naples. The data since 1861 refer to the areas that had formed the Kingdom of Naples before Italian unification.

Naples

DATE	ESTIMATE
Early 1200s	50,000
Early 1400s	45,000
Early 1500s	100.000+
1527	155,000
1547	212,203
Early 1600s	300,000+
ca. 1650	400–450,000
After 1656 plague	180,000
ca. 1700	250–300,000
ca. 1750	350–400,000
ca. 1790	400–450,000
1871	450,000
1881	493,000
1901	547,000
1911	668,000
1921	758,000
1931	839,000
1951	1,010,000
1961	1,182,000
1971	1,126,000
1981	1,210,000
1991	1,073,000

Sicily

DATE	ESTIMATE
1277	700,000
1375	300,000
1439	350,000
1478	500,000
1505	570,000
1548	804,000
1570	940,000
1583	989,000
1607	1,094,000
1636	1,137,000
1651	1,121,000
1681	1,142,000
1713	1,143,000
1747	1,359,000
1806	1,584,000
1831	1,941,000
1861	2,392,000
1901	3,568,000
1951	4,487,000
2001	4,969,000

NOTE: Naples was not usually covered by censuses until the modern period. For the eighteenth century especially, one problem with the estimates is that they do not always include residents who were not citizens (and who could number up to 100,000); also, estimates often do not include the *casali* of Naples, neighboring villages without administrative autonomy. For instance, in 1790 the city had about 450,000 inhabitants, and the *casali* about 135,000, for a total of almost 600,000 for what we may call the metropolitan area. The modern figures are from national censuses and refer only to the municipal borders; the number of inhabitants in the city's periphery was 1,125,000 in 1961; 1,483,000 in 1971; 1,732,000 in 1981; and 1,945,000 in 1991.

Genealogy Charts

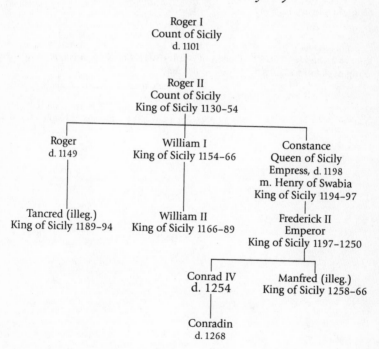

I. The Norman and Swabian Rulers of Sicily

Roger I
Count of Sicily
d. 1101

Roger II
Count of Sicily
King of Sicily 1130–54

Roger
d. 1149

William I
King of Sicily 1154–66

Constance
Queen of Sicily
Empress, d. 1198
m. Henry of Swabia
King of Sicily 1194–97

Tancred (illeg.)
King of Sicily 1189–94

William II
King of Sicily 1166–89

Frederick II
Emperor
King of Sicily 1197–1250

Conrad IV
d. 1254

Manfred (illeg.)
King of Sicily 1258–66

Conradin
d. 1268

NOTE: Conrad IV and Conradin were heirs to the Kingdom of Sicily, but neither was ever formally crowned as king.

II. *The Angevin Dynasty of Naples*

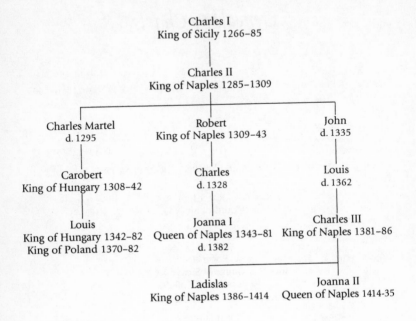

Charles I
King of Sicily 1266–85

Charles II
King of Naples 1285–1309

Charles Martel
d. 1295

Robert
King of Naples 1309–43

John
d. 1335

Carobert
King of Hungary 1308–42

Charles
d. 1328

Louis
d. 1362

Louis
King of Hungary 1342–82
King of Poland 1370–82

Joanna I
Queen of Naples 1343–81
d. 1382

Charles III
King of Naples 1381–86

Ladislas
King of Naples 1386–1414

Joanna II
Queen of Naples 1414–35

NOTE: This table simplifies the complex political history of the fourteenth century. The Angevins continued to use the title king (or queen) of Sicily, although they lost the island in 1282 to the Aragonese. The title king of Naples appears informally in the fourteenth century and comes into regular use by the sixteenth.

III. *The Aragonese Rulers of Sicily to 1479*

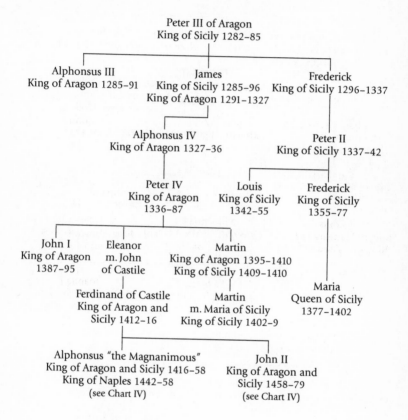

NOTE: The royal numerals are confusing: Frederick of Aragon, king of Sicily in 1296–1337, who was the second King of Sicily by that name, was often referred to as Frederick III, because Frederick II had ruled Sicily under his imperial numeral. Thus, his grandson (who ruled 1355–77) is also at times referred to as Frederick III. Nicknames are often used instead of numerals, and the latter king is unflatteringly known as Frederick "the Simple."

IV. *The Aragonese and Spanish Rulers of the South, 1458–1700*

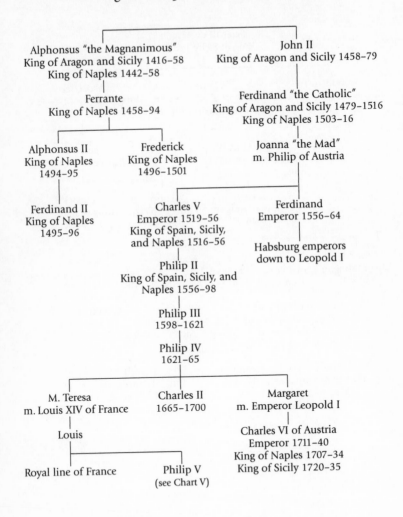

Alphonsus "the Magnanimous"
King of Aragon and Sicily 1416–58
King of Naples 1442–58

Ferrante
King of Naples 1458–94

Alphonsus II
King of Naples
1494–95

Frederick
King of Naples
1496–1501

Ferdinand II
King of Naples
1495–96

John II
King of Aragon and Sicily 1458–79

Ferdinand "the Catholic"
King of Aragon and Sicily 1479–1516
King of Naples 1503–16

Joanna "the Mad"
m. Philip of Austria

Charles V
Emperor 1519–56
King of Spain, Sicily,
and Naples 1516–56

Ferdinand
Emperor 1556–64

Habsburg emperors
down to Leopold I

Philip II
King of Spain, Sicily, and
Naples 1556–98

Philip III
1598–1621

Philip IV
1621–65

M. Teresa
m. Louis XIV of France

Charles II
1665–1700

Margaret
m. Emperor Leopold I

Louis

Charles VI of Austria
Emperor 1711–40
King of Naples 1707–34
King of Sicily 1720–35

Royal line of France

Philip V
(see Chart V)

V. The Bourbon Rulers of Naples and Sicily to 1861

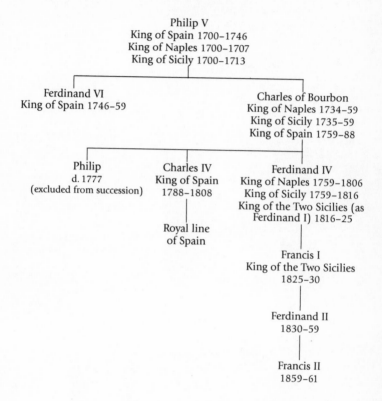

Philip V
King of Spain 1700–1746
King of Naples 1700–1707
King of Sicily 1700–1713

Ferdinand VI
King of Spain 1746–59

Charles of Bourbon
King of Naples 1734–59
King of Sicily 1735–59
King of Spain 1759–88

Philip
d. 1777
(excluded from succession)

Charles IV
King of Spain
1788–1808

Royal line
of Spain

Ferdinand IV
King of Naples 1759–1806
King of Sicily 1759–1816
King of the Two Sicilies (as
Ferdinand I) 1816–25

Francis I
King of the Two Sicilies
1825–30

Ferdinand II
1830–59

Francis II
1859–61

NOTE: Philip V lost Naples to Charles of Austria in 1707 (see Chart IV). In 1713 the Peace of Utrecht forced him to give Sicily to the duke of Savoy; Spain reclaimed the island in 1718, but another treaty gave it to Austria in 1720. In 1734–35 Charles of Bourbon took Naples and Sicily from the Austrians. Charles of Bourbon, once he became king of Spain in 1759, ruled there as Charles III; his numeral as king of Naples and Sicily was ambiguous (by most historians he was Charles VII of Naples), and thus was not used often during his reign there.

Source Notes

These notes give references for all quotations from sources. All translations from foreign sources are my own.

Chapter I

The Horace line is *Epistles* 1.1.83. The Cicero quotes are from J. D'Arms, *Romans on the Bay of Naples* (Cambridge, Harvard University Press, 1970), and E. Bradford, *Mediterranean* (London, Hodder and Stoughton, 1971). The quotes from Theodosius and Ibn Hawqal are in M. Amari, ed., "Description de Palerme," *Journal asiatique*, 4th series, tome 5 (1845), pp. 73–114.

Chapter II

I have quoted these historians for the Norman period: Amato di Monte-cassino, *Storia de' Normanni* (Rome, Tipografia del Senato, 1935), the major history of the Normans overall; Amato was an eleventh-century monk, but his text only survives in a fourteenth-century French version. G. Malaterra, *De rebus gestis Rogerii Calabriae et Siciliae comitis* . . . (Bologna, Zanichelli, 1928), focuses on Roger I; this edition includes the anonymous *Annales siculi*, which I have also quoted. Romualdo Salernitano, *Chronicon* (Città di Castello, Lapi, 1935); Romualdo was a bishop who wrote primarily about Roger II. Alessandro di Telese, *Alexandri Telesini Abbatis Ystoria Rogerii* . . . (Rome, Istituto Storico Italiano per il Medio Evo, 1991), is the main panegyrist of Roger II. *The History of the Tyrants of Sicily by "Hugo Falcandus," 1154–1169* (Manchester, Manchester University Press, 1998) is a modern edition of a work by the major historian of the later Normans; Hugo Falcandus is the traditional name for the unknown author of this text. This edition includes an appendix of additional documents, from which I have quoted the anonymous comment on the crisis of 1189. Other historians I have quoted on the Normans are the Byzantine princess Anna Comnena, *The Alexiad* (Baltimore, Penguin, 1969), and the great Enlightenment historian

Edward Gibbon, *The Decline and Fall of the Roman Empire*, 3 vols. (New York, Modern Library, [1932?]).

I have also quoted excerpts from other contemporary observers that I found in the works of other historians. Robert Guiscard's oath to the papacy of 1059 and Albert of Aix's description of Adelaide's arrival in Jerusalem are cited in J. J. Norwich, *The Normans in Sicily* (London, Penguin, 1992), one of the most engaging and accessible histories of the Norman kingdom. Robert's epitaph is cited in G. A. Loud, *The Age of Robert Guiscard* (London, Longman, 2000). The German writer's comment on the Normans, the Arab scholar Al-Idrisi's comment on Roger II, and the laws of Roger II are cited in H. Houben, *Roger II of Sicily* (Cambridge, UK, Cambridge University Press, 2002). Al-Idrisi's comment on Palermo's buildings is cited in D. Mack Smith, *Medieval Sicily 800–1713* (New York, Viking, 1969); his description of Naples, in P.-A. Jaubert, ed., *La géographie d'Édrisi* (Amsterdam, Philo Press, 1975). The Arab traveler Ibn Jubair's comments on traveling in Sicily and on the Martorana are cited in G. M. Cantarella, *La Sicilia e i Normanni* (Bologna, Pàtron, 1988), as is the thirteenth-century historian Riccardo di San Germano's comment on the memory of William II. Ibn Jubair's comment on William II's Muslim officials is cited in J. Johns, *Arabic Administration in Norman Sicily* (Cambridge, UK, Cambridge University Press, 2002), and his comment on women in A. Metcalfe, *Muslims and Christians in Norman Sicily* (New York, Routledge-Curzon, 2003).

The witness on Frederick II's youth is cited in E. Cuozzo, "L'unificazione normanna e il regno normanno-svevo," in G. Galasso and R. Romeo, eds., *Storia del Mezzogiorno*, vol. II.2 (Naples, Edizioni del Sole, 1989). Frederick's law on feudal succession is cited in N. Santamaria, *I feudi, il diritto feudale e la loro storia nell'Italia meridionale* (Naples, Marghieri, 1881). The Arab observers on Frederick II's Crusade are cited in F. Gabrieli, ed., *Storici arabi delle Crociate* (Turin, Einaudi, 1987). Frederick's 1231 laws are cited in Cuozzo, "L'unificazione," and in D. Abulafia, *Frederick II* (London, Allen Lane, 1988). The papal decree deposing Frederick is cited in N. P. Tanner, S.J., ed., *Decrees of the Ecumenical Councils*, 2 vols. (Washington, DC, Georgetown University Press, 1990). Frederick's statement on the sources of law is cited in G. Vallone, "Evoluzione giuridica e istituzionale della feudalità," in Galasso and Romeo, *Storia del Mezzogiorno*, vol. IX (Naples, Edizioni del Sole, 1991). Frederick's letter to the University of Bologna is cited in W. Tronzo, ed., *Intellectual Life at the Court of Frederick II Hohenstaufen* (Washington, DC, National Gallery of Art, 1994). Innocent IV's reaction to Frederick's death is cited in É. Léonard, *Gli Angioini di Napoli* (Milan, Dall'Oglio, 1967), while Manfred's letter to Conrad IV on the same occasion is cited in Cuozzo, "L'unificazione." Finally, the Franciscan chronicler commenting on Frederick's character is Salimbene in *The Chronicle of Salimbene de Adam* (Binghamton, NY, Medieval and Renaissance Texts and Studies, 1986).

Chapter III

Angevin period: The quotes on the Vespers are from the *Rebellamentu di Sichilia*, in *Rerum Italicarum Scriptores*, 2nd ed., tome XXXIV (Bologna, Zanichelli, 1917). The quotes on Amalfi are from Gibbon's *Decline and Fall*; from Ibn Hawqal as cited in H. Bresc et al., *La Méditerranée entre pays d'Islam et monde latin* (Paris, SEDES, 2001); and from the chronicler Guglielmo Apulo cited in Loud, *Age of Robert Guiscard*. Petrarch's description of the 1343 storm and his comments on King Robert are in F. Petrarca, *Prose* (Milan-Naples, Ricciardi, 1955). Boccaccio's comment on Naples is cited in Galasso, *Napoli capitale* (Naples, Electa, 1998). The comment on Joanna I's succession is from the Renaissance historian Angelo Di Costanzo, cited in Galasso, *Il Regno di Napoli* (Turin, UTET, 1992).

Aragonese period: I have used Masuccio Salernitano, *Il Novellino* (Bologna, Sampietro, 1968); on Emperor Frederick III's visit to Naples, Notar Giacomo, *Cronica di Napoli* (Naples, Stamperia reale, 1845); on the barons' conspiracy against King Ferrante, C. Porzio, *La congiura dei baroni* (Venosa, Osanna, 1989); and on Ferdinand II's return to Naples, R. Filangieri, ed., *Una cronaca napoletana figurata* (Naples, Arte Tipografica, 1956).

Chapter IV

On Pedro de Toledo: Minturno's verses are cited in C. J. Hernando Sánchez, "El *Glorioso Triumfo* de Carlos V en Nápoles y el Humanismo de corte entre Italia y España," *Archivio Storico per le Province Napoletane* 119 (2001); the inscription celebrating Charles is cited in T. Megale, " 'Sic per te gens inimica ruat.' L'ingresso trionfale di Carlo V a Napoli (1535)," ibid.; the comment on Toledo's curiosity about Naples's administration, in "Racconti di storia napoletana," *Archivio Storico per le Province Napoletane* 33 (1908); Charles's praise of Toledo is cited in Hernando Sánchez, *Castilla y Nápoles en el siglo XVI* (Salamanca, Junta de Castilla y León, 1994); the comment on Toledo's nature, in G. Rosso, *Historia delle cose di Napoli* (Naples, Giovan Domenico Montanaro, 1635); his biographer is S. Miccio, *Vita di don Pietro di Toledo* (1600), in *Archivio Storico Italiano* 9 (1846); the French historian's comment, in J. A. de Thou, *Historiarum sui temporis . . .* (1609–14), 7 vols. (London, S. Buckley, 1733); and G. A. Summonte, *Historia della Città e Regno di Napoli*, 6 vols. (Naples, Domenico Vivenzio, 1748–50).

The 1563 law barring the kissing of married women is in L. Giustiniani, ed., *Nuova collezione delle prammatiche del Regno di Napoli*, 15 vols. (Naples, Stamperia Simoniana, 1803–8). Aristocratic criticisms of Spanish rule are in G. C. Caracciolo, "Discorso sopra il Regno di Napoli," and F. Carafa, "Memorie," both in R. Ajello, *Una società anomala* (Naples, Edizioni scientifiche italiane, 1996). Francesco D'Andrea's memoir is *I ricordi di un avvocato napoletano del '600* (Naples, Lubrano, 1923). On the 1585 revolt, apart from de Thou and Summonte, I also quoted *Diurnali di Scipione Guerra* (Naples, Società Napoletana di Storia Patria, 1891). On Bartolomeo d'Aquino I quoted F. Capecelatro, *Degli annali della città di Napoli* (Naples, Tipografia di Reale, 1849). The comments of Poggio Bracciolini and Tristano Caracciolo on the Neapolitan nobility are in T. Caracciolo, *Nobilitatis Neapolitanae defensio,* in *Rerum Italicarum Scriptores,* 2nd ed., tome XXII, part I (Bologna, Zanichelli, 1935); the 1594 comment by the Tuscan agent is cited in "Narrazioni e documenti . . . ," *Archivio Storico Italiano* 9 (1846). On the Masaniello revolt I quoted the historians M. Bisaccioni, *Istoria delle guerre civili di Napoli* (1652; Florence, Centro editoriale toscano, 1991), and Giuseppe Donzelli as cited in M. Melchionda, ed., *Drammi masanelliani nel-l'Inghilterra del Seicento* (Florence, Olschki, 1988). Pepe's comment on Spain's rule is cited in Galasso, *Il Mezzogiorno nella storia d'Italia* (Florence, Le Monnier, 1977); Charles V's comment on the Neapolitans is cited in Galasso, *Mezzogiorno medioevale e moderno* (Turin, Einaudi, 1975).

Chapter V

The Belli case is cited in P. Scaramella, *I santolilli* (Rome, Edizioni di storia e letteratura, 1997); the source on the Waldensians, in Scaramella, *L'Inquisizione romana e i Valdesi di Calabria (1554–1703)* (Naples, Editoriale scientifica, 1999). The comment on Ochino is in Rosso, *Historia*; the quote on the tanners, in E. Novi Chavarria, *Il governo delle anime* (Naples, Editoriale scientifica, 2001). The comments on the Jesuits' missions are cited in ibid. and in J. Selwyn, " 'Procuring in the Common People These Better Behaviors': The Jesuits' Civilizing Mission in Early Modern Naples 1550–1620," *Radical History Review* no. 67 (1997). D'Andrea's *Ricordi* is cited earlier. The 1699 bishop's comment is cited in R. Martucci, " 'De vita et honestate clericorum': La formazione del clero meridionale tra Sei e Settecento," *Archivio Storico Italiano* 144 (1986). The sources on nuns are cited in F. Strazzullo, *Edilizia e urbanistica a Napoli dal '500 al '700* (Naples, Berisio, 1968), and Novi Chavarria, *Monache e gentildonne* (Milan, Angeli, 2001); on Giulia De Marco, in P. Zito, *Giulia e l'inquisitore* (Naples, Arte Tipografica, 2000); and on Orsola Benincasa, in H. Hills, *Invisible City* (Oxford, UK, Oxford University Press, 2004). The source on the Sicilian Capuchin is cited in V. D'Alessandro and G. Giarrizzo, *La Sicilia dal Vespro all'Unità d'Italia* (Turin, UTET, 1989). Tutini's 1631 narrative is cited in M. Niola, *Sui palchi delle stelle: Napoli, il sacro, la scena* (Rome, Meltemi, 1995); the other source on the eruption is G. C. Capaccio, "Incendio del Vesuvio," appendix to *Il forastiero* (Naples, Giovan Domenico Roncagliolo, 1634). The Enlightenment critic of devotion to the saints is P. M. Doria, *Massime del governo spagnolo a Napoli* (Naples, Guida, 1973). The comment on the 1710 procession is cited in "Racconti di varie notizie," *Archivio Storico per le Province Napoletane* 31 (1906). The source on Lecce is cited in M. A. Visceglia, *Territorio feudo e potere locale* (Naples, Guida, 1988). The quote from Alfonso de' Liguori's notebook is cited in F. Jones, *Alphonsus de' Liguori* (Westminster, MD, Christian Classics, 1992). The comments on popular devotion at the end of the chapter are in M. Polou, *Prima dioecesana synodus* (Naples, Nicola Migliaccio, 1730); cited in D. Gentilcore, *From Bishop to Witch* (New York, Manchester University Press, 1992); in M. De Gennaro, *Constitutiones* (Reggio,

Giuseppe Bisogni, 1673); and in J. J. Lalande, *Voyage en Italie,* 9 vols. (Paris, Veuve Desaint, 1786).

Chapter VI

In this chapter I have often quoted Capaccio, *Il forastiero,* a famous guide to the city written by the municipal secretary. The 1590 Tuscan agent's comment is in "Narrazioni e documenti . . . ," *Archivio Storico Italiano* 9 (1846). The bishop of Caserta's comment is from G. Coniglio, ed., *Declino del viceregno di Napoli,* 4 vols. (Naples, Giannini, 1990–91). Viceroy Toledo's initiatives on the Naples streets are in "Racconti di storia napoletana," *Archivio Storico per le Province Napoletane* 34 (1909). Viceroy Lemos's initiatives are in *Diurnali di Scipione Guerra,* as is the description of the 1624 feast of St. John's. The 1712 convent claim is cited in Hills, *Invisible City*; the 1728 episode with the Barletta nuns is in "Racconto di varie notizie," *Archivio Storico per le Province Napoletane* 31 (1906). The 1550 edict on vagrants is cited in G. Muto, "Il Regno di Napoli sotto la dominazione spagnola," in *Storia della società italiana,* vol. XI (Milan, Teti, 1989). Cervantes's quote is from *Don Quijote,* I.51. The quotes on Gesualdo are in C. Modestino, *Della dimora di Torquato Tasso in Napoli* (Naples, Giuseppe Cataneo, 1863). The visitor's comment on Piedigrotta is in Lalande, *Voyage.* The 1680 episode about the mad dancers is from the chronicler Domenico Confuorto as cited in M. Campanelli, "Feste e pellegrinaggi nel XVI e XVII secolo," in Galasso and Romeo, *Storia del Mezzogiorno,* vol. IX (Naples, Edizioni del Sole, 1991). On the Popolo, besides Capaccio, I have quoted C. Tutini, *Del origine e fundatione de' Seggi di Napoli* (Naples, Beltrano, 1644). The food edicts are in Giustiniani, *Nuova collezione.* The guild documents are in Archivio di Stato di Napoli, Cappellano Maggiore 1184 #24 (1710) Verdumari, and 1189 #15 (1720) Formellari di bottoni.

Chapter VII

The passage from Campanella is cited in Galasso, *Alla periferia dell'impero* (Turin, Einaudi, 1994). The comment on Imperato's museum is from G. B. del Tufo, *Ritratto o modello . . .* (Naples, Agar, 1959): this peculiar long poem, written around 1600, celebrates all the glories of Naples, from mozzarella to science. The comment from the member of the Academy about the scientific method is Francesco D'Andrea's as cited in B. De Giovanni, "Magia e scienza nella Napoli seicentesca," in the catalogue *Civiltà del Seicento a Napoli,* 2 vols. (Naples, Electa, 1984). The source on the trial of the atheists is cited in L. Osbat, *L'Inquisizione a Napoli* (Rome, Edizioni di storia e letteratura, 1974). All quotes about Giannone come from his autobiography, *Vita scritta da lui medesimo* (Milan, Feltrinelli, 1960). The archbishop's comment about the Naples nobles is cited in Ajello, *Una società anomala.* The university visitor's comment is in Lalande, *Voyage.* Genovesi's essay is "Discorso sopra il vero fine delle lettere e delle scienze" (1753), in F. Venturi, ed., *Illuministi italiani,* tome V (Milan-Naples, Ricciardi, 1962). The doctor commenting on the 1764 famine is Michele Sarcone as cited in F. Venturi,

"1764: Napoli nell'anno della fame," *Rivista Storica Italiana* 85 (1973). Kelly's memoirs are *Reminiscences*, 2 vols. (New York, Da Capo Press, 1968). The edition I have used of Filangieri's work is *La scienza della legislazione*, 6 vols. (Milan, Società Tipografica dei Classici Italiani, 1822). On Filangieri and Franklin I have cited the documents in A. Pace, *Benjamin Franklin and Italy* (Philadelphia, American Philosophical Society, 1958). Goethe's comments are in his *Italian Journey* (London, Penguin, 1970).

Chapter VIII

In this chapter I have quoted many travel accounts, some quite often, and I have also used excerpts I found in the works of other scholars. The sources I used directly are J. C. R. de Saint-Non, *Voyage pittoresque*, 4 vols. (Paris, Imprimerie de Clousier, 1781–86); Goethe, *Italian Journey*; Lalande, *Voyage*; G. Burnet, *Some Letters Containing an Account . . .* (London, J. Lacy, 1724); A. de la Vigne, *Le voyage de Naples* (Milan, Vita e pensiero, 1981); F. Petrarca, *Prose*; G. Sandys, *A Relation of a Journey Begun An: Dom: 1610* (London, W. Barrett, 1615); F. Moryson, *Shakespeare's Europe* (New York, B. Blom, 1967); S. Mazzella, *Parthenopoeia*, J. Howell, ed. (London, H. Moseley, 1654), with Howell's Addition; J. Ray, *Travels* (1664), in *Complete Collection of Voyages and Travels*, 2 vols. (London, John Harris, 1764); C. de Brosses, *Lettres familières écrites d'Italie*, 2 vols. (Paris, É. Perrin, 1885); J. J. Rousseau, *Oeuvres Complètes*, 5 vols. (Paris, Pléiade, 1995); C. Burney, *Music, Men, and Manners in France and Italy* (London, Eulenburg Books, 1974); Stendhal, *Rome, Naples and Florence in 1817* (New York, Braziller, 1960); P. Colletta, *Storia del reame di Napoli*, 3 vols. (1834; Naples, Libreria scientifica editrice, 1969); *The Memoirs of Jacques Casanova*, 12 vols. (New York, Venetian Society, 1928); A. de Jorio, *Gesture in Naples and Gesture in Classical Antiquity*, A. Kendon, ed. (Bloomington, Indiana University Press, 2000).

The excerpts are from the following sources: Charles VIII's comment, Montesquieu's, and Swinburne's are cited in A. Mozzillo, *Passaggio a Mezzogiorno* (Milan, Leonardo, 1993). Hamilton's nephew is cited in C. Knight, "Sir William Hamilton nella rivoluzione napoletana del 1799," in *The Hamilton Papers* (Naples, Associazione Amici dei Musei di Napoli, 1999). Winckelmann's comment is cited in M. T. Penta, ed., *Napoli in prospettiva* (Naples, Istituto Suor Orsola Benincasa, 1996). The 1765 comment on Naples's buildings is cited in Strazzullo, *Edilizia*. The 1801 comment about the South as Africa is cited in M. De Bonis et al., *Settecento calabrese* (Cosenza, Edizioni Periferia, 1985). Sade's comment is cited in N. Moe, *The View from Vesuvius* (Berkeley, University of California Press, 2002).

The eighteenth-century South has also been the subject of recent fiction and music studies: Anne Rice's novel *Cry to Heaven* (New York, Knopf, 1982) is the story of a castrato singer; Susan Sontag's novel *The Volcano Lover* (New York, Farrar, Straus and Giroux, 1992) takes place in Naples in the 1790s and includes among its characters the Hamiltons and Nelson; Daniel Heartz's recent survey of music in eighteenth-century Europe, *Music in European Capitals* (New York, W. W. Norton, 2003), devotes its first section to Naples.

Chapter IX

On the 1799 revolution, the main source is V. Cuoco, *Saggio storico sulla rivoluzione di Napoli* (1800; Milan, Rizzoli, 1999). I also quoted C. de Nicola, *Diario napoletano dal 1798 al 1825*, 3 vols. (Naples, Società Napoletana di Storia Patria, 1906); D. Pietromasi, *Alla riconquista del Regno* (1801; Naples, Il giglio, 1994); the Lecce miracle is cited in A. M. Rao, "La repubblica napoletana," in Galasso and Romeo, *Storia del Mezzogiorno*, vol. IV.2 (Naples, Edizioni del Sole, 1986); Queen Maria Carolina's letter to Lady Hamilton is in J. Santore, ed., *Modern Naples* (New York, Italica Press, 2001), a collection of documents from which I have also cited later comments by Metternich on Francis I, Luigi Settembrini on the Bourbons, and Lady Blessington on Naples. There are two novels on the women protagonists of the revolution: E. Striano's *Il resto di niente* (Naples, Loffredo, 1986) focuses on Eleonora Pimentel Fonseca while A. Dumas's *La Sanfelice* (serialized in the Paris paper *La Presse* in 1865) focuses on Luisa Sanfelice and has recently been filmed by the Taviani brothers.

On the later period I have quoted three major nineteenth-century Neapolitan historians: Colletta, *Storia del reame di Napoli*, who also cites Napoleon's comment on the Bourbons; N. Nisco, *Storia del reame di Napoli dal 1824 al 1860* (1884–94; Naples, Lanciano e Veraldi, 1908); and R. de Cesare, *La fine di un regno* (1894; Milan, Longanesi, 1961). F. Venturi, "L'Italia fuori d'Italia," in *Storia d'Italia*, vol. III (Turin, Einaudi, 1973), cites Metternich on the events of 1820, Gladstone's essay, and Maury's comments on the South. The 1847 comment on Sicily's economy is cited in D. Mack Smith, *Modern Sicily after 1713* (New York, Viking, 1968). The diplomatic documents are in H. R. Marraro, ed., *Diplomatic Relations Between the United States and the Kingdom of the Two Sicilies*, 2 vols. (New York, S. F. Vanni, 1951). The British critic's comment about art is in F. Napier, *Notes on Modern Painting in Naples* (London, J. W. Parker, 1855). The San Carlo censor is cited in F. Mancini, ed., *Il Teatro di San Carlo 1737–1987*, 3 vols. (Naples, Electa, 1987). The comments of various travelers and authors are in Stendhal, *Rome, Naples and Florence in 1817*; Percy B. Shelley, "Letters from Italy," in *Essays, Letters from Abroad . . .* , 2 vols. (London, E. Moxon, 1852); C. Dickens, *Impressioni di Napoli* (Naples, Colonnese, 1985; a bilingual edition); T. Gautier, *Jettatura* (Paris, Flammarion, n.d.); C. A. Mayer, *Vita popolare a Napoli nell'età romantica* (Bari, Laterza, 1948); A. Dumas, *Il corricolo* (1843; Milan-Naples, Ricciardi, 1950), a novel, titled after the type of carriage Dumas employed, that consists of varied sketches of Naples's life. On jettatura I have also used A. de Jorio, *Gesture in Naples*. The 1852 newspaper comment is cited in H. R. Marraro, *American Opinion on the Unification of Italy, 1846–1861* (New York, Columbia University Press, 1932). Finally, the comments by Nassau, Renan, Gregorovius, and Settembrini are in Moe, *View*.

Chapter X

The quote about the Bronte episode is cited in G. Pandolfo, *Una rivoluzione tradita*, 2 vols. (Palermo, Palma, 1985). Most of the comments by northern Italians about southerners that I quoted in this chapter are cited in Moe, *View*. The comments on the bandits and Niceforo's statement are in J. Dickie, *Darkest Italy* (New York, St. Martin's Press, 1999). Sonnino's comment on the election system is cited in M. Clark, *Modern Italy 1871–1995* (London, Longman, 1996). Nitti's comment on emigration is cited in the catalogue *Brigantaggio lealismo repressione* (Naples, Macchiaroli, 1984). The 1888 U.S. consul, Munthe, and the French consul are cited in F. Snowden, *Naples in the Time of Cholera, 1884–1911* (Cambridge, UK, Cambridge University Press, 1995). The 1852 comment from an American diplomat is from Marraro, *Diplomatic Relations*. I have quoted various passages from M. Serao, *Il ventre di Napoli* (1884; Cava de' Tirreni, Avagliano, 2002). Cook's 1884 guide is cited in *Lonely Planet Italy*, 5th ed. (Footscray, Australia, Lonely Planet Publications, 2002). S. Di Giacomo, *Poesie e prose* (Milan, Mondadori, 1977). P. Scialò, *La canzone napoletana* (Rome, Newton and Crompton, 1995), cites the text of *Zappatore*. Villari and Sonnino's works on the southern question are cited in the anthology by R. Villari, ed., *Il Sud nella storia d'Italia*, 2 vols. (Bari, Laterza, 1974). Fortunato is cited in F. Barbagallo, *Mezzogiorno e questione meridionale (1860–1980)* (Naples, Guida, 1980). Colajanni's comment is cited in M. Jeuland-Meynaud, *La ville de Naples après l'annexion (1860–1915)* (Aix, France, Éditions de l'Université de Provence, 1973). Verga's first major novel is usually translated in English as *The House by the Medlar Tree*; I quoted from *Mastro-Don Gesualdo* (Milan, Garzanti, 1987); there is an English translation of this novel by D. H. Lawrence, first published in 1925. I have quoted from F. De Roberto, *I viceré* (Milan, Garzanti, 1959); A. Gramsci, *La questione meridionale* (Rome, Edizioni Rinascita, 1951); C. Levi, *Cristo si è fermato a Eboli* (Milan, Mondadori, 1961); C. Malaparte, *La pelle* (Milan, Garzanti, 1978); and G. Tomasi di Lampedusa, *Il gattopardo* (Milan, Feltrinelli, 1959). The British soldiers are cited in Santore, *Modern Naples*; the comment on the mafia is cited in F. Renda, *Storia della Sicilia dal 1860 al 1970*, 3 vols. (Palermo, Sellerio, 1987).

Illustration Credits

Page 21: Reprinted with the permission of Cambridge University Press

Pages 37, 73, and 298: Courtesy of the Istituto Centrale per il Catalogo e la Documentazione, Rome

Pages 45 and 152: Images by Gregor A. Kalas

Pages 65, 74–75, 91, 92, 145, 146, 148, 156, 172–74, 176, 211, 217, 258, 268: Courtesy of the Soprintendenza Speciale per il Polo Museale Napoletano, Naples

Page 136: Image by the author

Page 194: Courtesy of the Biblioteca della Società Napoletana di Storia Patria, Naples

Pages 222, 227, and 241: Courtesy of the Library of Congress, Rare Book Room, Rosenwald Collection

Page 225: Courtesy of the Library of Congress, Map Room

Pages 234 and 299: Courtesy of Luciano Pedicini/Archivio dell'Arte, Naples

Pages 244 and 275: From Francesco de Bourcard, *Usi e costumi di Napoli*, vol. 2 (1858)

Index

Note: this index does not include Naples, Sicily, Italy, and southern Italy when used generally; it also does not include titles of works when they are only mentioned on the same pages as their authors.